THE EVIL WITHIN

THE EVIL WITHIN
Why We Need Moral Philosophy

Diane Jeske

OXFORD
UNIVERSITY PRESS

OXFORD
UNIVERSITY PRESS

Oxford University Press is a department of the University of Oxford. It furthers
the University's objective of excellence in research, scholarship, and education
by publishing worldwide. Oxford is a registered trade mark of Oxford University
Press in the UK and certain other countries.

Published in the United States of America by Oxford University Press
198 Madison Avenue, New York, NY 10016, United States of America.

© Oxford University Press 2018

Names: Jeske, Diane, 1967– author.
Title: The evil within : why we need moral philosophy / Diane Jeske.
Description: New York : Oxford University Press, 2018.
Identifiers: LCCN 2017057399 (print) | LCCN 2018023199 (ebook) |
ISBN 9780190685409 (online resource) | ISBN 9780190685386 (updf) |
ISBN 9780190685393 (epub) | ISBN 9780190685379 (cloth : alk. paper)
Subjects: LCSH: Good and evil. | Ethics.
Classification: LCC BJ1401 (ebook) | LCC BJ1401.J47 2018 (print) |
DDC 170—dc23
LC record available at https://lccn.loc.gov/2017057399

9 8 7 6 5 4 3 2 1

Printed by Sheridan Books, Inc., United States of America

To my mother, Barbara Franke:
Thank you for being my best friend

Contents

Preface

When I was eleven years old, my mother gave me a copy of *The Diary of Anne Frank*. At the end of the book was an afterword, explaining what happened to Anne and the other occupants of the Secret Annex after their capture by the Gestapo. This brief glimpse into the horrors of the Holocaust had a profound impact on me. I was young enough to be afraid that what had happened to Anne and her family could happen to me and my family. I wanted to alleviate this fear, and thus was led to find out more about the Holocaust and its origins in order to reassure myself that what had happened in Europe in the 1940s would never happen in the American Midwest of the late twentieth century in which I lived.

By the time I was fourteen, I had done more reading, including William Shirer's *The Rise and Fall of the Third Reich*. Gradually, the object of my fear had changed: instead of being afraid of being a victim, I had become afraid that I carried within me the potential to be a perpetrator. This fear was in part responsible for my interest in philosophy: I wanted to know how to be a good person, how to ensure that I would *be* and would *stay* the sort of person who would never, under any circumstances, be a perpetrator.

Not surprisingly, as I studied philosophy, my focus and interests changed. However, after I had tenure, I had more freedom and time to think about new sorts of courses to teach. My early concerns about the perpetrators of the Holocaust and a somewhat more recent interest in the history of American slavery led me to construct a course called *The Nature of Evil*, in which I used case studies of very bad individuals to examine various topics in moral philosophy. My teaching of this course has been one of the most rewarding experiences of my twenty-five years as a professional philosopher. Students have often been struck by their unexpected sympathy with perpetrators and with a stark realization that they just don't know what they would do if they found themselves in morally challenging circumstances. I have been gratified by the extent to which the grip of the first-person perpetrator narratives has resulted in the same sort of self-examination in my students that it has caused in me, and also by how those narratives can make what might otherwise have seemed to be merely abstract philosophical issues appear as what they really are: urgent questions that every person needs to confront for him or herself.

And so I began the writing of this book, using first-person narratives by perpetrators of evil to enliven and make accessible issues in moral philosophy. Gradually, however, I began to see the book as a way to demonstrate the importance, for everyone, of the study of moral philosophy. This motivation came as a result of spending six years as chair of my department, six years that commenced in 2008 just before the economic downturn that has resulted in so many cuts in higher education. Attempting to defend the autonomy of my department in opposition to an administration that wanted to merge us with other units, I was forced to constantly point to how well philosophy majors do on entrance exams for business or law school and how high the salaries of philosophy majors who end up in business are relative to those who majored in other fields. And I realized that we are all losing the most important point of a liberal education, an education to which philosophy is absolutely essential: the creation of citizens who can think for themselves, and can enter into civil debates on complex moral issues with others who have opposing positions, citizens who can analyze arguments, and perhaps most important, see when no argument has been forthcoming. The level of the "debate" in the 2016 American presidential election and the numbers of people seduced by terrorist propaganda have confirmed to me how much we need to ensure that we have citizens who can think beyond mere efficiency, self-interest, and slogans.

I am certainly not naïve enough to believe that a study of moral philosophy is either necessary or sufficient for creating the sorts of citizens we need in order to have a well-functioning democracy. But I do believe that incorporating the study of philosophy—in particular, of moral philosophy—into our standard curricula at all grade levels has the potential to contribute to the creation of such citizens. The best compliment I ever receive as a teacher is when a student thanks me for a course in political philosophy or ethics by saying, "I just never thought about these issues in this way before." I regularly see students questioning their beliefs, and questioning them in ways that are completely new to them. Most important, I see students coming to see complexities that they had never seen before, acknowledging that maybe, just maybe, there is more to think about with respect to their own views and with respect to the views of others than they had previously thought.

Studying philosophy can be a painful process, insofar as it has the very real potential to shake our deepest convictions and to cause us to view ourselves in a new and perhaps less gratifying light. I am firmly convinced that education must challenge students to confront uncomfortable claims made by others, and teach them how to engage in such debates in a civil and fruitful manner. We do not do that by limiting what we say to each other but, rather, by learning how to respond to each other and how to examine what we ourselves are saying.

The first and most important step we need to take in any attempt to find the truth is figuring out what we actually believe and why we believe it. This book is intended, in part, to provide the reader the kind of exercise in self-examination that I think is philosophy's most important product when it is successful. In my own case, I have never entirely convinced myself that I *absolutely* could not, under the "right" circumstances, become a perpetrator of evil. I do hope that my own study of philosophy has at least lessened the likelihood that I would become such a perpetrator, and I think that we have absolutely nothing to lose from launching an experiment to see whether widespread education in moral philosophy can help us to collectively prevent such "right" conditions from ever being realized.

Acknowledgments

The idea for this book grew out of my experiences teaching a course called *The Nature of Evil*. I would like to thank all of the University of Iowa students who have taken that course over the past several years for your enthusiasm and contributions to classroom discussions: you have helped me a great deal in thinking about the issues raised by this book. I would also like to thank the graduate students in my seminar *Ethics and the Holocaust* for provocative discussions of similar issues.

The final version of the manuscript benefited greatly from comments by David McNaughton, Lisa Tessman, and an anonymous referee for Oxford University Press. Richard Fumerton read and reread and then read yet again various drafts of this manuscript and, as always, provided incisive comments and critiques. Most important, he provided encouragement and advice at every step of the process as he has throughout my career, and this work, like all of my work, is far better than it would otherwise have been.

Finally, I would like to thank my editor at Oxford University Press, Lucy Randall, who has been enthusiastic and supportive from first submission to final product, and who provided valuable and insightful comments on the manuscript.

THE EVIL WITHIN

Learning from Evil

Thomas Jefferson and Edward Coles

In 1814, Thomas Jefferson, retired from public service after his two terms as president of the United States, was living the life of the genteel southern patriarch: ensconced in his mountaintop home, Monticello, Jefferson could indulge his passions for invention, correspondence, and university building because the day-to-day work of his plantation was performed by the men, women, and children he held in bondage. This human capital constituted a large portion of Jefferson's assets, against which he could borrow money to hold on to Monticello and to continue to engage in his intellectual endeavors, particularly those that would solidify his reputation with posterity. And this was how the revered author of the Declaration of Independence fully intended to live out the remainder of his days.

In that year, Edward Coles punctured the fabric of this southern idyll. Coles was a young man who had served as a private secretary to James Madison and was soon to inherit the means to live the southern upper-class male ideal on a neighboring plantation. But Coles had come to see slavery as wrong, as a blight on the South left over from colonial days. He knew that

Jefferson had, as a young man, spoken out against slavery, even including in his initial draft of the Declaration of Independence an indictment of England for having introduced such an institution on the soil of the New World.[1] Of late, Jefferson had been silent on the slavery question, but Coles recognized Jefferson's potential influence in moving Virginia toward a policy of gradual emancipation. He hoped to rouse Jefferson to once again speak out, unhesitatingly and without reservation, against the institution of slavery, thereby giving emancipation the support of Virginia's favorite and most revered son.

But Coles did not intend simply to sit back and see what Jefferson and the Virginia legislature would do. Coles could not control the fate of slavery in Virginia, but he did have immense power over the fate of his own slaves. He intended to sell his plantation, move with his slaves to the free territory of Illinois, and use his resources to establish farms for his then-freed bondsmen and bondswomen. Coles hoped to get Jefferson to endorse this plan, thereby encouraging other young men of Coles's position to follow his example. For Coles, recognition of the evil of the institution of slavery was *motivating*—it provided him with an impetus to action, an impetus that outweighed his own social and financial interests. He wanted to get others to see slavery's wrongness and to act on that perception, and he formulated a plan to extricate himself from complicity with the institution and to do what he could to help those who suffered under it.

Thomas Jefferson, however, did not intend to allow Coles's letter to puncture the fabric of his peaceful retirement. His response to Coles was twofold: first, Coles ought not to carry out the proposed move to Illinois because former slaves were as "incapable as children of taking care of themselves."[2] Given this fact, Coles's best strategy, according to Jefferson, was that which Jefferson himself had adopted: stay in Virginia and quietly (apparently, if we take Jefferson to be acting on his own advice, *very* quietly) work for gradual emancipation. Jefferson claimed that prudence dictated waiting for public perception to advance, because one would do more harm than good if one aimed for immediate change or tried to exhort people toward any moral improvement to which they were adamantly opposed. Jefferson, then, seemed to present himself as in fact taking the moral high ground by continuing to live a life financed by the sweat of his slaves.

Beyond these more general attempts to justify refusing to speak out in accordance with Coles's request, Jefferson also appealed to his advanced years. He told Coles that the work of emancipation was for younger generations, and that he was simply too old to undertake such an arduous task.[3] Coles must have found this a particularly weak excuse, given Jefferson's ceaseless and energetic commitments to invention, writing, and university building. In his response to Jefferson, Coles attempted to shame him by pointing to the continuing activism of the elderly Benjamin Franklin, a fellow Founding Father more than forty years Jefferson's senior. More important, Coles pointed out that Jefferson had a special obligation to take up the work of emancipation: Jefferson was one of the few "who have it in their power effectually to arouse and enlighten the public sentiment, which in matters of this kind ought not to be expected to lead, but to be led."[4] If the problem was public sentiment, then Jefferson, with the great respect and authority he carried, needed to work to change it. Coles might have added that by doing nothing, Jefferson was actually helping to solidify public opinion against emancipation, thereby making it more difficult for the younger generations to make that fight against slavery.

Edward Coles received no further communication from Jefferson. In 1819, he packed up his slaves and headed to Illinois. He not only emancipated those seventeen men, women, and children but he also established them on farms that they could gradually purchase from him at reasonable rates. Beyond the way in which he radically transformed the lives of his former slaves, he had an immense impact on the future of the nation that Jefferson had, in the previous century, helped to create. Illinois had entered the Union as a free state in 1818, but in 1824, pro-slavery residents tried to pass a constitutional amendment legalizing slavery. By then, Edward Coles was Illinois's governor, and largely due to his efforts, the pro-slavery forces were narrowly defeated. Illinois would remain a free state. In the 1850s, that state's Republicans would work to gain the party's presidential nomination for a resident of Springfield—Abraham Lincoln—who would finally complete the work done by early emancipators such as Coles.

The story of Edward Coles and Thomas Jefferson is that of two men who both claimed to believe the institution of slavery was morally wrong. Yet the actions of these two men were extremely different. This kind of situation—sharing apparently the same moral beliefs yet making radically different choices—forces us to ask several questions. Did Jefferson and Coles really share the same moral beliefs? Jefferson had certainly made antislavery assertions as a young man, and he continued, in private, to insist that slavery was morally wrong. Perhaps, however, we should read his actions as casting doubt on the sincerity of his assertions; after all, how can a man believe an institution to be seriously wrong and yet continue, with little apparent conflict, to remain complicit in it?[5] This question is particularly pressing with respect to Jefferson,[6] because he knew how much influence his name carried; merely by speaking out against slavery he could have had a major impact on the public debate in Virginia. If he had gone even further and emancipated his own slaves (or had ensured their emancipation upon his death, as George Washington had done), his actions would have had genuine potential to make gradual emancipation at the very least a real possibility. So why did Jefferson remain silent at such a crucial moment if he really believed slavery to be wrong?

One plausible explanation appeals to Jefferson's financial situation: he was in debt, he loved Monticello, and he wanted to preserve his estate for future generations of Jeffersons. There is little doubt that such considerations weighed heavily on Jefferson. But we need to keep in mind that we are talking about complicity in an extremely evil institution, the horrors of which are often papered over in schoolbook narratives of the lives of the founding fathers: men and women worked to death in disease-ridden swamps; families torn apart, never to be reunited; women and girls raped by powerful white men, backs scarred by the whip; and the endless degradation and humiliation of being denied education, self-governance, and basic self-esteem. Did Jefferson allow himself to see slavery as it was, or did he deceive himself into believing that it was not that bad after all? Did his own self-interest and his concern for his family cause him to ignore the realities of the institution that sustained his hobbies?

Perhaps he in fact, at least at some level, recognized the brutality of the institution of slavery, but in order to protect his own self-interest, he deceived himself into believing he really could do nothing about it and so he might as well just enjoy his life at Monticello. He seems to have convinced himself that he really did have "the wolf by the ears," as he famously described the South's situation with respect to slavery, and there was no way of letting go without causing grave harm to everyone involved. So maybe he did not even consider the merits of Coles's plan but, rather, willfully decided to ignore those merits so as not to mentally disrupt his own idyll. He had to convince himself that there really was no good antislavery option if he was to continue to perceive himself as a good man—even as the great man he so clearly wanted to be seen as by his fellow countrymen, both contemporary and in the future. And by continuing to cling to the belief that Americans of African descent were inferior to whites, Jefferson's own favored perception of himself was that much easier for him to maintain.

Now many might be inclined at this point to insist that Thomas Jefferson was a humane slaveholder, that he shielded his slaves from the worst aspects of the institution. Of course, Americans have been taught to believe that, and as a result we allow ourselves to maintain an idealized picture of Jefferson. In fact, Jefferson viewed slaves as commodities, advising friends to invest in black slaves in order to be financially secure. Jefferson himself authorized the whipping of young slave boys, and he employed an overseer of whose cruel reputation he was fully aware. He gave slaves as gifts to his daughter, knowing full well that in doing so he was separating families. All evidence points to his having taken a teenage slave girl, Sally Hemings, as his mistress, and any attempts to reinterpret this as a loving romance have to be reckoned with the immense power that Jefferson had over Hemings: her fate and that of her children (at least some of whom were most likely Jefferson's) was entirely in Jefferson's hands. In spite of this, Jefferson's own attempts to be remembered as a man noble in deeds as well as words have been all too successful.[7]

These reflections on Thomas Jefferson should be troubling to all of us. My goal is not to assassinate Jefferson's character. Rather, taking note of those aspects of Jefferson that are often ignored in American culture *should* trouble us, precisely because there can be no doubt about Jefferson's many extraordinary talents and accomplishments—talents and accomplishments that cannot be dismissed merely because Jefferson had so many of the flaws common to us all: he was surely vain, he had an immense sense of his own importance, and he was not always open to considering the merits of his opponents or of their views (witness his intractable dislike of and contempt for the at least as extraordinary and talented Alexander Hamilton). But Jefferson was intellectually gifted, highly educated, literate, scientifically minded, creative, and capable of deep affection and friendship, as well as having had cosmopolitan tastes and life experiences. How could such a man be so complicit in so much evil? More important, how could such a man have continued to maintain that his course of action or, rather, passivity was the morally best available? How could a man who had daily interaction with African Americans, and who moreover shared his bed with a slave woman and most likely fathered at least some of her children, have not come to seriously doubt the supposed inferiority of blacks? We cannot ignore the fact that Jefferson played a significant role in maintaining and benefiting from an evil institution, and we *should* not do so, because that fact raises important and pressing questions about moral belief, moral motivation, and moral action.

If Jefferson, with all his social and natural advantages, failed so miserably on such an important moral issue, we might be led to think that moral knowledge and the motivation to act in accord with such knowledge are terribly difficult to attain, especially under less than ideal cultural conditions. But it is for precisely this reason that I began with the story of Edward Coles and his letter to Jefferson. Coles was a product of the same social and cultural environment that produced Jefferson, and from the evidence that we have, there is no reason to think that Coles was Jefferson's superior, or even his equal, in intellectual capacity and accomplishment. Jefferson certainly was not devoid of personal courage: his authorship of the Declaration of Independence was an act of treason that would have exposed his neck to the rope if the British had won the war. So why did Coles attain the moral knowledge that slavery was wrong and the motivation to act on that knowledge, while Jefferson sat home and consoled himself with the thought that the Edward Coles of the world were hopelessly deluded idealists with no real understanding of African Americans?

One might think that these are questions of purely historical interest, and that we should leave it to the historians to sort out the tangled psychologies of long-dead figures. But the story of Jefferson and his response to Coles provides us with a valuable occasion for self-examination, an opportunity to ask whether we ourselves are guilty of engaging in precisely the sort of "justification" of our actions (or of our failures to act) as Jefferson was. Most Americans have tremendous admiration for Jefferson as a Founding Father; they view him as a "great man," and our country teems with streets, schools, towns, and the like that have been named after him. So we should all be willing to countenance the possibility that if Jefferson was capable of making certain kinds of mistakes, then so are we. And we should also recognize what a gift it would be to each of us to have an Edward Coles always to hand to help us see when we are making such mistakes. But we do not; we have to be our own Edward Coles. Further, we have to avoid responding to our own "inner Coles" in the way that Jefferson responded to the real Coles: we need to avoid defensiveness, self-deception, and self-pleadings. How can we accomplish these goals?

Thinking About Morality

There is no easy answer to the question just posed. However, the study of moral philosophy can provide at least part of the answer. My aim in this book is to use narratives such as those of Jefferson to give us entry into the sorts of mistakes not only that people engaged or complicit in evil often make in their reasoning but also of which we ourselves are or can be guilty. I hope to show how thinking in the ways that are characteristic of moral philosophy can be a tool for identifying and avoiding these types of mistakes. And, of course, I intend that the narratives of moral failure will serve as cautionary tales; that is, when common mistakes in moral reasoning collide with moral crisis, we can find ourselves committing morally heinous actions that make us complicit with great evil. I will also, at some points in what follows, suggest that we may already be complicit; indeed, one of the most difficult tasks of moral reasoning is to identify those morally loaded choices and situations.

I certainly am not making the claim that if we all study moral philosophy we will all become perfectly virtuous and no human-made evil will ever again contaminate the earth. Those, I am afraid, are unachievable goals. Many people who study moral philosophy remain morally indifferent or even quite nasty. Knowing how to approach thinking about moral issues is only one piece of a complicated puzzle: we need to have the desire to engage in the right sort of reasoning; the will to act on the conclusions we reach; and at least for most of us who are not quite as heroic as Edward Coles, the support and motivation a social group can provide. But making the study of moral philosophy widely available to people beginning from an early age can at least give us a start toward correctly placing one piece of the puzzle.

One important message I want to convey has to do with the ways in which philosophical reasoning can force self-examination. As we consider Jefferson's response to Coles, we cannot help but wonder whether Jefferson actually believed what he was saying. Was Jefferson opposed to slavery? Did he sincerely doubt the capacity of African Americans to live as free and independent people? Was his reluctance to promote Coles's plan due to his sense of being too old, or was it due to his desire not to impair his own financial and social position? I am not asking whether Jefferson was attempting to deceive Coles but, rather, whether Jefferson himself was any longer aware of his actual beliefs and motivations. If we are to make headway in our dialogue with others on moral issues, we need first to make headway with ourselves; and in what follows, I hope to show how philosophy can aid us in doing that.

In the chapters that follow, I use the narratives of bad people to highlight various sorts of impediments to thinking clearly about moral issues in order to show how moral philosophy can play a part in removing those impediments:

1. *Cultural Norms and Pressures*. One such impediment strikes everyone when they hear the story of Jefferson and Coles: cultural norms and pressures. Both Jefferson and Coles were born and raised in the upper class of the slaveholding American South, a class whose wealth and position depended upon the labor of those held in bondage. Many people in this society believed that the enslavement of Africans was morally justified and/or divinely sanctioned, while many others found it to their advantage to "accept" such justifications. The actions of Edward Coles surely met with profound disapproval from the vast majority of his social peers. While such societal disapproval can certainly affect one's ability to act contrary to it, it raises even more complicated issues. Many people are inclined to see some sort of connection between morally appropriate behavior and societal norms: they will excuse or even justify the conduct of Jefferson by saying something along the lines of "But it wasn't wrong for him to hold slaves—he lived in a different culture than we now do." What could it mean to make such a claim about Jefferson's actions? We need to know how to think about prevailing social norms in connection with morality if we are not to use the failures of those around us to provide facile excuses for our bad behavior (chapter 3).

2. *The Complexity of Consequences.* It is significant that Jefferson defends his rejection of Coles's plan by claiming that *it would be better in the long run* if Coles were to stay in Virginia and not free his slaves. It seems obvious that the consequences of our actions

are relevant to the morality of our actions. But *how* are they relevant? Is anything else relevant? How can we determine the long-term consequences of our actions? Suppose that Jefferson was correct in his predictions; would that have made Coles's actions wrong? Could either Coles or Jefferson justify holding his slaves in bondage by appealing to the good consequences to be gained by doing so? Some people will be thinking, "The ends cannot justify the means," or "It cannot be right to do wrong." But appeal to slogans only hides the very real complexities, both moral and nonmoral, that plague us in trying to make predictions about the future and in trying to figure out the moral import of the predictions that we make (chapter 4).

3. *Emotions*. We inevitably wonder how Jefferson could fail to empathize with the position of his slaves, given his own views about the importance of liberty and of education, and given the fact that he had a slave "mistress" with whom he fathered slave children. How could the emotions of slaveholders not be engaged by the sufferings of those they held in bondage? We all recognize that our emotions can, as we say, cloud our judgment, but we also expect our finer feelings, the "better angels of our natures,"[8] to urge us to the right course of action. Sorting through our emotions is a difficult task, and because morality is concerned with suffering and happiness, its subject matter inevitably calls forth our emotions, complicating the task of moral reasoning. Approaching and understanding our own emotions is an important part of moral thinking (chapter 5).

4. *Self-Deception*. I am confident that many of my readers will be inclined to say that Jefferson was engaged in self-deception when he claimed that doing nothing was preferable to Coles's plan. We all can identify times at which we actively seek to deceive ourselves: I often tell myself that I should put off working for (insert any one of a host of reasons here). But some kinds of self-deception are deeply entrenched and morally dangerous, as in the case of Jefferson. How can we try to root out and prevent self-deceptive strategies that impair our moral reasoning? (chapter 6).

I hope that use of the narratives in this book not only can convince you of the importance of thinking philosophically about morality but also show you how fascinating that thinking can be. While it can be difficult, there is great satisfaction in coming to know ourselves, to know what we sincerely believe to be worth pursuing, to be able to defend those beliefs, and to live our lives in accordance with those beliefs.

Moral Philosophy and Moral Education

Everyone agrees that moral education is important: we want to raise children to be morally good people, to make morally correct choices, and to have the strength to act on those choices even in the face of opposition. But the question is, How can we accomplish these goals? One approach that is sometimes advocated involves inculcation of precepts, such as the Ten Commandments. It has been suggested that we can create better people if we simply hang the Ten Commandments in schoolrooms around the country so that children will absorb them and guide their conduct by them.

It doesn't take much thought, however, to see how inadequate any such approach would be. First, and most obviously, there is no way in which we could provide children with precepts that would give them answers for every possible situation they might confront. At best, any manageable list of precepts would have to be rough-and-ready guidelines that require interpretation to apply in particular cases. Take the commandment "Thou shalt not kill." One might read that as a categorical prohibition on any form of killing, be it of human beings or of any other sentient beings. But most people immediately reject the implications of such a categorical prohibition; hardly anyone thinks it is morally impermissible to kill someone who is about to murder one's own child, just to take one of the most uncontentious of cases.

Another difficulty arises when there is conflict between precepts. Suppose your father is coveting his neighbor's wife, thereby breaking a commandment. You also acknowledge the commandment that you are to honor your parents. What is required of you in this situation? In order to decide, you would need to figure out what is involved in honoring someone: Does honoring your father extend to countenancing his wrongdoing? If not, does refusal to countenance wrongdoing take priority over honoring one's parents, or vice versa? Even very short catalogues of precepts such as the Ten Commandments will provide us with problems about both interpretation and prioritization.

So we need to know how to think, how to reason about morality. Two tasks are particularly important. The first we have already encountered: interpretation of moral assertions. What is it to "honor" someone, for example? Also, what is the scope of various precepts? When we are forbidden to kill, does that mean *all* killings are wrong? One danger is that without thinking through these questions about interpretation and scope, we will simply apply the precepts in cases where we like the results, and then insist that they do not apply in other cases. And then we find ourselves allowing our own self-interest to guide us, rather than morality.[9]

To engage in the interpretation of precepts, we need to, as it were, "think below" the precepts themselves: we need to ask, What justifies this precept? If I ask what is involved in honoring my parents, I need to figure out why certain sorts of behavior with respect to one's father and mother are appropriate. To understand which killings are forbidden, I need to think about why killing might be wrong, and then consider whether those wrong-making features are present in various sorts of cases. But these tasks, to be done properly, require me to evaluate what can be said for and against various interpretations, which involves evaluating what can be said for and against the precept itself.

In his classic *On Liberty*, John Stuart Mill defended freedom of expression in part because it promoted the kind of debate that could help prevent our beliefs from becoming what he called "dead dogma." He believed that if we do not have our beliefs challenged in such a way that we need to reconsider and reexamine their justification, we will not only lose our commitment to the beliefs but also will cease to accord them any real meaning: "not only the grounds of the opinion are forgotten in the absence of discussion, but too often the meaning of the opinion itself."[10] Consider an example: It is common for people in the United States to attack policies by saying, "But that would be socialism!" When I have students make this charge in discussions in my political philosophy classes, my first response is always, "What is socialism?" In most cases, students are stymied by the question or they equate socialism with communism. Before we can have real debates about a social policy, we need to understand the labels we attach to various policies, and then be ready to discuss why correct application of such a label is to count as an objection to a policy. Reducing morality and social policy to slogans entrenches our inability to think about these issues and to debate them with others, as I think most people, no matter their position on the political spectrum, would agree is evidenced by recent presidential politics.

Getting Prepared

My case studies are, with one notable exception, of slaveholders and Nazis. These people found themselves living in the midst of some of the most evil institutions ever created by human beings: African bondage in the American South and organized genocide of the Jews and others during the period of the Third Reich in Germany. In these sorts of situations, some people are perpetrators and some people are victims (and some may be both[11]). Of course, there are those, such as the Edward Coles, who resist the evil with which they are confronted, but for the most part, people remain passive as great evil is done by others around them. Even when I can convince myself that I would not be a perpetrator, when I read about American slavery and Nazi Germany, I find myself far from certain I would avoid being a bystander. So I try to do what I can to be the sort of person who would resist if she were to find herself in such morally demanding situations.

We all have a responsibility to prepare ourselves to, as philosopher Thomas E. Hill Jr. puts it, "make ourselves ready of mind and will to see what we must do [when faced with oppression or some other form of wrong-doing] and to follow through on our best judgment."[12] In his discussion of this responsibility, Hill identifies three duties that we each have:

- *Duty of Due Care in Moral Deliberation:* We need to be able to recognize that we are in morally dangerous situations—situations that require us to act in some way. And we have to be ready to deliberate about those situations, applying our more general beliefs to the situation, locating pertinent facts of both a moral and nonmoral nature.
- *Duty of Moral Self-Scrutiny:* We need to examine ourselves in order to avoid self-deception, to avoid convincing ourselves that our bad reasons for passivity are actually good reasons, that is, to avoid falling into the trap that Jefferson seems to have by the time he received the letter from Coles.
- *Duty to Develop Moral Virtue:* Of course, moral deliberation and self-scrutiny mean very little if we do not have the character to act on our moral commitments, so we need to become the sorts of people who take action when, after deliberation, we decide it is called for (or refrain from acting when we decide action would we wrong). We need to reflect

upon our emotions and the effect that those emotions have upon our beliefs and actions.[13]

The chapters that follow show how a study of moral philosophy can aid us in carrying out the first two duties of preparation that Hill identifies: the duty of due care in moral deliberation and the duty of moral self-scrutiny. Of course, we also need to have the character to act on our considered convictions, and I return in chapter 7 to reconsider that duty. For most of this book, however, I focus on how moral philosophy can help us arrive at those considered convictions and help ensure that we are being sincere in our commitments.

Moral Beliefs and Moral Reasoning

This book is about how philosophical thinking can aid us in our moral reasoning. But what is *moral* reasoning? Moral reasoning occurs when we attempt to support or undermine a particular moral claim or belief, that is, it is the process of finding reasons for or against the moral beliefs that we hold, that others hold, or that we are considering holding. Moral reasoning involves constructing arguments for or against our moral beliefs or evaluating arguments that others offer for or against particular moral beliefs. In the end, then, the goal of moral reasoning is to arrive at well-supported and well-defended moral beliefs.

What distinguishes our *moral* beliefs from our *nonmoral* beliefs? Importantly, moral reasoning involves both moral and nonmoral beliefs. Consider some reasons one might offer to undermine the moral legitimacy of the enslavement of Africans: persons of African descent are not incapable of taking care of themselves and their children; the enslaved endure great emotional and physical pain under the institution of slavery; all persons have a right to the fruits of their own labor; the world would be better overall without slavery; slavery breeds vices of character in the oppressors; people are not property that can be owned; race is not a morally relevant feature of persons. All these claims might figure as premises in an argument with the conclusion that slavery is morally wrong, but not all of them are moral claims. Most would be inclined to say that the first two are nonmoral claims, while the rest are moral claims. But why are we inclined to say this?

Moral philosophers spend a great deal of time analyzing what we take to be paradigmatic moral concepts: right and wrong, good and bad, virtuous and vicious, duty, obligation, and ought, to name the most obvious candidates.[14] Philosophers have widely varying views about how we are to understand these concepts and how the concepts relate to each other. We will see, for example, in later chapters that there are many proposed analyses of claims of the form "Slavery is morally wrong." However, for now, we have to begin from a shared set of paradigmatic concepts we take to be moral and the presence of which marks a claim or belief as moral.

But we all know that many words in English (and other languages) have more than one meaning or use. Banks can be places to deposit one's money, but banks may also be places where sandbags need to be placed to prevent flooding. If one fails to clean the litter box for several days, it will be stinky, but one can also do a really stinky job of cleaning the litter box. So when I suggest that good and bad are moral concepts, we need to immediately qualify that statement, because clearly there are some uses of the words *good* and *bad* that do not mark a statement containing them as a moral statement. Consider: Hitler was *good* at stirring up the German people with his speeches. The American Kennel Club holds that a *good* Shiba Inu has upright ears. Bleach is *good* for getting out blood stains. These claims that use *good* are not moral claims, and so belief in them would not be moral belief. The first and third claims—the ones about Hitler and bleach—are evaluations about means to ends: Hitler had abilities that allowed him to achieve a goal of riling people up, and bleach has properties that make it an effective stain remover. The second claim about dogs is a claim about what certain standards created by a group of people—in this case, standards set by the AKC—require.

But someone might say at this point, "Aren't moral claims about good really just claims about whether some person (Edward Coles), action (Coles's freeing of his slaves), or event (the abolition of slavery) is effective for achieving some goal or meets some standards set by, say, society or God?" Certainly some philosophers would answer yes to this question. I cannot here offer any definitive account of the moral without developing a complete theory of the nature of moral concepts and moral properties, and that would be an entirely different book. So all I can do is hope that my readers are in the same ballpark with me with respect to our shared paradigms of moral concepts and, thus, of moral claims or statements, that is, those which are such that when one believes them, one thereby has a moral belief.

Further, we probably have a shared conception of what morality, and thus moral concepts, are all about. Surely, morality has something to do with people and maybe nonhuman animals suffering or flourishing—that is, moral action and persons promote flourishing, immoral action and persons promote suffering or hinder flourishing. Morality has to do with people getting along; it somehow greases the wheels of social interaction in the "appropriate" manner. In some way, morality places constraints on an unbridled pursuit of our own pleasure and gain. This is all quite vague, but again, it puts some markers around our ballpark as we attempt to understand the nature of morality in a more precise, more philosophical way.

We all know that when we deliberate or argue about moral issues, we inevitably appeal to some nonmoral claims. Consider the following moral questions: Is abortion morally wrong? Are we obligated to care for our parents if they can no longer take care of themselves? Is it morally wrong to raise animals for human consumption? Do I have an obligation to loan money to a friend when she needs it? In attempting to answer those questions, we might find ourselves confronting some more questions: Has God endowed the fetus with a soul at the moment of conception? Do animals fear death? Did we consent to care for our parents or our friends by remaining in a certain type of relationship with them? So, moral reasoning will almost always involve evaluation of some nonmoral claims and will likewise involve thinking about what the relationship is between those nonmoral claims and various moral claims. If animals fear death, is that a reason to accept that killing them for food is wrong? If a fetus has a soul from the moment of conception, is it wrong to abort a fetus at any stage of development? Trying to figure out how nonmoral claims support or fail to support a particular moral claim is a major, and very difficult, part of moral reasoning.

There is no getting around the fact that moral reasoning is a complex matter—even figuring out what moral reasoning *is* is difficult! But as I've said, part of what I hope to do is to show how much more complex matters are than you might have thought. Philosophy has a way of humbling us, and in a divided society where debate can quickly become inflamed and acrimonious, such humility might very well have some "good" effects.

Bringing Together Theory and People

How does moral reasoning work? How can we justify our moral beliefs? How can we make ourselves into the appropriate sort of moral deliberators and moral actors? By examining throughout the book more examples, such as that of Jefferson and Coles, I hope to answer these questions. Both moral theory and real-life case studies will show us the importance of philosophical thinking for both moral deliberation and moral education.

I certainly hope that using detailed historical cases will make the discussion of ethical issues more lively and engaging but that is not my primary aim in using the cases. Philosophers have frequent recourse to what are known as "thought experiments," which are scenarios devised by the philosopher in order to illustrate a philosophical issue or to test a philosophical theory. Consider the following oft-used thought experiment:

> You are a transplant surgeon who has five patients in need of new organs: two need kidneys, one needs a heart, and two need lungs. These patients are running out of time: they need organs within the next couple of days or they will die. Lo and behold, you have a patient who has lovely kidneys, lungs, and heart, and who is, miraculously, a perfect match for all five of your patients who need a transplant. You can harvest the one's organs and save the lives of five, and you have the means to do this such that no one will be the wiser about how it was all accomplished. Ought you kill the one in order to save the five?

This thought experiment is used to ask questions about when or if it is permissible to kill in order to save a greater number. Of course, there are real-life cases that force people to confront this question, most obviously in warfare. But philosophers use the simpler case to focus attention on the relevant features with which they are concerned. Even some philosophers complain about these thought experiments, however, claiming that they are too divorced from real life to provide any insight on how we ought to behave, about what is right or wrong, or about how a virtuous person would act.

I think that the use of thought experiments is important for philosophical thinking about morality, and as I will argue in later chapters, thought experiments can be a valuable tool in moral education and deliberation. My real-life historical narratives serve as detailed thought experiments that allow us to put ourselves, through empathetic imagining, into situations of moral crisis. I think that their reality can do more to impress upon us the urgency of moral thinking than the simpler, merely hypothetical cases can. But I also hope that these narratives will demonstrate how philosophy, including its use of thought experiments—real or otherwise—can provide a corrective to the sort of thinking that often results in moral errors in both thought and action. The real-life examples show people making these sorts of errors and the sorts of actions (or inactions) to which those errors led. These narratives bring to life how important it is to know how to think about morality and to make ourselves the sort of people who are in the habit of thinking about morality. They reveal what can happen if we do not fulfill our duties of due care in moral deliberation and of moral self-scrutiny, and thus, I hope, show the importance of moral philosophy, insofar as I am successful in arguing that moral philosophy can aid us in fulfilling those duties.

Our Cast of Characters

I begin in chapter 2 with detailed expositions of my primary case studies. My case studies involve three Nazis, two slaveholders (including Thomas Jefferson who we have already discussed and who will not be discussed in chapter 2), and one psychopathic serial killer. The trio of Nazis consists of Albert Speer, Franz Stangl, and Rudolph Höss. Albert Speer was initially Hitler's architect and later his minister of armaments. Speer, we will see, was extraordinarily narrow-minded, not in the sense that he was intolerant of difference (although he was probably that as well) but in the sense that he was a person who thought only about a very narrow range of topics and rarely considered their moral significance. Did Speer know about the Final Solution? This is the question that has stood at the center of any discussion of Speer—ever since his memoir *Inside the Third Reich* was published. Speer himself spent a great amount of energy establishing, both to himself and to the public at large, that he knew nothing (or, at least, nothing significant or detailed) about the extermination of the Jews, and his need to establish his ignorance on this point becomes evident in his interviews with Gitta Sereny. I am certainly not going to try to resolve the question of what Speer knew, because not only am I as a philosopher and not an historian, not qualified to do so; but also because I think there is a more important question about Speer's character: Did he allow himself to develop any *moral* beliefs about a policy like the Final Solution, if only considered hypothetically? Given the anti-Semitism of the circles in which he moved, it seems that he should have considered the morality of various policies, and such consideration ought to have led him to monitor what was actually happening. If Speer did not know what was happening, that may be in part due to his unwillingness to think hard about moral questions, not the other way around. Unwillingness to canvass hypothetical possibilities, I will argue, poses a serious danger of not being able to see the facts that actually obtain. And consideration of hypotheticals is one of the tasks that philosophical training forces us to do.

My two other Nazi case studies were both commandants of Nazi concentration and/or extermination camps: Franz Stangl, commandant of Treblinka death camp, and Rudolf Höss, commandant of Auschwitz, the latter of which was composed of many subcamps, some devoted to labor and some solely to the killing of Jews, Gypsies, and other persons who were undesirable from the Nazi perspective. Stangl escaped to South America after the Second World War, but was eventually returned to West Germany where he stood trial for war crimes. He was sentenced to life imprisonment, and while in prison and just before his death, he participated in extensive interviews with Gitta Sereny, the same woman to whom we owe the interviews with Speer. Höss was captured at the war's end, and was eventually executed by hanging in front of the Auschwitz killing and cremation installation. While awaiting trial in a Polish prison, he composed his memoirs, describing his life before Auschwitz, as well as his work as death and labor camp commandant.

Stangl and Höss present very different pictures of themselves as men and as Nazis. While Stangl tries mightily to excuse and explain his actions in overseeing the deaths of approximately one million men, women, and children, Höss does nothing to attempt to get his audience to sympathize with him. Höss makes it clear that he accepted the Nazi worldview and accepted his work as a necessary part of the cleansing of greater Germany of foreign, infectious elements. Stangl tries to deny any kind of anti-Semitism and insists that he had no options but to do the work assigned to him by his superiors in the Nazi chain of command. Stangl will provide us with some striking parallels to Jefferson: both seem to have been self-deceived and to have artificially limited the options available to them. Höss, in contrast, presents a perhaps more straightforward picture of a man with false beliefs, both moral and nonmoral, that allowed him to engage in morally horrible endeavors with very little inner stress or strain.

In discussing Stangl and Höss, I think that it is essential to describe in some detail the reality of what these men encountered on an almost daily basis over the course of many months. I have mentioned that much of the excusing of Jefferson that we Americans encounter takes place against a background of sketchy accounts of American slavery. It is much easier to accept certain accounts of what was going on with Jefferson if we have a bland, almost picturesque image of slavery lurking in the backs of our minds. Once we bring to life the real horror of the institution, these explanations seem less compelling. Similar things can be said about the perpetrators of the Holocaust, particularly of those men who were not among the so-called desk murderers, such as Adolf Eichmann,[15] but were on the ground doing the daily work of genocide. Trying to comprehend cognitively what men like Stangl and Höss experienced will call forth certain emotions, and if we in our cozy and secure circumstances feel those emotions, what could we expect those men to feel? If they lacked those feelings, what does that say about them? Does it provide a clue to their failing to have moral knowledge?

I have already introduced the first of the slaveholder case studies, Thomas Jefferson. The other is Charles Colcock Jones, an antebellum American slaveholder who became known as "the missionary to the slaves" because of his work in trying to convert his slaves and those of neighboring plantations in Georgia. Jones is not someone whom we might at first be inclined to view as evil; however, we need to keep in mind that Jones spent his whole life supporting a highly evil institution, he benefited from that institution, and he was willing to ruin the lives of his slaves when doing so suited his needs. Jones, like Jefferson, was highly educated and had extensive exposure to the antislavery position.

Why did his study of that position not convince him and alter his motivations? Again, like Jefferson, early in his life, Jones professed to view slavery as a moral wrong. If he was sincere, how did he lose that belief? Or did he retain the belief but deceive himself into thinking that he had rejected that position? Is self-deception a real possibility? What has to happen, cognitively and emotively, for self-deception about moral matters to take place? Jones, like most educated, upper-class people in the nineteenth century, left behind an extensive correspondence that provides us with access to his self-understanding or, at least, to the ways in which he wanted others to perceive him. Erskine Caldwell uses these letters in his excellent biography of Jones, *Dwelling Place*, which I will rely upon for my discussion of Jones.

At the end of chapter 2, I turn to a case study quite different from those mentioned here: Ted Bundy, the notorious serial killer responsible for the deaths of somewhere between thirty-five and forty women and girls. (Some place the actual number of victims quite a bit higher.) Many people would describe Bundy as a sociopath or a psychopath.[16] The actual meaning and extension of these concepts is highly controversial, and although I will draw on both the psychological and the philosophical literature on sociopathy and psychopathy, I will not enter into the general debate on these concepts and their applications. I simply take it for granted that the label "psychopath" does in fact apply to Bundy. I recognize that some might find this aspect of my use of Bundy problematic, because of recent work that purports to show psychopaths have different brain functioning and/or structure than do those of us who are not psychopaths. If that is the case, we might wonder what we, with normal brain structures and/or functioning, can possibly learn from an aberration such as Bundy.

It is most likely true that Bundy and other psychopaths are born with certain types of incapacities that mark them as different from the rest of us, and it is also likely that these incapacities have some sort of physical basis in their brains, just as our "normal" capacities likely have some such physical basis. But I do not think that this means that we have nothing to learn from people like Bundy. Whatever deficiencies in thought and emotion characterized Bundy may also characterize "normal" human beings, even if the causal story about why Bundy had those deficiencies will be different from the story about why, for example, Stangl or Speer had those deficiencies. Even if one has the ability to think and feel in certain ways, it is still possible that one can lose or inhibit those abilities. Further, these capacities, such as empathetic engagement, occur on a continuum, so that we can make choices or perform actions that will lead to the weakening of our capacities. So, Bundy provides us with something of a barometer, an extreme case of a human being who, perhaps, couldn't help but be morally deficient, but who acts as a warning for those of us who could be morally deficient and provides us with insight about how to avoid such a fate.

Bundy, I think, failed to have moral beliefs not because, as with Speer, he failed to consider various moral issues but, rather, because while he seemed to be able, in some sense, to use moral terms, it is not at all clear he possessed the moral concepts. Bundy, I will argue, stands with regard to moral concepts in much the same way that most of us stand with regard to the concepts of quantum physics: we can construct sentences and assert claims such as "quarks are among the fundamental building blocks of matter" without much real sense of what a quark is or how objects such as cellphones, chairs, cats, and human beings are, or even could be, made up of quarks and other such particles.

If we are to engage in moral deliberation in a reasonable way, surely we need to understand the concepts involved in the claims we make. Understanding our moral commitments and making sure they are coherent and justified demands that we critically examine the concepts we are employing. We can learn from Bundy's conceptual handicaps precisely why we need to avoid thoughtless adherence to "beliefs" that we are unable to explain or justify if we are ever pressed to do so. We need to make sure we are not just mouthing words when we use the moral terms, and that we can attach meanings to those terms in a coherent and reasoned manner.

In my discussion of Bundy I have relied on the interviews that Hugh Aynesworth and Stephen G. Michaud conducted with Bundy while the latter was on death row in Florida. In fact, I have tried to use case studies of persons for whom we have some kind of first-person evidence, whether in the form of interviews, correspondence, or memoirs. It is important to try to get inside the minds of these persons, to try to understand how they understood themselves, either at the time of their engagement with evil or in looking back at such engagement. No doubt, these first-person narratives need to be taken with at least several grains of salt, but they provide information that no purely third-person narrative could. In the case of Bundy, we need to have examples of his own attempts to use moral language in order to sort out whether he possessed moral concepts, and if not, to what that lack was due. The way Bundy presents himself to his interviewers is significant precisely because we can be sure he is trying to put himself in the best light possible—part of what is disturbing about Bundy is what he takes to be a positive presentation of himself and of his actions and thoughts.

The case studies of chapter 2 then provide entry into the more theoretical discussions of chapters 3 through 7. As I said earlier, each chapter addresses a particular complicating factor or factors in moral deliberation: cultural norms (chapter 3), the role of consequences and probabilities (chapter 4), emotional responses (chapter 5), and self-deception of various sorts (chapter 6). In chapter 7, I return to Thomas Jefferson in order to bring all the various strands of the argument together, so as to state clearly my case for the importance of moral philosophy in moral deliberation.

As I argue for the importance of moral philosophy to moral education, one point I will stress is that philosophy is one of the best tools for self-examination and thus for self-knowledge that we have available to us. Philosophy forces us to confront the question, "But what do I really mean when I say that?" It forces us to think about the implications of our beliefs, thereby helping us to consider what we can really commit ourselves to. As mentioned, philosophers routinely employ thought experiments in order to test their theories; in so doing, we force ourselves and our readers to think about the entire range of possibilities, to open our minds to options that, when considered, often lead to a new understanding of the familiar and the routine. This sort of self-examination is not encountered in works labeled "self-help," where the end result is supposed to be some type of self-affirmation. Philosophical thinking can be uncomfortable, disconcerting, and even downright painful; after all, we might come to the conclusion that we are falling far short of moral virtue or perhaps that we don't even know what is involved in being virtuous. Philosophers seek truth, so moral philosophers seek moral truth, and perhaps the most important moral truths we will discover are those about our own characters and actions. That we might not like what we find is all the more reason to see the project as the most important one we will ever engage in.

Part of my intention in including real-life case studies is to show not only that moral theorizing is important to our actual lives but also to make it clear that moral philosophy is not dull and that engaging in it is not an odious intellectual chore. Examining how we ought to live is, as Socrates pointed out millennia ago, our most important task, but it is also a fascinating one, given that it allows us to consider our lives as a whole

and to place them in a larger context. Coming to understand ourselves can be painful, but it can also lead to a sense of living a
life guided by values that one fully endorses and for which one
can offer reasoned arguments. That sense provides an important
consciousness of purpose and meaning in lives that are rapidly
being swamped by technology, unstable and stressful work, a
chaotic political scene that seems to put our fates in the hands
of untrustworthy people, and petty routine demands that we
feel forced upon us. Having at least some understanding of what
our considered goals are and how to reach them in a rational and
morally acceptable way provides a stable core for lives inevitably
affected by so much that is out of our control. That is not to say
that doing philosophy will make us happy, but it can help us understand whether we are in fact happy and, if not, how to understand that unhappiness.

We begin our philosophical task of self-understanding
in chapter 2, with an examination of some very bad moral
deliberators and actors, who provide us with cautionary
examples. As you read the chapter, it is important not to pull
back from identifying with some features of those bad and perhaps even evil people. Part of what I hope to show is that moral
failings tend to take similar forms, so we need to be prepared to
encounter ourselves in the worst of our kind. Then we can use
whatever lessons we learn to strive to be better.

2

Just the Bad and the Ugly

Popular culture tends to present us with demonic and one-dimensional images of evil people. Hannibal Lecter, as played by Anthony Hopkins in the film *The Silence of the Lambs*, is the stereotypical psychopath: brilliant, entirely devoid of any human feeling, manipulative, and obsessively engaged in horrific acts of murder and cannibalism. The assassin in *No Country For Old Men*, portrayed by Javier Bardem, appears almost robotic and yet superhuman, defying all the devoted adherents of justice who pursue him. *Schindler's List* focuses its images of the horror of the Holocaust on Ralph Fiennes's camp commandant Amon Goertz, who amuses himself by shooting out his window at camp inmates.

Precisely because they are so one-dimensional with little to no understandable or familiar motivation for their heinous acts, we are reassured: evil is something embodied in aberrant human monsters, so obviously different from us that we need have no fear of descending to such a morally low level. Reality, however, is not as reassuring. Not all people who exhibit what are considered to be the hallmarks of psychopathy are homicidal maniacs; some experts claim that they can be found in all walks of life, while others claim that psychopaths just hold exaggerated

Them

versions of mainstream value systems.[1] Actual Nazis came from many sectors of society, and on careful study they often seem frighteningly normal or ordinary to us.[2] We are forced to wonder whether the only thing that keeps us from the evil of genocide or slaveholding is the good fortune of being born into circumstances in which such policies and institutions are frowned upon and punished rather than encouraged or rewarded. How would each of us fare if we were tested by difficult moral choices?

These kinds of issues raise the specter of what philosophers have come to call, following philosophers Bernard Williams and Thomas Nagel, "moral luck."[3] It seems plausible to most of us to assume that our worth as moral agents must be something that is under our control: if we are to be praised or blamed for the kinds of persons we are, it seems that it must be up to us what kinds of people we have become. But our circumstances are often beyond our control, so it seems to follow that difference in circumstances cannot be a factor in any assessment of our virtue or vice. So if I would have acted as Franz Stangl did were I in his circumstances, then I am just as bad as he is, or, put another way, Stangl—a man who oversaw the deaths of roughly one million innocent people—is no worse than I am morally.

In what follows I am not going to address the issue of moral luck directly. I do think, however, that it is important to see in the following cases that the errors of moral thought and/or emotion that lay behind the horrors are ones we all might make and often do make, without the misfortune of living in Nazi Germany or the antebellum American South. When we caricature evil, we inadvertently provide ourselves with a kind of comfort: see, we say to ourselves, I am not like *that*, so I am a good person. But moral virtue and vice are not all-or-nothing matters, and sometimes our moral flaws remain hidden until the time when we are tested. So we cannot wait for the crisis to strike before we straighten out our ways of moral deliberation; when the crisis comes, we need to be able to recognize that a moral choice confronts us, to think clearly about that choice, and to connect our deliberations with our motivational structures. (In fact, as I discuss in chapter 5, there may be crises confronting us right now that we are simply unprepared to recognize as such.) Studying the ways in which others were unprepared or blind is a good place to start our own moral work. The following case studies, then, provide us with motivation to take seriously our duties of due care in moral deliberation and of moral self-scrutiny and to find ways to act on those duties.

"Every man need only know what is going on in his own domain"

The title for this section is taken from the signs that were posted on the walls of every office in the Nazi bureaucracy, as reported to Gitta Sereny after the war by a high-ranking Nazi.[4] These office signs reminded the occupants of General Order No. 1 issued on January 11, 1940: "no member of a government or military agency was to be informed or seek to know more about secret matters than was required for the enactment of his or her duties."[5] Nobody lived this Nazi ideal of compartmentalization better than Albert Speer.

Speer was trained as an architect, and caught Hitler's eye in that capacity. In early 1942, Speer was appointed to the important post of Minister of Armaments and War Production. There is no contesting that Speer was brilliant at his job, a master of organization and planning. Speer was able to keep the German war machine running effectively much longer than almost anyone else could have: through his role in extending the war, Speer was responsible for an immense number of deaths, on the battlefield; in concentration, labor, and death camps; and among civilians.

Speer finally turned against Hitler in 1945, only because he could not comply with Hitler's orders to destroy infrastructure in Germany and various occupied countries: his final resistance had nothing to do with Hitler's policies of genocide, mass murder, and slavery.

The central questions in studies of Speer and in Speer's own work have been: What did Speer know about the genocide of the Jews, and when did he know it? Speer always insisted that he did not know what was happening at places such as Treblinka and Bergen-Belsen, although he also admitted to having had the means to attain such knowledge if he had cared to acquire it.[6] I am not interested in questioning Speer's denials or in trying to place him where he claimed he wasn't. However, it does seem likely that Speer avoided forming any moral beliefs about the atrocities being committed by the Third Reich. Whatever more general moral beliefs Speer might have had, such as "it is wrong to kill innocent children," don't seem to have been applied to the genocide occurring around him. Speer seems to have grasped moral concepts and had some moral beliefs, but he failed to form such beliefs about Hitler's treatment of the Jews. But how could he have avoided doing so? I will suggest that Speer managed by (i) evading knowledge about nonmoral matters with moral import[7], (ii) diverting his attention to avoid appreciating the import of what he did come to know, and (iii) shutting off imagination and feeling in ways that blocked the employment of his moral capacities.

Speer himself, in his memoirs, reported a meeting with Karl Hanke, Gauleiter of Upper Selisia, in which Hanke told Speer never to go to a certain camp in Upper Silesia:

He [Hanke] had seen something there which he was not permitted to describe and moreover could not describe. I did not query him. I did not query Himmler, I did not query Hitler,

> I did not speak with personal friends. I did not investigate—for I did not want to know what was happening there. Hanke must have been speaking of Auschwitz. . . . From that moment on, I was inescapably contaminated morally; from fear of discovering something which might have made me turn from my course, I had closed my eyes.[8]

Here Speer comes within the vicinity of knowing what is happening to the Jews. He is told by a reliable source whom he trusts that terrible things are happening at a camp in Poland. Given his position, he could most likely have fabricated a need to go to Auschwitz and thus have seen first-hand what was happening. Or he could have asked, as he points out, Himmler or Hitler (or any number of other members of the SS) what was being done in Upper Silesia. He could have talked with friends about the proper course of action. But Speer had projects in place concerning war production, and carrying out these projects was essential to maintaining his power and position. Further, if he learned about terrible things happening at the command of Hitler, he would have had to question his unthinking loyalty and devotion to Hitler, and thereby question his career and his life's direction and very purpose.[9] So Speer decided not to know, and he evaded knowledge by failing to gather evidence that would have forced him to have beliefs about what was happening in the Third Reich.

After the Nuremberg Trials of Nazi war criminals, Speer spent twenty years in prison. During that time he sought the help of Georges Casalis, a French Protestant minister who tended to the spiritual needs of the Nazis who drew prison sentences rather than death penalties. Speer understood Casalis as introducing him to modes of thought—introspection, abstraction—that were new to him.[10] Casalis described Speer as wanting to learn: "Not facts, but learn to expand his thinking into realms he had not yet entered."[11] These comments from Casalis and Speer point to both as understanding Speer previously having utilized his intellectual talents in an extremely narrow-minded way: he had goals, and he set out to achieve those goals, thinking of everything in terms of contributing to or hindering success in that achievement. Speer supports this interpretation in his comments about his reaction to Hanke's warning regarding Auschwitz: thinking about what was happening would only distract him and make him question his goals, neither of which would aid in their realization. So he just wouldn't think about it or attempt to acquire any information that would force thought.

Of course, the Nazi regime was designed to encourage this kind of narrow focus, as evidenced by the signs on the walls and by General Order No. 1. Speer's descriptions of himself suggest that he was a walking embodiment of what the Nazis wanted to achieve at the institutional level: just as various departments attended only to their own tasks and prevented anyone else from finding out the nature of said tasks, so Speer's mind focused on production goals, pushing to the shadowy limits any inquiry into the justification or questioning of those goals. Annemarie Kempf, Speer's personal secretary, when talking of Speer's being out of the loop with respect to intra-office romances, said "there were some long-standing relationships everybody knew about. But not Speer—he couldn't have taken knowing about such things, so he just didn't. . . . In a way, I think he felt that what he didn't know didn't exist."[12]

So how did Speer, as one of the highest-ranking members of Hitler's government and as close to a friend as Hitler had, achieve this extraordinary task of avoiding thinking about what many have plausibly argued was the central objective and driving force of that government's war policies, at least after 1941? Speer simply narrowed his focus, filling his mind with his "own domain" and driving himself to exhaustion in pursuit of the goals that defined his domain. Speer wrote that "our burying ourselves in work was an unconscious effort to . . . anaesthetize our conscience."[13] Speer succeeded so well in narrowing the range of his thinking that he was able to regard the Final Solution as being "outside my competence, . . . not my business."[14] He did not consider his actions from the perspective of a moral agent but, rather, from that of a minister in Hitler's government: his self-understanding and approach to the world were completely framed by his professional role. This explains Speer's ability to exhibit unquestioning deference to Hitler as an authority: he was professionally subordinate to Hitler, so he could cede his judgment to Hitler. For example, he said of his attitude toward Hitler's murder of Rohm, "I suspect all I would have thought, if I thought at all, was that as Hitler was doing it, it had to be right."[15]

But Speer's own domain was saturated with elements of the Final Solution; after all, Speer's war machine depended for its functioning on the use of slave labor involving Jews from all parts of the Reich and POWs, especially those of Russian and Polish (i.e., "Eastern," or, in Nazi eyes, "inferior") origin. For example, in 1941, Speer was in charge of mobilizing housing for Berlin residents rendered homeless by Allied bombing raids. Lo and behold, 1,000 "Jewish flats" were somehow available. (Speer himself used this phrase to describe the housing in a memo dated January 20, 1941.) Surely he must have asked himself how these flats had become available. But, Annemarie Kempf says,

> I don't think he would ever have realized that there *was* a moral aspect to this transfer of umpteen-thousand apartments. If he had noticed it, what he would probably have done is get rid of that particular assignment as being too troublesome, potentially embarrassing. He never looked

to take on things which were likely to create problems for him. After all, . . . what he wanted was success.

However, having said that . . . I have to tell you that the drama, the tragedy behind these orders, simply never entered one's mind. It was purely an administrative matter. . . . It simply didn't occur to us [to ask why these flats were suddenly available].[16]

Speer (and Kempf) conceived of the Jewish apartments only under the description "available housing for bombed-out residents," never under the description "vacated homes of deported Jews," because the latter description would have forced questions about where these people were sent and for what purpose.

Speer evinced the same attitude toward the treatment of Russian POWs put to work at the Krupp factories in Essen. When he visited these facilities, he discovered that "the Russian workers' rations were so minimal *that they couldn't work properly*."[17] In this case, he was able to convince Hitler to provide better rations. Notice, however, that Speer's concern is not really for the Russians themselves, as he does not seem to think of them as human beings but, rather, only as tools in the production process. In fact, he describes the treatment of these workers as not "really my business:"[18] he had a subordinate to deal with keeping workers productive, but he offered help in this instance because he had Hitler's ear in a way that hardly anyone else had. But, again, once he had achieved greater production from the Russians, he thought no more about them. More significantly, the ill treatment of these workers did not cause him to raise further questions about workers in the myriad camps all over Germany and the occupied territories: if it did not have an impact on his ability to get his job done, then he simply was not interested.

When asked by Sereny where he supposed that 40,000 Jews—families, not men suited for labor—mentioned in a memo carrying his signature were being sent, Speer replied "I'm afraid I really wouldn't have cared. My mind was entirely on getting labor, on keeping production going."[19] Narrow focus, then, allowed Speer to avoid reflecting on the moral import of facts that were brought to his attention; he conceived of those facts only in relation to his goals of war production. Nonetheless, he says, "I sensed . . . that dreadful things were happening with the Jews."[20] And, cryptically, he remarks: "I was blind by choice . . . but I was not ignorant."[21] This almost paradoxical claim suggests that Speer understood himself, at least in hindsight, as having had all the relevant nonmoral information at his disposal, but that he did not appreciate that information and worked at not getting to the point of appreciating it. Speer refused to take his nonmoral knowledge and put it side by side with various general moral beliefs that he (may have) held, and so he never arrived at the moral belief that what his regime was doing to the Jews (and many others) was wrong.

Certain features of Speer's character, established well before his appointment as one of Hitler's ministers, aided him in his ability to balance on the precipice between knowledge and ignorance. Speer was a man unfamiliar with the engagement of emotions, his own or those of others. Sereny describes Speer as "virtually incapable of expressing private emotions," and as being alone even though constantly surrounded by people.[22] Speer says that there was always a "wall" between him and other people.[23] One of Speer's remarks is particularly telling, especially given that he makes this remark in the context of trying to vindicate himself:

But anyway, as far as practicing anti-Semitism or even uttering anti-Semitic remarks, my conscience is entirely clear. I really had no aversion to them, or rather, *no more than the slight discomfort all of us sometimes feel when in contact with them.*[24]

Here Speer takes for granted his affective response of "discomfort," not even reflecting, years after the war, on the import of that feeling. Speer simply had no practice at or aptitude for reflection on his own inner life. So, given the habit of seeing and speaking of Jews in this manner, he remains in that habit without its causing him to stop and question himself.

And once he took over as Minister of Armaments, Speer, as described by Kempf, had "[n]o time to feel."[25] His reconceptualization of human beings as industrial tools kept emotions at bay, thereby allowing him to be hyper-efficient. His mind stayed in the present, on the task at hand, never wandering to putting himself in the other guy's shoes.[26] Speer said, "It was as if imagination had died in me."[27] Finally, in Nuremberg, Speer had nothing to do but to sit and absorb the testimony of those who had suffered.[28] "Being myself the father of young children, I have sufficient imagination to picture myself in their place,"[29] he claimed. Unfortunately, those imaginative capacities were shut down during the war, and this allowed him to foster his natural tendency to dampen emotion.

Nazis constitute a disproportionate part of my case studies. In part this is due to my own interest in the Third Reich (although I am no historian and am thus forced to rely on the work of those who are), and in part to the overwhelming amount of literature available on the perpetrators.[30] However, there is another reason: the more we learn about the perpetrators of the Holocaust, the more we understand the diversity among these men. Speer, as we will see, was very different from both Höss and Stangl, both of whom were very different from one another. Thus, these three men provide us with a more complex case study than any one of them alone could provide. As we will see, a variety of kinds of moral epistemic failures all conspired to produce one of the most horrific events in human history.

"[M]y professional ethos was that if something wrong was going on, it had to be found out"

The quotation heading this section comes from Franz Stangl, commandant of the Nazi death camp Treblinka, made in a series of interviews with Gitta Sereny in 1971 while he was serving a life sentence in a West German prison. How could a man who had overseen the deaths of roughly one million innocent men, women, and children claim, with a straight face, that he was someone who had to ferret out and confront wrong-doing—that doing that was just part of his job?

In this section I examine the moral thinking of Stangl and of Rudolf Höss, commandant of the Auschwitz-Birkenau camp complex. (The latter wrote his memoirs while in a Polish prison prior to his execution by hanging.) Although Stangl and Höss were clearly very different in many ways, they reveal striking similarities in their attempts to justify or excuse their conduct as overseers of genocide and slavery. (We will also see some similarities to Speer, which forces us to wonder what Speer would have done if he had been in the position of either Höss or Stangl.) Although Höss's anti-Semitism was more overt and virulent than that of Stangl, both men were dedicated to and focused on their jobs and careers, refused or were unable to experience either empathy or sympathy for their Jewish victims, had an almost absurd conception of duty, and narrowed the scope of their own moral responsibility to a very small range of conduct.

Stangl said that before the Nazis took control of Austria, he really wasn't very interested in them at all, unless they impacted his job in some way. His job in 1930s Austria was that of a police officer. By 1942, he still considered himself a police officer, but instead of being a member of the Austrian civil service, he now had a position within the hierarchy of the SS. He had initially been assigned to one of the Nazi euthanasia institutes,[31] but when that project was shut down in response to public protest, he was transferred to Sobibor and then to Treblinka, both in occupied Poland. The only function of both camps was murder: these were death camps, not labor or concentration camps. Out of each transport of Jews, only a handful might be kept alive, at least temporarily, as "work-Jews," to assist in sorting valuables and disposing of bodies after gassing. But Stangl clung to his identity, insisting that he told his superior, with respect to his acceptance of the command of Treblinka: "I would be carrying out this *assignment* as a police officer under his command."[32] And carry it out he did, supervising in the space of less than a year the murder of roughly one million men, women, and children (estimates of the numbers actually killed varies). He received recognition by his superiors as "the best camp commander in Poland" because, as he said, "Everything I did out of my own free will . . . I had to do as well as I could. That is how I am."[33]

This kind of focus on work is something that we have already seen with Speer. But this focus played a different role in Stangl's moral outlook and character than it did in Speer's. For Speer, as we saw, work was a way of diverting his attention away from questions that would have forced him to form beliefs about matters with moral import. But Stangl, given his position as commandant of a death camp, could not, short of outright insanity, avoid knowledge of what was happening to the Jews. So his focus on doing his job *as a police officer*

as well as he could allowed him to justify to himself his own
actions:

> What I had to do, while I continued my efforts to get
> out, was to limit my own actions to what I—in my own
> conscience—could answer for. At police training school they
> taught us . . . that the definition of a crime must meet four
> requirements: there has to be a subject, an object, an action
> and intent. If any of these four elements are missing, then
> we are not dealing with a punishable offence. . . . [I]f the
> "subject" was the government, the "object" the Jews, and
> the "action" the gassings, then I could tell myself that for me
> the fourth element, "intent" . . . was missing.[34]

Stangl insists that because protocol was being violated in the
handling of the valuables of those deported to the camps, that
tending to the handling of these valuables "had become a legitimate police activity," and he was able to separate that from the
gassings because his "specific assignment from the start had
been the responsibility for these effects."[35]

There are striking points throughout Sereny's interviews with
Stangl that speak to a kind of blankness in Stangl's mind that
we would expect to be filled with a consideration of the point
of view of the people whom he was systematically murdering.
For example, Stangl became notorious for overseeing the arrival
and disposal of transports while wearing white riding clothes,
adding a macabre and surreal element to the terror and confusion of those events. When Sereny asks him about his choice of
clothing, Stangl merely replies, "It was hot." How such clothing
would appear to the arriving prisoners remained something
that he simply didn't consider. Of course, one wouldn't attempt
to imagine oneself from the perspective of what one viewed as
"cargo," as Stangl admitted to regarding the Jews. (He reveals this

after telling Sereny that the one time he thought of Treblinka after the war was when his train pulled up next to the lot of a slaughterhouse—the cattle's eyes, he said, looked exactly like those of the Jews being herded toward the gas chambers.[36])

One episode, in particular, I believe, is emblematic of Stangl's lack of empathy with the Jews in the camp. Stangl begins by saying that he enjoyed "friendly relations" with the work-Jews, and that he really enjoyed these sorts of "human relations." One of these work-Jews, Blau, had, along with his wife, been given a privileged assignment. The following episode involving Blau is so striking that I relate it in full:

> There was one day when he knocked at the door of my office about mid-morning and stood to attention and asked permission to speak to me. He looked very worried. I said, "Of course, Blau, come on in. What's worrying you?" He said it was his eighty-year-old father; he'd arrived on that morning's transport. Was there anything I could do. I said, "Really, Blau, you must understand, it's impossible. A man of eighty. . . . " He said quickly that yes, he understood, of course. But could he ask me for permission to take his father to the *Lazarett* [a fake hospital where elderly or ill arrivals were shot] rather than the gas chambers. And could he take his father first to the kitchen and give him a meal. I said, "You go and do what you think best, Blau. Officially I don't know anything, but unofficially you can tell the Kapo I said it was all right." In the afternoon, when I came back to my office, he was waiting for me. He had tears in his eyes. He stood to attention and said, "Herr Hauptsturmführer, I want to thank you. I gave my father a meal. And I've just taken him to the *Lazarett*—it's all over. Thank you very much." I said, "Well, Blau, there's no need to thank me, but of course if you *want* to thank me, you may."[37]

Following this narration, Sereny asks Stangl what happened to Blau, to which Stangl replies "I don't know."

This incident is almost overwhelming in how obtuse it reveals Stangl to be. The situation in which Blau finds himself is one that is hard to conceive of as even bearable: seeing one's elderly father at a death camp, knowing that the best one can secure for him is a last meal and a bullet instead of a forced run to the gas chamber. Helplessness, hatred, desperation, despair: the sickening grief and confusion inevitably experienced by Blau is nowhere in Stangl's narration—he actually intends this little story to be taken as a sign of his kindness and "friendly relations" with one of the work-Jews. But if one had any sense of fellow-feeling with Blau, one would have to be driven to despair if one really believed that this was the best that one could do for another human being.

But we know perfectly well that Stangl could have done better—he was the most powerful man in Treblinka. He seems to be saying that work-Jews cannot be elderly: that's a rule and there is nothing that he can do about it. This rule-bound way of thinking comes out even more clearly in another episode that would be darkly comical if it were fiction rather than history. Stangl relates an incident in which a Jew just off the transport to Treblinka makes a complaint to him: a guard had promised the Jew some water in exchange for a gold watch. Not surprisingly, the guard took the watch but did not give the Jew any water. Stangl says,

Well, that wasn't right, was it? Anyway, I didn't permit pilfering. I asked the Lithuanians then and there who it was who had taken the watch, but nobody came forward. Franz [Stangl's second-in-command] . . . whispered to me that the man involved could be one of the Lithuanian officers . . . and that I couldn't embarrass an officer in front of his men.

Well, I said, "I am not interested what sort of uniform a man wears. I am only interested in what is inside a man." Don't think *that* didn't get back to Warsaw in a hurry. But what's right is right, isn't it? . . . Once a complaint is made it has to be investigated.[38]

When Sereny asks him what happened to the man who complained in the first place, Stangl replies "I don't know." Of course, this is an odd story for Stangl to relate, given that his whole attempt to excuse his actions is an appeal to his fear of superiors. But he is willing to face their disapproval in order to enforce the rules. What is even more absurd is that the Jew's next stop is the undressing barracks where all of his possessions, including any gold watch that he might have had, would have been stolen from him. But, of course, the theft would have been in accordance with the rules, and so it is no theft at all in Stangl's eyes. Both this story and the one involving Blau reveal to us that neither of the Jews is any concern of Stangl's: he claims not to know what happened to them. The point of these stories is to build up Stangl himself, both in our eyes and in his own. In attempting to do this, he inadvertently reveals his complete lack of compassion and empathy.

While Stangl himself insists that he resorted to "compartmentalizing" his thought in order to continue to live while doing his job in Treblinka,[39] there are clues that Stangl's approach to the world, developed long before his arrival at the death camps, made it extraordinarily easy for him to compartmentalize (if he really had to do it at all). When Sereny asks him whether, during his time at the euthanasia institute, he ever considered "what if this were happening to my loved one," he just replies, "they told us immediately that there were four groups who were exempt," and one of those groups was "relatives of Euthanasia Aktion staff."[40] Later, when Sereny asks him what he would have done or felt if he had been assigned to carry out the gassings, he responds, "I wasn't. . . . That was done by two Russians."[41] Imagination was clearly not Stangl's strong suit.

These two exchanges between Sereny and Stangl have parallel structures: Sereny asks Stangl to consider a hypothetical situation, and he responds with a denial that the hypothetical was the actual situation. Of course, his response is no response at all: the whole point of a hypothetical is the consideration of an alternative possibility that may or may not have been or ever be actualized. Stangl reveals that he simply did not let his thinking range beyond the actual. Of course, if one does not think beyond particular actual situations, one will easily miss the significance of those actual situations. By refusing to consider himself in the position of relatives of those "euthanized" or of those assigned to carry out the actual gassings, he refuses to think about the feelings and conflicts of those who are in those positions. Stangl's focus is very narrow, indeed.

This inability or unwillingness to entertain hypotheticals is intimately related to Stangl's narrow conception of the alternative courses of action open to him. After receiving an order to kill Jews at work constructing Sobibor if they do not work quickly enough, Stangl heads off to see his superior. The latter instructs Stangl to just go back to his task at Sobibor. Stangl concludes, "What else could I do?"[42] He says that all he could try to do was to get a transfer: until that came through, he just went on with "construction work" to complete a death camp. When Sereny finally asks him why he did not stand up and protest, he replies, "If I had sacrificed myself . . . if I had made public what I felt, and had died, . . . it would have made no difference. Not an iota. It would all have gone on just the same, as if it and I had never happened."[43] So we are supposed to be led to believe that all Stangl could hope for was to get as far away from Sobibor and Treblinka as he could.

Of course, what Stangl was aiming for was a transfer, possibly to a unit involved in fighting partisan guerillas. So his protest of horror at what was happening in the Polish death camps is feeble, at best: the option he prefers is to fight for the regime engaged in the genocide, but at a safe distance from the day-to-day operations of mass murder.[44] Once again, we are hard pressed to find, in Stangl's inner life, any real signs of concern for the Jews. After all, alternatives involving helping the victims or undermining the regime are not in his array of possibilities. He insists that if he had publicly protested, nothing would have changed. But there is no suggestion that he really thought of various alternative ways of resisting and aiding. Imagination is required to contemplate alternatives and hypotheticals, and if Stangl had imagination, he certainly did not exercise it.

Narrowness of thought is a theme that runs through all our Nazi case studies. At the conclusion of his memoirs, Rudolph Höss issues a *mea culpa*: "I have never personally mistreated a prisoner, or even killed one. I have also never tolerated mistreatment on the part of my subordinates."[45] This is a statement made by the man who was in charge of Auschwitz, a camp to which around 1.3 million people were deported, of whom 1.1 million were murdered. How could he attempt to absolve himself with such a claim?

Höss took his focus on work even further than Stangl did, saying "I saw only *my work, my duty*. All human feelings were pushed aside by this."[46] So Höss simply identified work with what he ought to do. And so work, his job, became his only perspective on the world,[47] allowing him to evaluate all means in relation to the ends set by his superiors without ever questioning the nature of the ends themselves. This approach came quite naturally to him because, as he says, he was brought up to view deference and assistance to those in charge as his "highest duty."[48] As he got older, he continued to identify his duty with his role: "I had to obey, because, after all, wasn't I a soldier?,"[49] again never going beyond that role to ask questions about the goals of the army of which he was a part.[50]

Of course, once an agent conflates his moral duties and his obligations of role or position, he has thereby greatly narrowed his scope of responsibility: one carries out one's orders or assignment, and that is the end of the matter. Höss says that when the extermination order came down, "I wasted no thoughts about it. I had received an order; I had to carry it out. I could not allow myself to form an opinion as to whether this mass extermination of the Jews was necessary or not."[51] This is a truly extraordinary claim—Höss regarded consideration of the order to kill hundreds of thousands of men, women, and children as a waste of time, a matter concerning which he did not have the luxury of forming an opinion! But Höss only says overtly what Stangl could allow himself to say only indirectly. Recall that in describing the four requirements of a crime, Stangl manages to write himself completely out of the equation: the subject or agent of the genocide is the "government," and he understands that organization to be something distinct from himself despite his position in the SS. Who did he conceive of himself, as a police officer, as working for? In the end, it does not seem to matter: Stangl, like Höss, narrowed his understanding of what he was responsible for to such an extent that he was able to spend months engaged in mass murder on a daily basis.

Höss takes the narrowing of his own responsibility to the point of blaming the prisoners at Auschwitz for many of the camp's horrors, as though if only the inmates had cooperated more, Auschwitz would not have been nearly as bad as it was. With respect to the Polish prisoners—that is, the non-Jewish Poles—Höss claims "There was only one question. Who would be lucky enough to survive the imprisonment?"[52] He thereby deflects responsibility from himself onto blind chance, even though he goes on to list execution and mistreatment at the hands of the guards as possible causes of death. When it comes to the Jewish prisoners, Höss does not hesitate to implicate what he takes to be the very nature of Jews: "Of course, the Jews protected themselves in the typically Jewish way, by bribing their fellow prisoners. . . . Mostly they were tormented by people of their own race, whether they were Kapos or block seniors."[53] He goes on to claim that the "Jews did damage to each other whenever they could. Each tried to get an easy job for himself," and they were willing to sell each other out to do that.[54] Höss sums up:

> From what I observed, I firmly maintain that the death rate of most of the Jews was caused not only by the unaccustomed work [as though it was only Jews who were not used to working from sunrise to sundown (or longer) on a starvation diet], or the inadequate food, or the overcrowded living conditions and all the other unpleasantness and poor conditions of the camp, but mainly and most importantly because of their psychological condition. The death rate of the Jews was not much lower in other places of work in other camps under much more favorable conditions. It is significant that it was always relatively higher than the death rate of other prisoners.[55]

This passage raises significant questions about the relationship between Höss's anti-Semitism and his lack of sympathy or empathy for his Jewish victims. He never considers that the psychological condition of Jewish prisoners might be the result of knowing that other members of their families have been gassed, or by the obvious contempt felt for them by camp personnel.[56]

Höss claims that he purposely shut down his affective responses in order to be able to do his job properly. He describes his one-time superior, Inspector of Concentration Camps Eicke, as saying that "[a]ny compassion at all towards the ENEMIES OF THE STATE would be unworthy of an SS officer. . . . He said he could use only hard and determined men who would obey every order, no matter what the cost to themselves."[57] We have already seen that Höss's understanding of duty was as a matter of deference and obedience to superiors in the chain of command. Here is a particularly stark statement of his view: "As leader of the SS, Himmler's person was sacred. His fundamental orders in the name of the Führer were holy. There was no reflection, no interpretation, no explanation about these orders. They were carried out ruthlessly, regardless of the final consequences."[58] Höss claims to have experienced "inner doubts and depressions," "deep human emotion," and "pity" in overseeing the gassings of women and children, but claims that he stifled those feelings, not allowing them to show in his behavior or demeanor, in order to steel his subordinates to their tasks.[59] He stated that "only iron determination could carry out Hitler's orders and this could only be achieved by stifling all human emotion."[60]

Höss's reactions to his own affective responses (pity, compassion, etc.) are complicated in a way that he himself is unable to see, given his determination not to reflect on his emotions and feelings. On the one hand, he presents his emotions as nothing more than potential hindrances to the doing of what he takes to be his duty (the carrying out of the orders sent down the SS chain of command), thus dismissing them as unpleasant accompaniments to an important task. On the other hand, he seems to regard his emotions as presenting him with objections to the carrying out of the orders of Hitler and Himmler; for example, he describes "doubts which uprooted [his] deepest inner feelings," even going so far as saying that "these human emotions seemed almost like treason against the Führer."[61] There is some dim recognition that his emotions are not unconnected to his moral beliefs—that is why he not only regrets them, as one would regret chronic indigestion that made one's job unpleasant, but also fears them as in some way revelatory of disagreement with the "sacred" and "holy" persons of Hitler and Himmler.[62]

"Conscience is better than money"

It is difficult to find literature with more scattered references to self-deception than that concerning antebellum American slaveholders. And no wonder: here were men and women supposedly committed to ideals of liberty and equality, who nonetheless held men, women, and children as property. In earlier eras, such as ancient Greece or Rome, slavery did not produce so much anxiety and tension, because it did not conflict with liberal, progressive ideals in the way that it did in the southern states of the Union. How did American slaveholders reconcile or live with the inability to reconcile such conflicting commitments?

In the first chapter, I introduced the issues considered in this book with the story of Thomas Jefferson's epistolary exchange with Edward Coles. But now I want to consider a lesser known southern slaveholder—Charles Colcock Jones. Jones was born to a prominent slaveholding family in Liberty County, Georgia, in 1804. Jones is a good case study of conflict because, as a young man, he not only studied in northern schools but also befriended members of prominent abolitionist circles, including Harriet Beecher Stowe, the author of *Uncle Tom's Cabin*, the abolitionist novel that drove many southerners to infuriated defense of slavery while simultaneously garnering northern support for the impending war. Jones, then, was exposed to radical ideals—ideals at the other end of the spectrum from those of his conservative planter neighbors.

And his initial reaction was an endorsement of antislavery ideas. Jones was studying to be a minister, so it is hardly surprising that the endorsement grew out of his understanding of Christian teachings. As he wrote to his future wife, Mary, "Our souls [those of blacks and whites] are the same. God is no respecter of persons."[63] This religious conviction about the equality of all souls before God led to a belief that slavery was wrong: it was, he claimed, "high time that our country was taking some measures of some sort whose ultimate tendency shall be the emancipation of nearly three million of men, women, and children who are held in the grossest bondage, and with the highest injustice."[64] Slavery, he proclaimed to Mary, "is unjust, contrary to nature and religion."[65]

He acknowledged that his position in life was due to the labor of those held in bondage: "How often do I think . . . of the number of hands employed to furnish me with those conveniences of life of which they are in consequence denied—how many intellects, how many souls perhaps, withered and blasted forever for this very purpose."[66] Thus, Jones was in a very different position from those northern abolitionists with whom he interacted: he himself, and his entire family, was deeply implicated in and dependent upon the institution that he judged so wrong as to be evil. So Jones seemed to face a situation requiring decision: either continue to live off his slaves' labor or emancipate his slaves, thereby removing himself from the people and places he loved most in the world.

Jones could not tear himself away from Mary and the rest of his kin, and so he had to find a way to continue living as a privileged planter while soothing his conscience and ego. So he begins to look for a way of understanding his duty, both secular and religious, that did not require anything so drastic as emancipating his slaves:

> But the question is, in my present circumstances, with evil on my hands entailed from my father, would the general

interests of the slaves and community at large, with reference to the slaves, be promoted best, by emancipation? Could I do more for the ultimate good of the slave population by holding or emancipating what I own?[67]

Thus, Jones begins to look for some course of action by which "the best interests of the coloured population and the approbation of the whites may be secured."[68] Jones wants to soothe his conscience without alienating his social circle, so he convinces himself that doing his duty by the slaves requires the approval of the white planters. It is interesting that he can make these mental maneuvers while at the same time writing to Mary that the human heart "is deceitful above all things and desperately wicked and nothing short of the sovereign grace of God can subdue it."[69]

At the same time as Jones is convincing himself that no act that lacked "the cordial consent of the owner[s]"[70] would be for the benefit of the enslaved, he absolves himself of responsibility, by viewing slavery as something thrust upon him against his will. We have already seen him, in a quotation earlier, as claiming that slavery is an evil "entailed" upon him by his father. The implication is that previous generations bear the guilt, not he. (This assertion should remind us of Jefferson's insistence that slavery as an institution was forced upon the colonists by the British king, who also prevented them from abolishing it.) In a letter to Mary, Jones further portrays himself as a victim: "What I would not give . . . if our family were not freed of this property and removed beyond its influence!"[71] He thrusts the responsibility for extricating himself from slavery onto some unnamed forces, with the clear implication that it is something he himself does not control. Of course, Edward Coles would not have had much sympathy with Jones's lament, because Coles *freed himself and his slaves* and removed all of them to Illinois.

Jones decides that he can improve the condition of the slaves with the approbation of the whites by becoming a missionary to the slaves. He insisted to the planters (and to himself) that "the salvation of one soul will more than outweigh all the pain and woe of their capture and transportation, and subsequent residence among us."[72] (Is Jones here acknowledging that the slaves suffer under their bondage?) The nature of Jones's preaching reveals how much weight he gave to the opinion of the white planters. While insisting that "Jesus is able to save *all* who come to him" regardless of "*colour*" or "*condition*," he makes it clear that the way to Jesus is not the same for all: he devotes four pages of his *A Catechism for Colored Persons* to the "duties of masters and servants."[73] He composed a series of sermons that had as their goal to "inculcate respect, obedience and fidelity to masters, as duties, for the discharge of which they as servants would have to account to God in the great day."[74] There is no sign of how or whether he reconciled the claim that slaves owe duties to their masters with the claim that slaves are being held as slaves unjustly and against moral and religious principle: How did he think that kidnappers came to acquire legitimate claim to the obedience of their captives? Jones's claim about slavery being justified by the salvation of just one soul provides a clue: like many slaveholders, he might very well have told himself that God had designed the institution to bring Christianity to a heathen people. If so, he is pushing responsibility not only on to his earthly father but also on to his heavenly father.

Some of the content of Jones's sermons to the slaves reveals his ability to disguise from himself or to fail to see the conflict between his moral and religious ideals and commitment of any kind to slavery. Two of his constant themes were the sanctity of the Sabbath as a day free from work and the sacredness of the marriage contract.[75] Jones preached that marriages were indissoluble, that only death or adultery constituted grounds for separation, that husbands ought to provide for their wives, and that all marriages should be contracted lawfully. But all this ignores some all too obvious facts: slaves were not allowed to marry legally in antebellum Georgia; slaves could have their spouses sold away at the whim of a master; and slave husbands were not free laborers who could negotiate better living conditions for their families. One way that some slaves could provide for themselves was by hiring themselves out or by working small plots of ground given for their use by their owners. But such activities had to take place during their leisure hours—and Sunday was the only day off from their master's bidding. Thus, counseling slaves to keep the Sabbath sacred by resting was to encourage them not to avail themselves of independent economic opportunities— opportunities which were their only possible bid for freedom or for just a shred of independence within the confines of slavery. And Jones effectively forbid any form of rebellion by insisting that slaves ought not do anything to make their masters angry, thereby leading those masters from the good and the right.[76] So slaves were supposed not only to work for their masters but also to bear the burden of the virtue of those masters. Jones's preaching, then, put demands on slaves that either seemed incompatible with the institution of slavery or were only able to be met by acquiescing in one's own oppressive bondage.

Jones had entered into his mission to the slaves as an attempt to fulfill his duty to those whose bondage he viewed as unjust while avoiding alienating himself from the family and social circle the members of which he loved dearly. Events of 1856 show that, by that time, the effort had undone him morally. Charles and Mary had had difficulties with a particular slave family, and the escape and recapture of Jane, a daughter of that family, led them to a decision to sell the "whole" family: "We have concluded to dispose of the whole family, but not in Savannah nor in the low country. They must be sold up the country, where they will not come back. It is very painful, but we have no comfort or confidence in them, and they appear unhappy themselves—no doubt from the trouble they have from time to time occasioned."[77] Here Jones reveals that his entire concern is with himself and his family, not with his slaves—if his slaves cannot add to his family's comfort, then they must be gotten rid of. The unhappiness that he most likely correctly sees in the slaves is attributed to their inability to please him and his family—he pictures his slaves' emotional lives as revolving around their white masters. This is probably why Jones is frustrated and mystified when Jane's parents do nothing to help him locate her after she has run off.[78]

In making the decision to sell off a group of his slaves, Jones never seems to consider how much more traumatic such a sale will be for all his slaves than it will be for himself or for Mary. As he deliberates with Mary about the potential sale, he tells her that he does not want her "subjected to any inconveniences in [her] domestic arrangements whatever."[79] He soothes any moral qualms he might have felt by congratulating himself on insisting that the entire family be sold as a package rather than broken up; after all, he says "[c]onscience is better than money."[80] But, of course, the family was broken up: Jane's mother, Phoebe, had another daughter, Clarissa, who in turn had four children of her own.[81] This was a fact conveniently ignored by the Jones family, who decided where family lines were to be drawn among their slaves.

Phoebe's family was sold together, but to a trader: they ended up in the slave markets of New Orleans, where their ability to stay together as a family was seriously imperiled. How did Jones respond to this news? Well, they had not knowingly sold to a trader—as he put it, "We were endeavoring to do the best we could."[82] Charles had traveled a long way from his early flirtations with abolitionism. Harriet Beecher Stowe summed it

up: studying Jones's writings shows us "painfully how the moral
sense of the finest mind may be perverted by constant famil-
iarity with such a system."[83]

The Psychopath as Case Study

Ted Bundy is an anomaly among my case studies: he was a serial
killer whose actions were contrary to law and to established social norms of his time and place. Many people would label Bundy
a "psychopath." However, as I indicated in chapter 1, whatever
the source or cause of Bundy's moral failings, those failings can
still be instructive to those of us who are not psychopaths. For
example, if it is the case that Bundy lacked a capacity for sympathy or empathy, he can provide us with a glimpse of what can
happen if we do not exercise our capacity for sympathy or empathy. Bundy, perhaps in part in virtue of his emotional deficits,
also had some cognitive deficits, including, in the words of Eve
Garrard, "an inability to grasp the presence of reasons of the first
importance."[84] It seems to me that the subjects of the other case
studies either were able but failed to grasp such reasons or made
themselves gradually into people who lacked the ability to grasp
such reasons. Just as with Nazis and slaveholders, we should not
caricature psychopaths because, for all their differences from us,
there may be some frightening similarities. Bundy is the most
cautionary of cautionary tales.

And we need to be cautious as we listen to Bundy talk about
himself. Bundy was, without a doubt, a master manipulator, and
he treated truth and lies as only different tools for serving his
purposes, whatever they happened to be. But, with Bundy even
more than with my other case studies, I am not concerned with
the truth or falsity of what he says but, rather, with the fact that
he chooses to say it. I think that he is clearly trying to impress

his interviewers with his insight and intelligence, and so what he chooses to tell them is revealing of his character. However, I have to grant that my interpretation of Bundy's remarks is much more speculative than is my interpretation of the remarks of the other case studies. Nonetheless, I hope to show, throughout my discussion of him, that Bundy is useful to those of trying to understand the moral life.

Ted Bundy once described himself as "the most cold-blooded son of a bitch you'll ever meet" and that description is all too accurate. Stephen G. Michaud and Hugh Aynesworth spent hours interviewing Bundy while the latter was on death row. Because Bundy had not yet exhausted his appeals options, he was unwilling to confess his crimes, although he did so once his execution was a fait accompli.[85] Michaud and Aynesworth did get Bundy to talk, however, by asking for his insight into the mind of someone who was capable of committing the crimes of which Bundy had been convicted. So although Bundy talks in the third person, it is absolutely clear that he is talking about himself. Thus, Michaud and Aynesworth have provided us with an invaluable record of the inner mental workings of a man guilty of well over thirty rapes and murders; of a man who had sex with the corpses of his victims; of a man who managed, in spite of his crimes, to appear normal to those with whom he interacted (excluding, of course, his victims).

The interviews, however, very quickly dispel any air of normalcy that Bundy might have managed to convey to the casual observer, as over and over again he makes remarks that pull the reader up short. For me, none of Bundy's moral-linguistic faux pas is as telling as the following remark, made as an attempt to explain how some "mass murderers" would think about their victims: "they [the murderers] might also say, 'Well, there's so many people, they won't be missed.' So what's one less? What's one less person on the face of the planet? What difference will it make a hundred years from now?"[86] "To say that perhaps this person won't be missed. I mean, there are *so* many people. This person will never be missed. It shouldn't be a problem."[87]

What is so striking about these remarks of Bundy's is their telling lack of perspective, at just the moment that Bundy himself might very well be trying to get us to put his actions in what he perceives to be the *correct* perspective and thereby to justify or, at least, excuse them. Notice that Bundy says that his victims "won't be missed." He uses the passive voice, thereby evading any particular agents who might be doing the missing. No matter how many people there are in the world, a mother will miss her daughter, a brother will miss his sister, and a husband will miss his wife. Human beings are not fungible commodities, such that the loss of one can be compensated for by finding another to play the role of the one lost. And the value of a life is not diminished by the fact that its loss may not register in anyone's subjective experience one hundred years from now. What Bundy manages to do in this single statement is to demonstrate his extreme detachment from other human beings and his inability to understand the nature of intimate human ties. He has here given us an important and substantial clue to the nature of his psyche.

Consider another remark of Bundy's that might seem just plain comical, but, I think, deepens our understanding of him:

I'm very close to my feet. Right now. I'm lying on my back with my foot propped up on the bars. And I'm studying my toes. For a good portion of the night. They're probably the most attractive feet you've ever seen.

Socks are such a serious part of my life. They're so very important to me. They kept reading the list of socks and all [in court] and I felt proud. Honestly, it didn't even begin to occur to me that people might wonder why I had all those socks. I just felt proud that *I* owned all those socks. Like a man who stands at the back of his ranchhouse and looks out over the range and sees all them cattle.

The only time that I began to have a little bout of sheepishness was when I read about a white sock with a blue band and green stripe on the toe. Those are odor eaters—and that was getting too personal.[88]

At this point Bundy has just been returned to his cell during his second Florida murder trial. Why in the world is he talking about his feet and how attractive they are? Surely Bundy's reputation is more likely to be tainted by a murder charge than by his owning "odor eaters." Most important, is anyone really concerned with the kinds of socks Bundy had, given the horrific nature of the crimes of which he was accused? Bundy here shows a kind of self-absorption that is nothing short of extraordinary—perspective on the world is the last thing that this man has.

Bundy did, at several points during the interviews, claim to feel remorse for what he had done. But we need to look very carefully at those statements:

What he had done terrified him. Purely terrified him. And he was full of remorse and remonstrating with himself for the suicidal, uh, nature of that activity—the ugliness of it all— and, you know, he quickly sobered up, as it were.

It was clear to him, I think, that the course of conduct that he had engaged in on that first, monstrous, occasion, as it were, was totally inappropriate. Fraught with danger, badly thought out.

The guilt and remorse were most prevalent, if they were prevalent at any time, during that period when the individual was uncertain about the results of the police investigation.[89]

Bundy always connects remorse to the possibility of being found out—the feeling would only last until he was able to convince himself that the police were not on his trail. It is as though Bundy is able to grasp that remorse is a negative or unpleasant feeling that people experience after having done something that society judges "wrong." He does have some unpleasant feelings after his killings, but these are feelings of fear and anxiety about being apprehended by the police. So it seems that he is using the language of remorse when he is really talking about something else entirely—at one point, he comes very close to equating remorse with "fear of capture."[90] His focus always remains on his own well-being, not on the pain and suffering he has inflicted on others. His negative feelings are not related to any moral assessment of his actions but, rather, to a prudential assessment of those actions and their potential impact on his own interests.

Bundy was forced to think about his victims at some point—namely, during the commission of his crimes, which involved the rape and killing of his victims. During one episode, Bundy put his arm in a sling, and asked a young woman at a lakeside park to help him get something into his car. He then kidnapped her, took her home with him, raped and killed her, and stuffed her body in a closet. Bundy then returned to the same park, kidnapped another young woman, then took her home and raped and killed her—with the other young woman's body still in the closet. He was a master of manipulation and deceit, carefully planning, until his very last crimes, how to get what he wanted without getting caught. At one point he describes his victims as *"problems"* and as "threats." He says that for him they were "symbols," and that once they ceased to have "symbolic value" they simply became something needing to be disposed of.[91] Bundy stresses that he needed to engage in conversation with his victims in order to gain their trust, but he needed to do so in a way that allowed him to maintain his detachment from them, to maintain his lack of a sense of them as persons.[92] He compares his killing activities to deer hunting or to the collecting of automobiles,[93] thereby equating his victims with nonhuman animals and even with inanimate objects. He also compares the gratification he derived from killing to that which someone might derive from bowling a perfect 300 game.[94] He says, with respect to his victims, that

> They would be depersonalized sufficiently so that he was not able to muster that natural, normal ability to feel compassion for that individual to also place a high value on the sanctity of life.
>
> Oddly enough, this person (in) normal circumstances would place a high value on life. And on the goal that people should be free from suffering, and so on. But he would not allow himself to feel those emotions for the victim.[95]

Tellingly, Bundy talks about being unable to "muster" compassion and related emotions, thereby making it clear that such responses did not come to him spontaneously or naturally. He said of himself that "I don't care about the great mass of people out there. I care about people I know and come in contact (with) and how they feel about me."[96] Given this remark, we are forced to wonder if he had any idea of what compassion is or what it is to value another human being. If he does not care about people, how could it be that he places a high value on life? Surely one has some concern for what one takes to be of great value. It is natural to wonder if Bundy really knows what he is talking about when he uses the term "value." Even when he talks about the people he supposedly does care about, the discussion ends up focusing on him—he cares about how they feel with respect to him. Ted's thoughts never stray far from Ted.

Bundy's far-from-perfect grasp of language, and in particular of moral language, comes across in his choice of grossly inadequate vocabulary for his crimes: he says that he worried about the "correctness of his conduct," that he refused to let himself consider the "propriety or impropriety" of his crimes, and that he saw that one of his first acts of assault was "totally inappropriate."[97] The terms of criticism that Bundy chooses here are at home in discussions of indiscretions, social faux pas, or crude and vulgar behavior, not of brutal assault, rape, and murder. Imagine how ludicrous it would be for Rudolf Höss, the commandant of Auschwitz, to have written that he had wondered about the "propriety" or "appropriateness" of gassing to death innocent men, women, and children by the thousands on a daily basis. Serial murder and rape, and genocide and torture require different terms: *wrong, wicked, evil, vicious, cruel, inhuman*, etc. It is as though Bundy hasn't grasped the moral difference between forgetting to say "thank you," and bashing someone over the head with a hunk of wood. (The latter was Bundy's first violent crime, or at least the first of those that he "admitted" to Michaud and Aynesworth.)

Much of Bundy's difficulty lies in his apparent failure to grasp how other people, in and of themselves, provide him with any sorts of reasons for action. Consider, for example, Bundy's attempt to "justify" his conduct:

> As far as remorse over the act, that would last for a period of time. But it could all be justified. The person would attempt to justify it by saying "Well, listen you, you fucked up this time, but you're never going to do it again. So let's just stay together, and it won't ever happen again." Why sacrifice this person's whole life?
>
> And so, the focus then became on surviving and modifying behavior. A sort of optimist [*sic*]. Sort of finding the silver lining, you might call it. Or in some way justifying what had taken place.[98]

The rationalization that Bundy here provides is of a familiar type: for most of us, it is the sort of thing we say to ourselves if, for example, we have broken a diet and want to maintain our self-esteem and get back on track with our weight-loss goals. In other words, it is the kind of pep talk we might give ourselves when we have deviated with respect to a purely self-regarding project, such as dieting, quitting smoking, or getting out of bed when the alarm goes off. Bundy, however, treats rape and murder in the way that I might regard having a cinnamon roll: a slight misstep that I shouldn't beat myself up about. We just resolve to learn from our mistake.

Further demonstrating that he egregiously underestimated the scale of his wrongdoings, Bundy describes an attempt to "compromise" with himself. To go back to the earlier comparison, when I'm dieting and find myself assailed by powerful cravings for that cinnamon roll, I try to find a midway option: I'll have some baked apples spiked with cinnamon to quell my sweet tooth while remaining in the realm of the healthy and low-fat. Bundy, again speaking in the third person, attempts a similar midway option:

Uh, and so he, in sort of a, uh, a compromise decided that rather than go out and inflict this mortal injury on a someone he would search out a victim in such a way that there would be no possibility of detection and he would not be forced into a position of having to kill. In essence he compromised into just going out and performing an act of rape, as it were.[99]

Bundy claims that "his intent with this victim was not to harm her," just to rape her! He does end up killing her because she wouldn't stop screaming: he had "to throttle her into unconsciousness," but he goes too far.[100] The victim plays a very small role in this story—she's nothing more to Ted than his version of cinnamon-flavored baked apples. Bundy just disregards the pain and suffering that he has caused others—for him, it is all about Ted. He is locked into a conception of reasons that makes no reference to the well-being of anyone other than himself.

The entirely self-regarding nature of Bundy's thought is made more evident by the way he treats his killing "activities," to borrow his term for his murders. He comments to one of his interviewers: "with enough study and interest, . . . you, too, could become a fairly effective mass murderer." Referring to the opportunistic nature of his crimes, he goes on, "Anyone has the capacity, and it (doesn't) take a great deal of skill or thought to do it . . . it's a relatively easy crime to get away with."[101] Bundy is talking about serial killing as I might talk about cycling: with a little study of bike repair and safety, anyone can become a fairly good cyclist, because it is a sport that requires only basic motor coordination and places to cycle are easily accessible from almost any location. Bundy describes his killing as "just a small, small portion of what was predominantly a normal existence,"[102] just as cycling can be a pastime that forms a small part of a person's life. The moral significance of his choice of "activity" does not seem to register for Bundy: becoming a serial killer just involves mastering disposal of bodies and assessment of situations in terms of risk. Anyone can do it.

Earlier I referred to Bundy's claim that with respect to one victim, he didn't intend to harm her, but only to rape her. He insists that even when he put his hands around her throat to "throttle her into unconsciousness," he was "still intending not to harm her." Consider also the following claims that Bundy makes about himself:

> He received no pleasure from harming or causing harm to the person he attacked. He received absolutely no gratification from causing pain and did everything possible, within

reason—considering the unreasonableness of the situation—not to torture these individuals, at least physically.

We still have to remember that the individual—at least not on a conscious level—has no desire or implements no design with the goal of terrorizing or torturing the victim. And he ordinarily would not want to inflict any unnecessary violence or pain to the girl.[103]

There are two features of these remarks worth commenting upon. First, Bundy seems to equate harm with physical damage or bodily death: raping a girl does not constitute harming her, and torture other than the physical sort is waved aside, as though it is insignificant. There are different ways of understanding these remarks. Bundy might be trying to make himself look better. Or, perhaps, he has so little concern for his victims as persons that the individual feelings of this particular girl are lost behind his absorption with his ego. Another possibility is that Bundy completely objectified and dehumanized his victims: they are parts of his "activities," like a collector's automobiles or a bowler's shoes and ball. He views them entirely from the outside, paying little if any attention to their inner lives—he seems to not even consider their terror as one of the most significant harms that he imposes upon them.

Second, given this disregard of his victims' mental lives, perhaps we need to take more seriously than we might be inclined to do Bundy's claim that he did not receive satisfaction from causing pain to his victims. If he is unable to acknowledge or grasp in any robust fashion that his victims are beings with inner lives similar to his own, it is difficult to see how he could derive pleasure from their pain. Bundy's attitude toward his victims might be akin, then, to Michael Vicks's attitude toward the dogs he bred for fighting: complete indifference except insofar as they play a role in a fantasy or a money-making scheme, respectively.

Whatever happens in and to the psyches of the girls and the dogs is just a by-product of what these men were aiming at.[104]

The final comments of Bundy's to examine are those he makes on the subjects of conscience[105] and guilt. Here again, Bundy uses moral language—the conscience, after all, is a faculty for or ability to recognize actions as wrong. Bundy insists, "I *do* have a conscience. It may have gaps in it, but I have a very *strong* conscience." When Aynesworth presses for explanation, Bundy elaborates:

> Well, we all have gaps in our conscience. Some people feel guilty if they don't come home right after work. Others don't care if they stop off for a few beers. Some don't care if they pick up a little something at the supermarket without paying for it. Some people wouldn't be able to handle it. I, uh, stole textbooks when I was going to college. Some people couldn't handle that.[106]

So Bundy, like us all according to him, had some gaps in his conscience—that is, there were some actions for which he failed to feel guilt, supposedly because he did not acknowledge them as wrong or, at least, not so wrong that one needed to beat oneself up over them. Just as some people fail to feel guilty for using workplace computers for internet shopping, Bundy didn't feel guilty for stealing textbooks or for raping and killing young women.

Bundy is trying to present himself here as no different from the rest of us who stop for a few beers after work or shop on the internet during work hours. For Bundy, gaps are gaps, no matter what the subject matter that falls into the gap. Bundy seems to have no sense of moral proportion: he equates killing and raping with pocketing some batteries at the supermarket. I would suggest that the reason for this is that Bundy cannot think of morality as any different from, or as anything other than, any other set of rules that allow, forbid, and require certain forms of conduct. A breach of a rule is a breach of a rule no matter what the rule's subject matter, so moral character is to be evaluated by how many rules one disregards. Reasons and justifications for the rules and for breakings of the rules do not enter into Bundy's thinking, because he fails to think of the rules as expressive of deeper facts about value and of right and wrong. As a result he has no way of thinking about conflicts between moral rules or between moral rules and considerations of self-interest. Bundy's thinking about morality is so superficial that it fails to really constitute moral thinking at all, because he never penetrates the "do's" and "do nots" to get to the "whys" and "why nots." One theme of this book is the importance, for all of us, of making sure we penetrate beyond the superficial in our moral thinking.

Bundy presents himself as a man who is psychologically healthy, a man who is not plagued by the pathological and useless emotion of guilt (which, given Bundy's understanding of conscience, seems to suggest that everything has fallen into one huge gap for him). Consider the following claims he makes:

> I've learned to live absolutely and completely and totally in the *here and now*. I don't worry, think or concern myself with the past, or, for that matter, with the future, except only to the extent necessary. . . . Well, whatever I've done in the past, you know—the emotions of omissions or commissions—*doesn't* bother me. Try to touch the past! Try to deal with the past. It's not real. It's just a dream! In fact, it's as real as the future.
>
> Guilt? It's this mechanism we use to control people. . . . It's a kind of social control mechanism—and it's *very* unhealthy. . . . And there are much better ways to control our behavior than that rather extraordinary use of guilt. . . . I guess I am in the enviable position of not having to deal with guilt.

There's just no reason for it. . . . You don't need guilt to do the right thing. You don't have to feel bad about the past to be able to do well right here and now. And it's the here and now that carries us to the future.[107]

Bundy's comments actually raise serious questions about the nature of guilt—questions that I will address in more detail in chapter 5. Is guilt just a bad feeling, like nausea or back pain? Or is guilt more complex, perhaps partially or even wholly constituted by a judgment about the wrongness of one's past conduct and/or a desire to somehow make amends or take one's justly deserved punishment? Bundy rejects any role that guilt might play in reflection on one's moral character. For many of us, it serves as a catalyst for improving our characters and/or for repairing relations with people whom we have wronged. But Bundy cannot conceive of guilt in this way because, no surprise, he is only thinking about his own subjective well-being: guilt feels bad, so why deal with it? Ironically, Bundy's own conduct serves to refute his claims: without guilt, there was nothing to deter him from his murderous rampage. And the interviews do not give us any confidence that the future Bundy, if released from prison, would become a productive and harmless member of society.

There are a lot of issues raised by Bundy with respect to his relationship to moral belief. Did Bundy have moral beliefs—for example, the belief that killing for sexual gratification was wrong? Perhaps he did have such beliefs but was amoral—that is, he didn't care about whether he behaved in accordance with morality. This would provide an explanation as to why he didn't need to engage in the complicated psychological mechanisms of a Jefferson or Stangl: unlike those men, he acknowledged his wrong-doing and it simply didn't bother him. Another possibility is that Bundy didn't really have moral beliefs at all: he recognized that other people made claims involving moral

language and that if you were caught engaging in actions labeled "wrong," you would be subject to bad consequences. In
chapter 5, in the discussion of the emotions, I will suggest
reasons to suppose that the latter is the case—that is, that
Bundy lacked moral beliefs because he simply lacked the capacity to grasp moral concepts.

What can we learn from a serial killer, some Nazis, and a
couple of slaveholders? Of what interest are the stories of these
men to us, either as philosophers or as moral agents? There is
no doubt that these are examples of people who failed with respect to all three of the duties I discussed in chapter 1: the duties
of due care in moral deliberation, of moral self-scrutiny, and to
develop moral virtue. As I said in that chapter, I am concerned
with the first two of those three duties, and I believe that we can
use the cases of failure to aid us in seeing where we ourselves
can and sometimes do go wrong. If we are willing to take these
case studies to heart, we can take advantage of their obvious
errors to locate and correct our perhaps more subtle and less obvious (at least to us!) errors. In trying to understand the errors
of Jones, Höss, and company, we can force ourselves to locate
moral questions and to isolate areas where we need to exercise
greater care in own moral deliberations. I think that it is difficult
not to engage in moral self-scrutiny upon reading of these men's
attempts to justify their actions to us and to themselves, and we
can use this self-scrutiny to spur us on to develop or strengthen
our own moral virtue.

Culture and Moral Evaluation

Cultural Norms and Moral Assessment

Thomas Jefferson and Charles Colcock Jones lived in the antebellum American South, a society that culturally and legally
sanctioned slavery. Franz Stangl, Albert Speer, and Rudolf Höss
lived in the Third Reich, a society that both culturally and legally
sanctioned anti-Semitic attitudes and actions. We[1] in the twenty-
first century do not condone, either culturally or legally, African
American slavery or anti-Semitism. What role should these facts
about cultural and legal norms play in our moral reasoning?
In what way are they relevant to the moral assessment of the
actions of others and of ourselves? Are cultural norms guides to
good behavior? Are cultural pressures and norms impediments
to effective moral deliberation?

One prominent way of answering these questions is defended
by historian and Jefferson scholar Douglas L. Wilson in his 1992
article "Thomas Jefferson and the Character Issue."[2] Wilson's article was prompted by the charges made most prominently by
Fawn Brodie that Jefferson had had a sexual relationship with
his slave Sally Hemings and had fathered several children by her,
children whom he had continued to hold in slavery.[3] At the time

Wilson wrote his article, the DNA evidence that has now with a high degree of likelihood supported Brodie's contentions was not yet available, and Wilson was determined to "debunk" Brodie's claims by an appeal to what he regarded as undisputed facts about Jefferson's character and his relationships with his (white) family and their attitudes toward him.

But any attempt to defend Jefferson's character must contend with the undoubted fact that Jefferson was a slaveholder. Further, he was a slaveholder who loudly and often proclaimed the natural rights and equality of all men. As Wilson acknowledged, the question must arise as to whether Jefferson was a hypocrite. And if he was a hypocrite, why not suppose that he had a relationship with Hemings, even if such a relationship was, as Wilson contends, in conflict with standards of moral decency to which Jefferson was apparently committed?

Wilson attempts to save Jefferson from the charge of hypocrisy by defending Jefferson on the slavery issue. He does this by pointing to what he sees as a mistake commonly made in popular attempts to understand the fact of Jefferson's holding slaves:

> "Presentism" is the term that historians use for applying contemporary or otherwise inappropriate standards to the past. An awkward term at best, it nevertheless names a malaise that currently plagues American discussions of anything and everything concerning the past: the widespread inability to make appropriate allowances for prevailing historical conditions.[4]

Wilson claims that we ought not, in our moral assessments of Jefferson, appeal to our own beliefs on the moral status of slavery. When we take into account the milieu in which Jefferson was raised and lived, we should instead, according to Wilson, find the fact that Jefferson ever came to see slavery as wrong as astounding and admirable. (Not surprisingly, however, we have no mention of Edward Coles in Wilson's defense of Jefferson.)

The quotation from Wilson uses the expressions "inappropriate standards" and "inability to make appropriate allowances" when talking about contemporary Americans applying their own moral standards in appraisals of Jefferson as slaveholder. But Wilson does not tell us what makes these standards inappropriate or why certain allowances would be appropriate. Clearly, Wilson thinks that the cultural (and perhaps legal) norms that governed slavery in Jefferson's society need to be taken into account, but how are they to be taken into account? This question is important not only in our assessment of historical figures but, more significantly, in our assessments of ourselves and in our moral deliberations about how we ought to act. Are claims about our cultural norms important premises in our moral arguments? Are claims about cultural norms themselves moral claims? How are claims about cultural norms related to moral claims and beliefs?

Issues about the relationship between cultural norms and moral assessment are not limited to questions about the character and actions of historical figures such as slaveholders and Nazis. In the Western democracies today, these issues arise in cases of immigrants whose cultural norms, including expectations of legality/illegality, are in conflict with the dominant norms of Western culture and of Western democratic legal systems. For example, what is known as female circumcision, which "involves removal [and/or the closure] of some or all of a woman's external genitalia," is still widely practiced in Africa and the Middle East.[5] For various reasons, members of the relevant cultures regard this practice as necessary, and desire to continue to engage in it when they move to, for example, the United States or Canada.

Contemporary Westerners view the practice of female circumcision as abhorrent, highly disapprove of it, and believe it ought to be prohibited. What we have, then, is a conflict between the cultural norms of the immigrants' new country and the cultural norms of their country of origin. What implications does this have for the moral assessment of the actions of the immigrants who attempt to circumcise their daughters or other female relatives? Ought we to make different moral assessments of an immigrant who engages in such actions and an American or a Canadian whose family has been in the United States or Canada for many generations who engages in such actions? Are immigrants who engage in this practice morally justified in doing so, or do they at least have an excuse not available to the American or to the Canadian? If either is the case, should we allow such people to have a justification or an excuse in a court of law?[6]

In order to answer these questions, we need to understand the relationship between morality and cultural norms. What role should claims about an agent's cultural norms play in her own moral deliberations and in others' moral assessments of her behavior? This is not only important from a third-person perspective as we try to engage in moral evaluation of Nazis, slaveholders, and people committed to female circumcision, but also from the first-person perspective: we need to consider the role that the cultural norms of our own cultures ought to play in our moral thinking.

These issues are quite complicated and messy, because there is no doubt that culture has a deep impact on each of us—it affects what we care about, how we interact with others, what motivates us to act in various circumstances, and what we disapprove or approve of, among many other things. And it seems right to suppose that morality is somehow tied to what people care about, how they interact with each other, their actual and possible motivations, their attitudes, and so on. So no matter what the ultimate relations are between cultural norms and morality, there is no doubt that there are myriad connections between the two. But we need to sort out these issues, both so that we do not fail to excuse ourselves and others when cultural factors can legitimately provide such excuses and so that we do not give ourselves or others easy moral passes by appeal to culture.

Justification and Knowledge

In the previous section, I talked about justification for actions and excuses for actions. Relevant to assessing whether an agent was either justified in or had an excuse for acting in a particular way, we need to assess not only whether the agent acted rightly or wrongly but also what the agent knew or was justified in believing about the situation in which she acted. So I need to make a few remarks about knowledge and justification for belief before we can continue.

Let's begin by considering the following hypothetical case: Martin is a wealthy landholder in twelfth-century Britain, and Richard is a peasant working Martin's land. Martin and Richard both believe that the sun orbits the earth. Martin also believes that the square root of 9 is 9, while Richard has no beliefs about the square root of 9, because he does not possess the concept of a square root. How we evaluate Martin and Richard as epistemic agents—that is, as believers or knowers—depends on what sort of evaluation we are making and on various features of Martin and Richard. We will certainly judge that Martin and Richard had false beliefs about the earth's relationship to the sun, Martin has a false mathematical belief, and that Richard lacks a certain class of mathematical beliefs. But we will certainly not blame them, in their capacity as scientific thinkers, for their false beliefs about the orbits of the sun and the earth: the evidence available to them was limited, and they made what certainly seems to be a reasonable inference from the evidence that was available. In other words, it seems plausible to suppose that both Richard and Martin were *justified* in believing the sun orbits the earth; that is, they had justified false beliefs about the orbits of the sun and the earth. However, we might assess Martin and Richard differently in their capacity as mathematical thinkers. After all, the evidence available to them about the square root of 9 is exactly the same as the evidence available to us now. However, Martin was educated, whereas Richard was not; further, Richard had no time to engage in any mathematical reasoning unnecessary for plowing the fields and putting food on the table. So even if there is some sense in which the evidence for the square root of 9 being 3 is available to both Richard and Martin, there is also a sense in which we can expect Martin to reach the correct conclusion on this matter while it is unreasonable for us to expect Richard, an uneducated peasant, to do the same.

This imaginary case of Richard and Martin illustrates some important things to keep in mind when we talk about bringing present standards to bear on historical figures or bringing one's own cultural norms to bear on members of a different culture. First, we need to distinguish between the *truth* or *falsity* of the agent's beliefs, moral or otherwise, and the *justification that the agent had* for her beliefs, be they true or false. As we have seen, an agent may have false beliefs that are nonetheless justified relative to the evidence available to her.[7] So, in the case of Jefferson, the relevant question would be: Were his beliefs about African Americans and the institution of slavery justified, even if false? Facts about the particular agent need to be examined, given that different agents in the same cultural and historical milieu may reasonably be held to different standards. Here education, intellectual capacities, time for reflection, and reasonable priorities all seem relevant to a global assessment of an agent's situation as a knower. So we might reasonably, it seems, demand more, both epistemically and morally, of a Thomas Jefferson than of a poor white southern farmer. Further, we might expect Jefferson to expend more energy thinking about the moral status of his slaves than he would expend in thinking about making, for example, a revolving bookcase (one of his actual inventions), just as we would expect an engineer to expend more effort in designing a bridge than in putting together a salad for a dinner party: when serious consequences for other people are looming, our expectations of epistemic agents rightly increase.

But of course, there is an important feature of moral knowledge or belief that differentiates it from theoretical scientific or mathematical knowledge or belief: moral judgments are judgments about an agent's duties, obligations, reasons for action, the relative status—that is, inferiority or equality—of various groups of beings, and so on. In other words, moral judgments have practical import; moral reasoning is reasoning about how to act, what goals to pursue, how to live one's life and to treat other people, animals, the earth, and the like. Typically, when we are evaluating historical agents, we are evaluating their choices and actions. For example, in the case of Thomas Jefferson, Wilson is concerned with the ways in which contemporary Americans judge him, given the fact that he was a slaveholder. And, as we have seen, by the end of his life, he was a slaveholder who had become completely passive with respect to undermining the institution; further, he had an affair with one of his slaves and had at least one child with her, a child that he continued to regard as a slave. What pressures were there on Jefferson to continue to comply with such evil?

Wilson is at pains to point out that Jefferson was subject to forces and pressures that only full engagement with historical reality can allow us to understand and appreciate. We cannot dispute that an *explanation* of Jefferson's beliefs and actions is a task that requires a detailed understanding of Jefferson's cultural and historical placement.[8] Similarly, members of cultures that advocate female circumcision are subject to pressures very different from those to which I am subject. But we are, or at least ought to be, concerned with more than mere explanation of an agent's actions—we are concerned with *evaluation*. And it is obvious that explanation and evaluation (or justification) can come apart. I have often spent an evening watching reruns of the TV series *Law & Order* when my time would have been better spent doing some work. In such a case, we certainly have an explanation of my behavior: I am lazy and also really like *Law & Order*. But I am not justified in my behavior—my balance of reasons supported my getting some work done in order to prepare for the next day's classes or to make progress on my research projects. Not every explanation offered provides a justification for an agent's imprudent or immoral behavior.

Sometimes, however, we say that while an agent was not justified in acting as she did, she had an excuse for her behavior. The law makes a distinction between justification defenses such as self-defense and excuse defenses such as insanity. But in morality the distinction is a contentious one, because how one understands it, if one accepts it at all, depends on how one understands the nature of right or wrong action. Consider, for example, the case of a medieval Christian who sincerely believes that heretics pose a threat to the souls of all who encounter them, and the only possible way to redeem such heretics and to protect others from heresy is to torture any who profess heretical doctrines. Is this Christian justified in torturing heretics? She might very well, given her cultural placement, be justified in her beliefs, so perhaps the right action for her is to torture heretics. Or do her justified but false beliefs merely excuse her—that is, make her less blameworthy for doing the wrong thing than if she did not have those beliefs?

I am going to sidestep these questions in what follows by simply stipulating a particular understanding of justified action and excusable action. I will suppose that an agent was justified in acting as she did if she had a justified belief that the action she performed was the right action,[9] and that excuses arise in cases where the agent is less than fully blameworthy (culpable, responsible) for failing to act in a justified way. This understanding of justified action parallels that of justified belief in two ways. First, just as one can have a justified false belief, one can perform a justified and yet wrong action. So we might say that our medieval Christian acted wrongly and yet was justified in doing so, because she was justified in her beliefs about the salvations of souls. Second, just as one can have an unjustified true belief, one can perform a right action that is unjustified. Suppose, for example, I send a large sum of money to the ASPCA because my horoscope told me that being charitable today would lead to my finding my true love. It might very well be that sending money to help animals in need is the right action for me given my circumstances, but I am unjustified in performing that action: I act on the basis of advice from a very unreliable source, one that I have no good reason for regarding as reliable.

If, for example, we were to offer an excuse for Jefferson's behavior, we would need to examine his epistemic condition (What did he know? What could he be expected to know, given his situation? What was he justified in believing?) and also the sorts of pressures that were peculiar to his personal and social situation, in order to determine if he was less than fully culpable for doing wrong in holding slaves. Taking this route would surely demand an examination of Jefferson's cultural milieu. However, we would employ our own moral standards in determining that he in fact did the wrong thing.

Notice that understanding the distinction between justifications and excuses as I am understanding it is relevant to the important distinction between the moral evaluation of an action and the moral evaluation of the agent who performs that action. Consider our medieval Christian who is sincerely concerned about the souls of the orthodox and of heretics, but who mistakenly believes that the torture of heretics is the way to care for the souls of all. We might very well say that the Christian is justified in acting as she does, but that she acts wrongly because her actions produce such great suffering without a sufficient counterbalancing gain in well-being. And, given her beliefs, she may spend a good portion of her life engaged in wrong action. On the one hand, we might judge that this Christian is a good person: she does her best to determine what is right, she cares deeply about other people, and she has the courage to act on her convictions even when doing so is unpleasant. On the other hand, we can imagine someone who always does the right thing, but does so on the basis of her horoscope dictating these actions as the best way to find romance—we would be unlikely to judge her a good person. So even if Jefferson, Jones, Höss, et al. did morally abhorrent things, we cannot immediately assume they were bad men; to reach that conclusion, we would have to examine their beliefs, their justifications or lack thereof for their beliefs, and their motivations for doing what they did.

But I want to begin by examining an approach to moral theory that might very well provide a justification for the actions of at least certain Nazis and certain slaveholders, an approach that identifies moral standards with cultural norms and standards. Perhaps the rightness or wrongness of, for example, Jefferson's actions is a function of the moral standards of his culture, because in fact there are no culture-independent moral standards. If this is so, then it might very well be the case that Jefferson was justified, not merely excused, in holding slaves. The cultural relativist offers a view that identifies moral standards with cultural attitudes.[10]

Cultural Relativism and Moral Disagreement

Many people are struck by what appears to be an incontrovertible fact about morality: people disagree about it. Even within a particular culture at a particular time, people take radically opposing sides on moral questions; just consider the debates on abortion and gay marriage in twenty-first-century America. But across cultures at a time, and particularly across time, the disagreement seems even more pervasive and deep. In 1930s and 1940s Germany, there were a significant number of people who thought that morality not only permitted but also required the extermination of Jewish men, women, and even children. In the antebellum American South, many people regarded African slavery as morally preferable to emancipation of the slaves. In many places in Africa and the Middle East, it is regarded as morally impermissible *not* to circumcise your daughter. Given this widespread disagreement which doesn't ever seem to go away, many people find themselves wondering whether there is any morality independent of cultural norms that we can use to evaluate those cultural norms. Maybe, they begin to think, when we are talking about morality, we are really just talking about cultural norms. If this is so, then moral evaluation of a person is just to evaluate her as either acting in accordance with or acting contrary to the norms of her culture.

How can we navigate these difficult and important issues? We need to begin by distinguishing between two different relativist theses.

Descriptive Relativism: People in different cultures often have different moral beliefs.

Descriptive relativism is a thesis about what beliefs people actually hold, not about the truth or falsity or even about the justification of those beliefs. So descriptive relativism is an anthropological claim, which can be verified or refuted only by going out and observing people in various cultures or by studying historical documents. But the second form of relativism, cultural relativism, is a philosophical thesis about the nature of morality.

> *Cultural Relativism*: For person S to judge that X is right (or good) is for S to judge that X is approved of by members of the relevant culture.

So, X here could be a state of affairs (for example, the state of affairs of Thomas Jefferson's holding slaves), an action (Jefferson's having sex with Sally Hemings), or some character trait (Jefferson's arrogance). The cultural relativist is asserting that facts about goodness or rightness are just facts about the relevant people's attitudes toward certain features of the world. Who are the relevant people? Americans in Jefferson's lifetime? Americans now? We will consider these options shortly.

So cultural relativism provides us one way of understanding what people mean when they say "Morality is all just subjective!" Cultural relativism tells us that facts about morality are really just facts about how people subjectively feel about various things. And we all know that what people like or dislike, approve of or disapprove of, will vary across time and across cultures. So if we were to accept both cultural relativism and descriptive relativism, we would get the conclusion that what is right or wrong or good or bad will vary from one culture to another.

But now we need to clarify the cultural relativist thesis. How do we determine which is the relevant culture for the assessment of a given action? Consider the case of Jefferson's being a slaveholder. Suppose I make the judgment that it was wrong for Jefferson to hold slaves. Which is the relevant culture for assessing the truth value (i.e., the truth or falsity) of my judgment—mine or Jefferson's? This question suggests two variants of cultural relativism:

good pt

1. *Cultural Relativism with Speaker-Relativity*: For person S to judge that person T's doing X is right (or good) is for S to judge that *members of S's culture* approve of T's doing X.
2. *Cultural Relativism with Agent-Relativity*: For person S to judge that person T's doing X is right (or good) for T is just for S to judge that *members of T's culture* approve of T's doing X.[11]

According to cultural relativism with speaker-relativity, when a speaker makes a judgment about some action or state of affairs, she is saying something about the attitudes of people in *her* culture to such actions or states of affairs, regardless of the cultural membership of those performing the action or participating in the state of affairs. According to cultural relativism with agent-relativity, in contrast, when a speaker makes a judgment about some agent's action, she is making a judgment about the attitudes of *the agent's* culture toward that action as performed by one of its members.[12] So cultural relativism with speaker-relativity and cultural relativism with agent-relativity would yield different assessments of my judgment that it was wrong of Jefferson to hold slaves; according to cultural relativism with speaker-relativity, my judgment is true because members of *my* culture disapprove of slaveholding, but according to cultural relativism with agent-relativity, my judgment is false because it seems that *Jefferson's* culture approved of slaveholding.[13] If we are cultural relativists with agent-relativity, then presentism would be a serious error: according to cultural relativists with agent-relativity, each agent is to be evaluated by the norms of her place and time. However, if we are cultural relativists with speaker-relativity, presentism is not an error, because cultural relativists with speaker-relativity evaluate the agent against the background of the speaker's own place and time.[14]

Many people will say of, for example, Jefferson or Höss, "It was right of him to hold slaves [or to exterminate Jews]." Sometimes, in making such a claim, such people are employing a theory such as cultural relativism with agent-relativity in their moral evaluations of the actions of Jefferson or Höss. Sometimes, however, what they mean when they say "It was right of Höss to participate in the Final Solution" is really just "Höss believed that it was right of him to participate in the Final Solution." The last claim is just a claim about what Höss believed, not about whether Höss actually did the right thing. Consider as an analogy saying of our peasant Richard, "For him, the sun orbited the earth." In this case, clearly we just mean that Richard believed that the sun orbited the earth, leaving it open whether Richard's belief was true—that is, whether the sun actually orbits or did orbit the earth. We can accept that, for example, Höss believed he was acting rightly at Auschwitz without committing ourselves to the truth of any version of cultural relativism or, for that matter, to any particular account of the nature of right action. In this section, I am discussing cultural relativism and, in particular, cultural relativism with agent-relativity, according to which the rightness or wrongness of an agent's actions is determined by the norms of the culture of which she is a member. If one accepts cultural relativism with agent-relativity, then in saying "It was right of Höss to participate in the Final Solution," one is saying that Höss's actions are the right actions for him to perform, and so he was morally justified in behaving as he did. But if one really just means that Höss believed it was right of him to participate in the Final Solution, then it is quite possible that Höss had a false belief and that it was, in fact, wrong of him to participate in genocide. Similarly, if cultural relativism with agent-relativity is true, then the member of the resistance who believes that it is wrong of people like Höss to participate in genocide would have a false belief. My discussion of Martin and Richard illustrates, however, that people can have false yet justified beliefs, and that one's social and cultural placement can provide the explanation for one's having those false beliefs and also for one's having justification for those false beliefs.

In a later section of this chapter, I will discuss the possibility that culture can provide an excuse for morally wrong action insofar as it explains one's justified false beliefs about what morality either requires or permits one to do. But for now, I want to focus on cultural relativism with agent-relativity and examine what can be said in its favor. As I said at the beginning of this section, an important driving force behind the popularity of cultural relativism is what appears to be prevalent and persistent moral disagreement.

Just consider again our own case studies: educated men and women in the antebellum American South believed that it was morally legitimate to regard persons of African descent as property, and wide segments of German society in the 1930s and 1940s believed that morality permitted or even demanded the elimination of the Jews from Europe (if not from the planet). In today's world, there are groups of people who believe that morality requires them to mutilate the genital organs of their female children and young women. In our own current American "culture,"[15] there is widespread disagreement about the moral status of same-sex sexual activity, some regarding such activity as on a moral par with heterosexual sex while others seeing it as a sinful perversion threatening the very foundation of American society. How can we explain such disagreement?

Well, those drawn to cultural relativism point out that moral disagreement seems to follow, at least roughly, cultural divides, whether they be temporally or geographically drawn: in the antebellum United States, debate over slavery mirrored sectional divides between the North and South.[16] Debates about female genital mutilation within the United States today are debates between those whose communities have practiced female circumcision as part of their religion, often bringing that tradition with them or inheriting it from relatives who brought it with them from the Middle East or Africa, and those in communities who revile female circumcision and yet take male circumcision for granted. Debates about same-sex sexual relations seem to follow cultural boundaries that are religious in nature, although the boundaries of this debate are constantly shifting owing to a broad-based and effective LGBTQ advocacy movement.[17] There is absolutely no doubt that part of the socialization process involves educating children into what those doing the educating take to be the correct moral norms, and more often than not, it is assumed that the correct moral norms are those taken for granted within the social group in which the educator was raised. Thus, it is not surprising that moral differences trace other sorts of differences, such as religious difference, ethnic difference, difference in national origin, and even difference in socioeconomic status.

So how are these facts about the natural history of disagreement supposed to support cultural relativism? After all, other differences in belief—for example, religious belief—also follow lines defined by upbringing, but few would attempt to reduce religious facts to facts about human attitudes of one sort or another.[18] Further, even beliefs about the natural world—that is, scientific beliefs—are often the result of our socialization and education, which can vary by religion (think of the intelligent design/evolution debate), social class, national origin, and many other factors. Few of us have justification for our beliefs about, say, the solar system beyond having been taught various claims in school and hearing those claims reiterated on the Discovery Channel or in *Scientific American*. So if the defender of cultural relativism intends to have disagreement in belief that follows lines of socialization support her view, she is going to be forced to support relativist views about just about everything (perhaps even about relativism itself!). Given that most defenders of cultural relativism do not want to take such a line—they standardly want to say that morality is subjective, but science and religion are objective[19]—they need to point to something distinctive about *moral* disagreement as opposed to *scientific* or *religious* disagreement.

Let's leave aside religious belief—which raises enough difficulties of its own—and focus on the supposed contrast between *moral* disagreement and *scientific* disagreement. John Mackie, in his well-known *Ethics: Inventing Right and Wrong*, makes the following claims about the differences between moral disagreement and certain other types of disagreement:

> [I]t is not the mere occurrence of disagreements that tells against the objectivity of values. Disagreement on questions in history or biology or cosmology does not show that there are no objective issues in these fields for investigators to disagree about. But such scientific disagreement results from speculative inferences or explanatory hypotheses based on inadequate evidence, and it is hardly plausible to interpret moral disagreement in the same way. Disagreement about moral codes seems to reflect people's adherence to and participation in different ways of life. The causal connection seems to be mainly that way round: it is that people approve of monogamy because they participate in a monogamous way of life rather than that they participate in a monogamous way of life because they approve of monogamy. . . . In short, the argument from relativity [disagreement] has some force simply because the actual variations in the moral codes are more readily explained by

the hypothesis that they reflect ways of life than that they express perceptions, most of them seriously inadequate and badly distorted, of objective [i.e., culture-independent] values.[20]

Mackie is agreeing that we can find plenty of correlations between cultural divides and disagreements in various areas. However, he argues, we need to ask when it is plausible to suppose that the cultural divides are what cause the disagreement and when it is some other factor that coincides with the cultural divide that causes the disagreement. In the case of scientific disagreement, he claims, the latter is the case: people across temporal and geographical space have varying access to equipment and leisure that allow one to collect and assess the data relevant to both developing and testing scientific hypotheses. But, he asserts, that cannot be the explanation for moral divergence; rather, he insists, the most plausible explanation for that divergence is the attitudes and practices of those with whom one is socialized.

But should we agree with Mackie that the most and only really plausible explanation of moral disagreement is preexistent commitment to rules of conduct in the society in which one is raised and educated?[21] Mackie seems to be assuming no one would assert that moral disagreement could plausibly be explained by "speculative inferences or explanatory hypotheses based on inadequate evidence." It is not at all clear, however, why that is not a plausible explanation of moral disagreement. On almost any moral view other than cultural relativism, the well-being of human beings (and perhaps of other sentient beings such as cats and pigs) is at least one source of our moral reasons for action. Questions about what will make human beings suffer and what will make them do well, however, are causal questions. Even if we were all to agree about what constitutes the best life for human beings, we would need to know how to create the social conditions optimal for living such lives. Further, trying to determine what constitutes the best life for human beings is a complicated question requiring consideration of options for forms of living and an understanding of how human beings respond to various social and natural environments. And these are questions to be addressed by the various social and natural sciences.

So whatever disagreement infects scientific belief is going to leech into and have an effect on moral disagreement. Thus, whatever explains scientific disagreement is, at least in part, also an explanation of moral disagreement. The points that I made in the previous paragraph give us reason to deny an implicit assumption of Mackie's argument: that it is not plausible to think that some social conditions are better than others with respect to the acquisition of true moral beliefs. Just as John Stuart Mill thought that the "marketplace of ideas" was optimal for the acquisition of true beliefs in general, so we might say that the "marketplace of ways of life" is optimal for the acquisition of true beliefs about how it is best for us to live. If one lives in a society that offers few options in terms of how to live, one has few choices and little evidence to justify deviation from the norm. In some societies—those for whom mere survival is never a given—the assignment and fulfillment of traditional roles may be required in order to ensure that the group has sufficient material resources for survival. Further, in such societies, there is little time for moral debate, and there may be very good reason not to tolerate such debate: we cannot allow some to opt out of necessary tasks because, if we do, none of us will survive.

So disagreement does not give us good reason to accept cultural relativism. (In fact, there are lots of reasons to think that the extent of moral disagreement is highly overstated by those who offer the argument from disagreement, but I will not get into that point here.) However, one might use the fact of moral disagreement in a different way to support cultural relativism. It might be said that when there is so much divergence of opinion, we ought to be tolerant of those who disagree with us, and cultural relativism is the moral theory best placed to value tolerance appropriately. So let's now consider a commitment to toleration as motivation for cultural relativism.

Cultural Relativism and the Importance of Toleration

The second prominent motivation for accepting cultural relativism with agent-relativity is a desire to promote tolerance of different cultures and of the members of those different cultures. This is in many ways an admirable desire: misunderstandings between cultures can lead to horrific violence, and often these misunderstandings might have been avoided or differences resolved if patience and empathy had been employed. Many people seem to think that if we accept cultural relativism with agent-relativity, we will see that people's actions can only be morally evaluated against the background of *their* cultural norms, not against our own cultural norms. Thus, we will see that, for example, those engaging in female circumcision are acting rightly, and that we, as a result, have no basis for moral criticism of those who engage in the practice, regardless of the fact that our cultural norms condemn female circumcision. If we have no basis for moral criticism, the reasoning seems to go, then we ought to be tolerant of the actions and of those who perform them.

However, it is important to see that the conclusion of that reasoning—that we ought to be tolerant of the actions of members of different cultures—is itself a moral claim. But if we accept cultural relativism with agent-relativity, what each of us ought morally to do is determined by what people in our own culture approve or disapprove of. So the fact that, for example, a Somalian immigrant does nothing morally wrong in circumcising her daughter is irrelevant to whether I ought to tolerate her or her behavior. The only relevant fact in determining the moral status of my actions is the attitude that others in my culture would take to it. Thus, if others in my culture approve of being intolerant of immigrants and of immigrants' cultures, then it would be *wrong* of me to be tolerant of those immigrants or of their cultures. The cultural relativist with agent-relativity is committed to the possibility that it is right of me to be intolerant of people even if those people are doing the right thing!

Cultural relativism with agent-relativity is itself neutral with respect to the value or rightness of tolerant attitudes and conduct. Consider Nazi attitudes toward Jews and other "inferior" persons such as Gypsies and Slavs. If those Nazi attitudes were those of German culture of the 1930s and early 1940s, then what was right or good for a member of that culture would be relative to anti-Semitic and other bigoted attitudes. So toleration of Jewish, Slavic, and Gypsy culture would have been wrong or bad for an "Aryan" member of the culture of the Third Reich. For the cultural relativist, tolerant conduct and attitudes are to be morally evaluated in the same way that genocide, slavery, lynching, and rape are to be morally evaluated: relative to the culture of the persons engaged in that conduct.

It is extremely important for us, as moral thinkers, to assess whether a particular moral view really does the work we think that it does. Many people, I believe, have accepted cultural relativism with agent-relativity on the basis of the mistaken view that only cultural relativism with agent-relativity can avoid intolerance toward differences. However, cultural relativism is in fact singularly unsuited to promoting toleration, because cultural relativism makes morality a matter of cultural attitudes, and the sad continuing history of humankind is a history of bigotry, hatred, fear, and intolerance.

Of course, besides seeing whether a moral view really gets us the conclusions we want to get, we also need to consider whether we really ought to want to reach those conclusions. In order to assess the claim that we ought to be tolerant of different cultures and of members of different cultures, we need to think about what toleration would involve. I am sure that as you read my case studies of Nazis and slaveholders, you were not inclined to think we ought to be tolerant of such evil if what that means is not interfering or condemning. To refrain from interfering or condemning might very well amount to being complicit in great evil, to standing back as innocent people suffer horribly. And we would also have to be tolerant of people in our own culture, which, again, if that means not interfering or condemning, would lead to refusing to change bigoted, sexist, and racist attitudes in America.

But perhaps by advocating toleration, what we really want to promote are attempts at understanding and empathizing with one another. As I said earlier, people in different times and places are subject to different pressures. Our views are inevitably shaped by whomever is taken to be an authority in our culture. As children, we trust and believe what we are told by the adults around us, especially our parents and our teachers. If we do not attempt to understand a person's situation at the time of acting, we might not be willing to offer excuses where excuses are warranted. So even if cultural relativism is an incorrect view about the nature of morality—even if there is some culture-independent standard of morality that we can use to morally evaluate cultural norms—it might be that people who act wrongly but in accordance with the norms of their culture have an at least partial excuse for their behavior such that they are not to be regarded as fully responsible for their wrongdoing. So let's consider some arguments in favor of such excuses.

Reasons, Motivation, and Sanity

There are certain beings whom we do not hold morally responsible for their actions. In fact, we do not even think it is appropriate to make certain kinds of moral judgments about these beings. Consider, for example, domestic cats. These animals are predators: their bodies are set up in such a way that they need animal proteins in order to live, and they respond by hunting creatures such as mice, rabbits, and chipmunks. We are often struck by how our cute and cuddly pets can apparently taunt and play with their prey before finally eating it. But it seems wrong to blame cats for their behavior, or to say that cats are acting wrongly. Making these kinds of judgments seems misguided because we do not think that cats can be motivated by certain considerations, such as the suffering of their prey, to abstain from certain kinds of behaviors. They do not and, further, are unable to see the suffering of a mouse or a chipmunk as providing a reason to refrain from "playing with" their food. Certain facts about the nature of cats exempts them from moral evaluation.

We also exempt very small children from moral evaluation. As children grow we attempt to inculcate in them norms of behavior, such as "don't beat up other children in order to take their crayons," and eventually, we hope to get them to see the reasons behind such norms by, for example, fostering their empathy with other people. But, of course, the norms that children internalize and the reasons they accept for acting in accordance with such norms depend upon the cultural environment in which they are raised. While most of us in twenty-first-century America try to teach children to disregard race in their treatment of others, in the Jim Crow South, white children were taught to treat the races very differently, and this behavior was enforced by, for example, taking children to lynchings, where they were taught the reasons behind the norms (the purported hyper-sexuality and depravity of black men, and their insatiable desire to defile white women). So it seems to be obviously true that cultural environment affects the reasons one sees oneself as having and, thus, how one will be motivated to act. Without a certain kind of environment, one will not acquire certain sorts of motivations or see certain considerations as reasons to act, and thus we might think it would be inappropriate to make one the object of certain kinds of moral evaluation.

Even, then, if we reject cultural relativism as an account of the nature of morality,[22] we might think that being raised in a particular culture exempts one from certain forms of moral evaluation. The cases of nonhuman animals and small children show us that the possession and development of certain capacities is a prerequisite for moral evaluation. Even if the vast majority of human beings, no matter their social and cultural placement, have the requisite capacities, the development of those capacities plausibly requires a certain kind of upbringing and education—after all, we are certainly not surprised by the fact that feral children—children raised without human contact—lack the kind of moral responsiveness that you and I have. Thus, in this section I am going to examine considerations derived from the arguments of two philosophers who both claim that some kinds of moral evaluation are inappropriate when applied to agents raised in certain kinds of environments. Our case studies will help us to see that the claims of both philosophers are problematic when applied to a range of real-life examples.

In his well-known article "Moral Relativism Defended," Gilbert Harman defends a sophisticated version of cultural relativism. I am not interested here in exploring Harman's view itself. Rather, I want to examine the considerations he raises in attempting to defend his view. Harman claims that, for example, if some cannibals eat a shipwreck survivor, we will not insist that they ought not to have eaten her (or that it was wrong of them to have eaten her), although "we will speak of the primitive morality of the cannibals and may call them savages."[23] Similarly, Harman insists, it would be odd to say of Hitler that it was wrong of him to order the extermination of the Jews or that he ought not to have ordered their extermination. What, according to Harman, explains the inappropriateness of judging the cannibals and Hitler in these particular ways? He argues that certain types of moral judgments—what he calls "inner judgments"—have implications with respect to the motivations of the agent about whom we are making the inner judgment. Inner judgments take one of the two following forms: (i) S ought (ought not) to have done P; or (ii) it was right (wrong) of S to have done P. As we will see, Harman is not making any claim about other sorts of moral judgments, and the reason is that, unlike inner judgments, they have no implications about S's motivation to act (or to refrain from acting). However, Harman claims, we "make inner judgments about a person only if we suppose that he is capable of being motivated by the relevant moral considerations."[24] Harman thinks that the reasons we cannot say that Hitler ought not to have ordered the extermination of the Jews is that "we suppose that in acting as he did he shows that he could not have been susceptible to the moral considerations on the basis of which we make our judgment."[25] We can judge that Hitler was evil, but he was "beyond the pale" of moral motivations available to us and so inner judgments do not apply to him. In fact, Harman insists, it is somehow "too weak" to judge of Hitler that it was wrong of him to order the extermination of the Jews, because that suggests that certain moral considerations actually carried weight for him when, in fact, he was well beyond the motivational reach of those considerations.

For Harman (and for many other philosophers), all reasons have their source in the agent's "goals, desires, or intentions," and some of our aims and intentions are the result of our enculturation and of the aims and intentions of those around whom we were raised and live. It is simply not at all surprising that people raised in the same sort of environment develop the same sorts of motivations and thus, according to philosophers like Harman, the same sorts of reasons to act. Many of the habits and dispositions that express and/or constitute these shared intentions and reasons will be formed at an early age without conscious awareness; we may not even be able to linguistically describe these intentions. Thus, in making Harman's inner moral judgments about any agent, we need to consider what sorts of motivations her culture instilled in her and what motivations we think it is possible for her to have given that enculturation. Only then, Harman insists, can we know what sorts of reasons that agent actually or potentially has.

Let us suppose that Harman is right about the oddity of making inner judgments about the cannibals and about Hitler. Before we make any generalizations from these two cases, we can notice that they are unusual cases: the cannibals, we suppose, are an isolated group who have not confronted persons who oppose their dietary practices; and Hitler had various narcissistic and phobic pathologies that seemed to make him unable to consider alternative viewpoints in a rational manner. Does the plausibility of exempting the cannibals and Hitler have any implications for the appropriateness of making inner judgments about, for example, our American slaveholders, Thomas Jefferson and Charles Colcock Jones? Both acted in ways that are plausibly understood as having been endorsed by most of the people of their social class and regional affiliation, and both were raised in an environment in which racial prejudice was deeply entrenched. But neither Jefferson nor Jones had lived an isolated existence that insulated them from antislavery sentiment—both had received educations that exposed them to opposing viewpoints and to persons who espoused those opposing views.[26] Further, neither man exhibited any cognitive or affective pathologies; they were both men who were capable of forming deep and lasting bonds with friends and family, and both were able to think about conflicting positions in a rational way. We have no reason, then, to suppose that Jefferson and Jones were not susceptible to the moral motivations that drive those of us who regard property in human beings as morally abhorrent.

In their cases, other motivations—primarily self-interest—triumphed over those moral motivations. Jones, for example, could not bear the thought of being estranged from his extended kin network in Liberty County, Georgia. As a result, as we have seen, he engaged in a lengthy and ultimately successful process of cleansing himself of the antislavery notions he had acquired through his northern religious training. He found a way of appeasing both his conscience and his pro-slavery neighbors: he became a missionary to the slaves on his and on nearby plantations. Jefferson, concerned with his reputation and with his dire financial straits, hoped to live a life devoted to activities, such as architecture, inventing, and university building, that were suited to the twilight years of a great statesman and nation builder. In so doing, he would do his best to preserve something of his estate for his descendants and to remain the revered icon that he had become for many Americans, particularly those among the southern slaveholding gentry. Rocking the moral boat in the way urged by Edward Coles simply did not fit into Jefferson's agenda. We can certainly understand why both Jones and Jefferson did what they did, but the availability of such an explanation does not exempt them from moral judgment: if we start exempting people from certain forms of moral evaluation because their self-interest was stronger than their moral motivation, then it seems most of us will be exempt from such moral evaluation.

Our Nazis—in particular, the death camp commandants Höss and Stangl—don't provide any better examples of persons about whom we are unable to make inner judgments. Stangl presents himself as repulsed on his first exposure to the functions of Sobibor and Treblinka, gradually learning ways to cope with his environment and with his assignment. Like Jones and Jefferson, it seems he was capable of loving relationships and of sympathetic responses to the plight of strangers. Even Höss, arguably the "hardest" of them, presents himself as having to overcome a natural resistance to the gassings and willing to work to overcome that resistance because he believed it was a form of treason against the Führer. So these men seemed quite capable of being moved by the considerations that move us not to engage in torture and murder and, thus, there is no reason to suppose any of the Nazis of our case studies are beyond the reach of our inner judgments.

Which leaves us with Ted Bundy, our psychopath/sociopath. As we will see in chapter 5, there are serious questions about Bundy's affective capacities, and given certain connections between morality and emotion, Bundy's affective flaws may have impaired his capacities for moral cognition. Thus, there are reasons to wonder whether Bundy was capable of being motivated by paradigmatically moral considerations. There is no doubt that prudence and self-interest were capable of acting as restraints on Bundy's behavior, at least to a certain extent—we saw that his desires to possess and dominate women were often too strong for his more rational self to control. If anyone, then, fits Harman's description of someone "beyond the pale," it is Bundy. But if Bundy is beyond the reach of certain moral considerations, it is because he lacks certain capacities, just as domestic cats and very small children lack those capacities; in other words, it is because Bundy, in virtue of his inability to grasp moral concepts, is not a moral agent.[27] Unless, however, we think that some kinds of enculturation render persons psychopathic, it does not seem that we can make any generalizations from the fact that some wrong actions are culturally endorsed to the claim that persons raised in that culture are exempt from moral evaluation when they perform such actions.

However, that does suggest another category of persons to whom we offer excuses when they act wrongly—namely, those suffering from certain kinds of insanity. Consider the familiar type of insanity that provides an excuse in a court of law: a psychosis with a delusional character. If someone has auditory or visual hallucinations, she is unable to grasp or to understand the nature of the world; her hallucinations provide her with data that lead her to conclude the external world is different from the way it actually is. Typically, mental disorders such as schizophrenia impair an agent's ability to assess this evidence, because disordered thinking and reasoning is a common accompaniment to psychotic delusions. Further, the psychotic are afflicted with inappropriate and disproportionate affective responses, causing their fear, anxiety, and distrust to be abnormally intense and overwhelming. The facts of their condition—misleading delusional data, disordered reasoning patterns, disproportionate affective responses—provide us with good reason to believe such psychotics have either a partial or a complete excuse for their wrongful actions in relevant circumstances.[28] Such persons cannot get at the way the world is, and as a result, they often are led to false beliefs about how they ought to behave—false beliefs that may very well be justified, given the data provided by their delusions.

In her well-known discussion of the conditions of moral responsibility, "Sanity and the Metaphysics of Responsibility," Susan Wolf argues that having been raised in certain kinds of cultures provides an excuse for wrongful behavior for the very same reason that clinical insanity does. What the clinically and legally insane lack is "the minimally sufficient ability to cognitively and normatively recognize and appreciate the world for what it is."[29] So sanity "involves the ability to know the difference between right and wrong, and a person, who, even on reflection, can't [for example] see that having someone tortured because he failed to salute you is wrong plainly lacks the requisite ability."[30] This last is a description of a hypothetical case study described by Wolf, but we could instead say that someone unable to see that genocide or slavery is wrong lacks "the ability to know the difference between right and wrong." Wolf, in fact, thinks that we should "give less than full responsibility to persons who, though acting badly, act in ways that are strongly encouraged by their societies—the slaveowners of the 1850s, the German Nazis of the 1930s":

These are people, we imagine, who falsely believe that the ways they are acting are morally acceptable. . . . But their false beliefs in the moral permissibility of their actions and the false values from which these beliefs derived may have been inevitable given the social circumstances in which they developed. If we think that the agents could not help but be mistaken about their values, we do not blame them for the actions which those values inspired.[31]

Wolf is making very strong claims here, saying that it was *inevitable* that Nazis and slaveholders have false moral views, that they *could not help* but be mistaken about right and wrong action. All it takes, of course, to show these very strong claims to be false is one person who did avoid the false moral views while existing in the same cultural milieu—that is why it is so important to bring Edward Coles into any discussion of the character of Thomas Jefferson. But Wolf's point would be strong enough if she simply claimed that it is very difficult, under certain cultural conditions, to develop the requisite moral capacities, and thus, people raised under those conditions ought not to be held to the same moral standards as those of us raised in conditions more conducive to the acquisition of moral truth. To what extent can culture render those raised in it unable to tell the difference between right and wrong?

If we take the case of delusional psychosis as our paradigm of an excusing condition, we can approach other cases by attempting to see in what ways they are similar to our paradigm. Consider the case of Bundy: Is there some feature of Bundy that constitutes a partial or complete excuse for his behavior? The answer to this question clearly depends on how we interpret Bundy's character. First, however, we can set aside any appeal to delusions—Bundy did not experience any auditory or visual hallucinations that would have warped his understanding of the external world. Second, it certainly seems that Bundy was quite capable of standard means–end reasoning, even if his strong impulses often made him act imprudently relative to his ends. But, of course, we are all capable of imprudent behavior owing to temptation, but we do not think that such is sufficient to constitute an excuse for wrongful behavior: no matter how much I want the expensive necklace on display in the department store, I possess no excuse for stuffing it in my bag and attempting to leave the store with my treasure undiscovered. The law in many U.S. jurisdictions allows for a defense of "irresistible impulse," but the distinction between a literally irresistible impulse and an impulse that is merely not resisted or only feebly resisted is impossible to make from the third-person (and perhaps even from the first-person) perspective. In any case, we have no reason to think that Bundy's impulses were any less resistible than those of the rest of us.

If Bundy differs from us in any distinctive way (other than in the content of his desires), it is with respect to his affective capacities. As I will argue in chapter 5, Bundy's moral-linguistic faux pas are plausibly seen to be the result of a lack of understanding of the inner lives of other human beings. Bundy seemed incapable of grasping moral concepts that rely for their application and meaning on facts about human well-being and suffering, because he couldn't seem to grasp that other people have inner lives like his own. So unlike the delusional psychotic who has data that lead her to posit nonexisting beings in the external world or to posit nonexistent motives and intentions in other actually existing persons, Bundy suffered an affective failure due to his inability to grasp actually existing mental states in other persons. Whether Bundy has an excusing condition depends on the extent to which his affective failure can be attributed to his own doing or is the result of some endemic structural defect in his brain or blood chemistry over which he had no control.[32]

Finally, we are ready to turn to our cases of, if Wolf is right, insanity caused not by psychosis or tumor but by cultural environment. Wolf is surely right that if a being is such that he is incapable of recognizing the wrongness of certain actions, then he is exempt from at least certain forms of moral evaluation, just as a shark or tiger is so exempt. But do we really think that many people in Nazi Germany, the slaveholding American South, or cultures that practice female circumcision lack the capacity to grasp moral truth? The vast majority of people in these cultures had or have plenty of interactions with other people—interactions both of an intimate kind (e.g., with friends and family) and of a less than intimate kind. Many received a basic education that equipped them to make comparisons and draw analogies. We can also presume that they were able to grasp that other human beings experienced emotions and had projects and plans for their lives. So it seems that they had all the tools they needed to recognize that their actions caused suffering to other human beings, and that those others suffered just as they would have if they had been in that position. Wolf might insist, however, that these people's upbringings led them to have a warped perspective on the data, that they were unable to see the *significance* of the suffering of their victims: they were unable to value African Americans or Jews as they deserve to be valued. In other words, they were unable to move from their recognition of certain nonmoral facts to the moral facts.

But let's consider the example of a slaveholder of the antebellum South. Here I will use a hypothetical example, because both Jefferson and Jones were extraordinary in terms of education and contact with northern antislavery contingents. The average slaveholder had a very small number of slaves, perhaps two or three, and he worked his land alongside his slaves. Even those with larger holdings interacted with their slaves on a near-daily basis, unless they were absentee landowners. They enlisted slaves to cook their meals, clean their houses, and, most important, care for their children. They allowed their children to play with slave children, and male slaveholders often took female slaves into their beds, siring children by them. No doubt these men and women of the slaveholding class were raised to believe that blacks were inferior to them, that blacks were akin to children and would be unable to care for themselves if they were set free, that blacks did not feel as deeply as whites would the separation of family members that was such a pervasive aspect of the trade in human beings. Further, these whites socialized only with persons of like mind, and so were taught that those who opposed slavery were "fanatics" who did not understand blacks and their natures in the way that southerners did.

Nonetheless, these white men and women had plenty of data that even the smallest amount of reflection would have revealed as undermining their cherished theories: Why did slaves react with violent outbursts of emotion when they were separated from family members? Plenty of freed blacks made their way on their own in an extremely hostile environment, and slaves themselves carried out complex tasks for their white masters.[33] White claims about black laziness and lack of initiative were undermined by blacks who, in their little free time, cultivated garden plots or raised livestock in order to make some money of their own. However, whites formed their views through the filter of their own self-interest: they viewed blacks as lazy because the latter had to be forced to work for the former. But did the whites never ask themselves, "How motivated would I be to work for another person's interests?" It is plausible to suppose that the white slaveholders simply kept themselves from reflecting on facts that were right before their eyes—they skated over the surface, as it were, with their self-interest acting as a thin sheet of ice keeping them from falling through into the icy water of reality.

So it is no doubt true that there were barriers that needed to be overcome in order for slaveholders to acknowledge the wrongness of their actions. But barriers exist for virtually every human being on the planet; each of us is guided to a great extent by self-interest, and we all have distractions in the form of financial pressures, familial demands, and peer pressure. Nonetheless, these distractions and temptations are not in and of themselves an excuse for our not attempting to ascertain our moral duties and fairly assessing the value of other

still wd've of a
been more of a
feat for them

human beings and animals. If we have moral concepts at all, we have all that we need to engage in moral deliberation (assuming that we have a certain minimal level of cognitive and affective capacities).

Slaveholders had moral concepts and grasped the nature of moral deliberation—if they hadn't, then they would not have engaged in lengthy polemics designed to justify their participation in the practice of human bondage. Perhaps an entire society of psychopaths would be one in which no one had any moral concepts. However, someone raised by psychopaths and only by psychopaths would likely be akin to the feral children raised by wolves, but we certainly do not want to compare members of cultures with false moral beliefs to feral children. My point is simply that the vast majority of human beings who have moral concepts thereby have the tools for critique and evaluation of their actions. If they do not undertake such critique, whether because of peer pressure (think of lynch mobs in the postbellum South), self-interest (antebellum slaveholders), or plain old selfishness, then they are culpable for their failure to do so. Our inclination to suppose that we might behave in exactly the same way under similar conditions is no reason to excuse such agents; rather, it is reason to suppose that we are also morally weak and have only good fortune to thank for not having as many temptations or hurdles. While we may not have performed the same number of wrong actions or wrong actions of such seriousness, we may be no better people than the agents engaging in genocide or slaveholding. Thus, even if we accept Wolf's thesis about the conditions for moral responsibility, it is unclear that it has any significant implications for how we assess agents in different historical and cultural contexts.[34]

However, an issue is left hanging here. What seems relevant about at least some Nazis and some slaveholders is that they quite sincerely thought what they were doing was morally right.

Could some of them have had justified false beliefs that what they were doing was right? If so, how do we morally assess the actions that resulted from justified yet false moral beliefs? How much effort are we required to expend rationally evaluating our moral beliefs and collecting data about situations to which those beliefs might be relevant? This is the issue to be addressed in the next section.

False Belief and Moral Culpability

There are cases in which it seems quite clear-cut that an agent's false belief or beliefs absolves her of or diminishes her responsibility. For example, suppose that Hannah has started to have an allergic reaction to her meal. She asks her dinner companion, Grace, to retrieve Hannah's medication from her bag and to give her an injection. Grace does as asked, giving Hannah an injection. However, unbeknownst to Grace, Hannah had accidently put in the wrong syringe that morning, and given her current allergic reaction, the wrong medication has a fatal effect on her. Grace, it seems, is not morally blameworthy for Hannah's death, because she was justified in believing she was acting in a way that would save Hannah's life, not kill her. Further, given her limited time, it was reasonable for her not to seek further verification that Hannah had put the correct syringe in her bag—she has no reason not to trust Hannah, and she has to act quickly. So Grace is in no way to blame for performing an action that leads to Hannah's death.

Consider another sort of case. Suppose that Bernhard has grown up in an isolated rural village in Germany in the years between the World Wars. Everyone who Bernhard knows and respects—parents, teachers, clergy, village officials—is anti-Semitic and they convey this anti-Semitism to the young people of the village. The only books available to Bernhard portray Jews as greedy, scheming, and determined to destroy "Aryan" culture and to rape "Aryan" women; there are no actual Jews in the village for Bernhard to meet to compare with the images in the books. Not surprisingly, Bernhard grows up to be anti-Semitic, and when he gets news of Hitler's agenda, he wholeheartedly supports it.

The case of Bernhard certainly appears to be one in which the culture in which he was raised provides him with justification for false beliefs about Jews. Further, given that Bernhard is justified in believing that Jews are dangerous, it seems that his false but justified beliefs about the nature of Jews give him justification for his false moral view that Germany needs to act to contain the Jews in some way. And, in order to reach this conclusion, we do not need to think that Bernhard, in virtue of the culture in which he is raised, is incapable of the moral motivations you and I have or that he is not capable of knowing the difference between right and wrong. All we need to suppose is that our moral beliefs rely on many nonmoral beliefs for their justification, and that it is possible for our cultural situations to provide us with justification for false nonmoral beliefs. And it seems quite obvious that our cultural situations can do that.

The most important features of cultural situations that can provide us with justification for false beliefs are facts about authority and testimony. Much of what we believe about the world is a result of the testimony of other people—that is, it is the result of what other people tell us. And as we grow up and mature, we take most seriously the testimony of persons who seem to be authorities on various matters: we listen to our teachers as they teach us math, science, and history; we listen to clergy as they tell us about God and the afterlife; and we listen to what our parents tell us about how we ought to behave. In the case of Bernhard, everyone he encountered in positions of authority taught him that anti-Semitism was morally required; he had no competing testimony or evidence to balance against what these authorities told him, and he had no reason to suspect that his authorities were not in fact experts on the matters on which they purported to have knowledge.

It is important to see that the mere fact that one's moral belief is the dominant view in one's culture does not constitute justification for that belief. In order for others' holding a belief to constitute justification for my holding the belief, I must have justification for believing that I can trust others on the subject matter of the belief. And this is where the fact of moral disagreement is relevant. If I am aware that different cultures adhere to different moral views, then I have good reason to question the truth of my own culture's moral code, because I can see that I would most likely accept the code of whatever culture I was raised in. Why should I regard the people around me as somehow morally expert in ways that people in other cultures are not? In attempting to answer this question, I am forced to think about the nature of moral knowledge and of the conditions best suited to its acquisition. In other words, even to assess the authority of the people around me, I have to engage in some independent moral reflection. My imaginary Bernhard was not in a position to do this, because he was not exposed to competing positions, or even to the fact that there were competing positions. And this is one reason why it is important to incorporate instruction about other cultures into moral education: children must be raised in full awareness of diversity, so that they can be provided with reasons to call into question the moral authority of those around them. Only when moral agents have been raised to question the cherished values of their cultures in a critically reflective way can we hope to make moral progress. But we cannot be afraid of also engaging in critical evaluation of the cherished values of other cultures; neither our own dominant moral view nor those of other cultures should be immune from critical evaluation.

It is, however, certainly true, as I pointed out in my example of Hannah and Grace, that we often face constraints in the acquisition of evidence and in reflection upon evidence. We have only so much time, and practically speaking, we cannot devote most of our days to moral thinking (unless we are lucky enough to have jobs as professors of philosophy). We need to pay the bills, do our jobs, take care of our friends and families, and do all the other mundane tasks essential to keeping ourselves going in the world. Morality is a complex matter of the nature of human well-being, the ways to bring about well-being without thereby causing injustice, and the nature of moral personhood and moral agency. Just as I am forced to rely on the testimony of others for many of my beliefs, so it might be said that practical constraints make it rational for us to rely on the moral testimony of others for at least some of our moral beliefs. Can we really be expected to call our culture's values into evaluation wholesale? Surely we need to at least start from some of our culture's basic moral presuppositions.

I think there is much truth in such a claim. Here it is important, though, to think about what counts as basic moral presuppositions. While many defenders of cultural relativism support their view via an appeal to moral disagreement, we can question how much disagreement there is at the basic or fundamental level. How many cultures have moral codes that do not understand moral rules as aimed at the promotion of human well-being? What differs from one culture to another are beliefs about how to promote well-being and the nature of well-being. Thus, within every culture, moral deliberators are confronted with dominant views about the best ways of life and how to promote those ways of life. They are also confronted with claims about who stands where in the moral hierarchy and which beings are outside the realm of moral concern altogether. In the ante-bellum South, for example, whites were raised to believe that the system of black slavery functioned to the benefit of both the whites and the blacks, and that other systems posed serious danger of undermining the well-being of both classes of persons. These moral claims were backed up by theories of the differing natures of blacks and whites.

It takes very little reflection upon human nature to recognize the human tendency to view the world through the lens of self-interest and to rationalize various actions and practices that benefit oneself. So whenever a social practice involving hierarchy is justified by appeal to the best interests of the subordinate class or classes, one should see the need to question the justification for such a practice, especially if one is a member of a dominant group. We often take scientific hypotheses on authority, and there is no reason not to do so when human well-being is not at issue; thus, I have little reason to do independent investigation about the nature of black holes. But the "scientific" theories purporting to show the inferiority of blacks were put to work to justify keeping blacks in bondage. Acting on such theories, then, carries with it grave moral risk. In such a case, I am far less justified in simply taking such theories to be true based on testimony. Further, I, as a member of the slaveholding class, could have acquired relevant evidence without going out of my way; all that I had to do was to try to interact with my slaves in an open-minded way.[35]

Even if moral agents take the dominant beliefs of their cultures as a starting point, they are rationally required to reflect on those beliefs, given that moral beliefs are about our reasons for action. So we need to be able to discern what our moral beliefs are, whether our moral beliefs cohere with one another, upon which nonmoral beliefs they rely for justification, and how those beliefs came to be dominant in our culture. We need to reflect in this way all the while keeping in mind the potential biases involved in our reasoning about the relevant matters. There is never any guarantee that we will not go astray in our moral thinking, and so there may be cases in which the most conscientious, reflective, and concerned moral agent acts wrongly, perhaps very wrongly. In such a case, her culpability may be diminished or eliminated. But we have seen no reason to think that the mere fact she acted in ways approved by her culture renders her situation to be such.

We can return to John Stuart Mill for some interesting remarks on this issue. In *The Subjection of Women*, Mill argues that the Victorian system of making women second-class citizens had no justification in spite of its deep entrenchment in the culture of which Mill was a member.[36] Given its deep entrenchment, how could Victorian men be expected to see that it was unjust? Mill pointed out that every male had a vested interest in maintaining the system: it bolstered his self-esteem and eliminated half the population as competition. Every man could lord it over all the women in his life and feel justified in doing so. As I have said, whenever a system benefits the class of which we are a part, we are obligated to attempt to consider open-mindedly whether it really does benefit the subordinated class or classes.

Also, whenever a system is justified by an appeal to the nature of members of the subordinate class relative to the natures of the members of the dominant class, we need to reflect on the evidence for the inferiority of the former class. Women in Victorian England were denied educational opportunities available to men, and they were raised to believe that the whole success of their life depended on attracting a suitable male. How, then, could any rational person think he had sufficient evidence for concluding that women were frivolous creatures, concerned only with hair and dress, without interest in or talent for science, government, or the professions? Similar considerations could also have been raised about the supposed inferiority of blacks.

It is of course true that if one were raised in a culture where morality had nothing to do with human welfare, no one had ever noticed the human tendencies to bias evidence on the basis of self-interest, and no one ever reflected on the nature and coherence of their beliefs, that person would have little if any culpability for wrong action. But it is questionable whether such a being is really a moral agent at all. If we refuse to deny that members of other cultures are moral agents, and we refuse to accept that their cultures are that radically defective and empty, then we are forced to hold their members accountable for their wrong actions based on certain false beliefs. Respect for them as persons demands that we blame them when they act badly and, also, that we blame ourselves when we are in similar situations.

Humility and Conviction

I began this chapter by considering Wilson's cautions about using our present-day standards of moral behavior to evaluate Jefferson: Wilson claims that it is "inappropriate" to do so. So the question arose: Is it inappropriate to evaluate Jefferson by using our own moral standards, and if not, why not? The question is important for us as moral agents and deliberators, because we need to know what role our own cultural norms and expectations ought to play in our moral thinking both about how we ought to behave and about how we ought to evaluate others and ourselves. Our case studies of Nazis and slaveholders provide stark examples of the dangers of not thinking clearly about cultural norms or in using those norms as excuses for passivity or for following along. If we are to act on our duty of due care in moral deliberation, we need to be able to think about the appropriate place of cultural norms in moral deliberation. And our duty of moral self-scrutiny requires us to see how our own habits, dispositions, and assumptions are derived from our cultural placement, and then to evaluate those habits, dispositions, and assumptions to the best of our ability.

We can now see ways in which Wilson is quite right if we take him as urging us to be sure to pay attention to an agent's cultural placement before we morally assess her or her actions. Culture is a matter of how people in a community behave and what they believe, and there is absolutely no doubt that what each of us is justified in believing is, at least in part, a result of what we are told by those in our community who are taken to be experts. But once we become aware of human fallibility and diversity of opinion across time and space, we acquire a responsibility to question even the most revered among us; after all, Thomas Jefferson claimed that blacks are inferior to whites and many scientists and other scholars in Nazi Germany accepted false racial theories; these should be cautionary tales for us, warning us to never casually accept the word of experts when doing so potentially has grave consequences for the well-being of others or of ourselves. Albert Speer decided that Hitler was an appropriate authority to whom to defer, as many of his time and place did, demonstrating that even widely accepted beliefs can be radically false.

Unless we accept cultural relativism—and we need to find better reasons to do so than the mere fact of disagreement or its purported support of the virtue of toleration—we cannot appeal to cultural norms, in and of themselves, as justification of our actions or of the actions of others. We also have to be cautious before we give either ourselves or others an easy pass for wrongful behavior by appealing to culture as an excuse. Recognizing the difficulties in questioning the authorities of our time and place should breed a certain humility in us as we judge the actions of those from other cultures, but our slaveholders and Nazis also show us that such humility cannot be allowed to become passivity. We need to push ourselves and others to question our assumptions, even the ones deeply embedded in our ways of life. Trying to find the appropriate balance between humility and understanding in judging others and an unwillingness to tolerate wrong and injustice, to act upon our convictions while remaining open-minded, is one of the greatest challenges of the moral life.

Finally, the examples of the slaveholders and the Nazis show us how important it is to pull apart our own reasoning or that of others in order to see what sorts of nonmoral claims are being used to support a moral belief. As I pointed out in our discussion of disagreement, whatever disagreement there is on, for example, scientific matters can have an impact on moral disagreement. At some point, we may very well have to take some experts at their word, but we need to make sure we have done all that we reasonably can to assess the status and claims of those experts. Sometimes it is easier to just take the "experts" at their word, particularly when doing so allows us to go along with the dominant norms of our culture. But easiness is not an excuse for wrongful behavior.

Do the Ends Justify the Means?

Moral Deliberation and the Consequences of Our Actions

As I pointed out in chapter 1, our moral deliberations often involve an appeal to various nonmoral claims and, in particular, to claims about the consequences of proposed actions. So in fulfilling our duty of due care in moral deliberation we need to (i) be prepared to deliberate about the consequences of the various alternative actions available to us, and (ii) have some conception of the role that the conclusions about consequences ought to play in our reasoning about right and wrong action. To set up some of the complications that arise in approaching (i) and (ii), let's remind ourselves of some examples from our case studies of appeals to consequences to justify choices and actions.

The Choice to Run a Death Camp

Franz Stangl ran a death camp, where he oversaw the death of roughly one million men, women, and children. We naturally find ourselves wondering how one could live with oneself after having been engaged in such horrific endeavors, about how one would have to think about such events in order to go on with one's life. Stangl apparently did so by claiming that he chose the best of a bad set of options. Stangl, over and over again throughout the interviews with Sereny, insisted that he did what he did out of fear of the consequences of refusal, a fear that both he and his family would suffer if he did not comply with orders.

But his fear for himself raises a further question about how he could live with what might be seen as his own cowardice. At one point during the interviews, Sereny confronts Stangl about just these sorts of issues:

> There were *people in Germany who stood up for their principles; not many, it is true, but some. Yours was a very special position; there were less than a dozen men like you in all of the Third Reich. Don't you think that if you had found that extraordinary courage, it would have had an effect on the people who served under you?*
>
> He shook his head. "If I had sacrificed myself," he said slowly, "if I had made public what I felt, and had died . . . it would have made no difference. Not an iota. It would all have gone on just the same, as if it and I had never happened."
>
> . . . *But even so, don't you think somewhere, underneath, it would have affected the atmosphere in the camp, would have given others courage?*
>
> "Not even that. It would have caused a tiny ripple, for a fraction of an instant—that's all."[1]

Here Stangl seems to be attempting to justify his actions by saying that nothing would have been better if he had opted out: he would have suffered, presumably someone else would have gotten his job, and the work of genocide would have continued as before.

Sereny contrasts Stangl's behavior with that of the few "who stood up for their principles." So we have a supposed contrast between those who adhere to their principles and those who do not, for whatever reason. Here we find ourselves naturally in agreement with Sereny, praising those who stood on their principles versus Stangl, who participated in genocide. But what, if anything, is wrong with Stangl's reasoning? Did he fail to act on principles, or was he really just acting on different principles than he would have been doing if he had refused his assignment or publicly protested? Did he act on the wrong principles, or did he act on the right principles but misapply them in the situation in which he found himself?

Stangl presents his deliberations as weighing the risk of harms to himself and to his family (he had a wife and two small children) against what he saw as the meager, if any, good that would come from his protest. Most of us agree with Stangl that morality requires us to take care of our loved ones, particularly our children. But how much weight are we allowed to accord to the good of our loved ones as opposed to the good of strangers? Can one be justified in killing others, perhaps a great many others, to protect those whom one loves?

A further issue that arises when we consider Stangl's deliberations is whether one could ever justify doing something like running a death camp. Are there certain kinds of activities that, no matter what the consequences, one ought never to take part in? A worry is that if we say this, we are showing more of a concern with keeping our own hands clean than with helping others—maybe sometimes we have to get ourselves down in the muck, no matter how awful the deeds, if getting our hands dirty means helping people.

Taking Account of One's Own Interests

While on death row, during his interviews with Michaud and Aynesworth, Ted Bundy repeatedly claimed to experience remorse after committing murder. But, of course, Bundy never considered turning himself into the police in order to prevent himself from killing again. In fact, he suggests that he didn't do so because he convinced himself that that would have been pointless:

> As far as remorse over the act [the killing], that would last for a period of time. But it could all be justified. The person [Bundy] would attempt to justify it by saying, "Well, listen you, you fucked up this time, but you're never going to do it again. So let's just stay together, and it won't ever happen again." Why sacrifice this person's whole life?
> And so, the focus then became on surviving and modifying behavior. A sort of optimist. Sort of finding the silver lining, you might call it.[2]

As with Stangl, here we have Bundy attempting to justify his actions, which seem to us in this instance clearly unjustified, by pointing to the better consequences of not turning himself in. Bundy, it seems clear, is primarily concerned with the consequences for himself, but aren't we all? So we need to consider how much risk or suffering one is required to assume or undergo in order to help or to protect others. How does one weigh one's own benefits and burdens against those of other people? Which consequences of our actions are the morally relevant ones, and how do we weigh those consequences against each other?

Bundy's situation also raises again the issue of standing on principle with which Sereny confronts Stangl. While I am going to assume that none of us has committed crimes on the level of Bundy's, we have all made moral mistakes of one kind or another, and some of these moral mistakes affect other people. When are we required to "come clean"? Can we have a duty to do so even if the result will be only suffering for ourselves and for other people? Is it morally important to be, for example, honest, even if no good will come from being honest? Is it morally important to "see justice done" regardless of the costs?

Taking Everyone into Account

Charles Colcock Jones, the Southern slaveholder, was a man who took what he regarded as his moral duties very seriously. As we saw in chapter 2, Jones studied in northern schools and became well acquainted with abolitionists and their views. In a letter to his future wife, he expressed the belief that slavery was unjust, and that it was wrong for him to live a comfortable life financed by slave labor. But Jones's entire life—the people and places he loved—were bound up with the institution of slavery. How much change in the social situation was he morally bound to bring about? Was he morally required to attempt to change his family and friends? How much might he be expected to sacrifice?

Jones begins to consider whether he could find a course for his life that would promote "the best interests of the coloured populations" without disturbing or upsetting his white neighbors, friends, and family. Having studied to be a minister, it is natural for him to choose to minister to the souls of the slave population. By doing so, he believes, he will lead them to God and bring some good out of their enforced servitude. He believes that he has found a solution that will allow him to do the most good for himself and his family, and for the white and black populations of Liberty County, Georgia.

Jones, like Stangl, is trying to weigh his own good and that of his family against that of the enslaved population. He decides that he can satisfy everyone by preaching to the slaves. The same questions arise in Jones's case as arose in Stangl's case: Is Jones acting on the right principles but misapplying them? Or is he misguidedly allowing his own good and that of the people he loves to play too large of a role in his moral deliberations? How much is he required to sacrifice for the sake of "justice"? Is justice something different from trying to do the best for everyone involved? If so, what is it?

We judge Jones's slaveholding to have been wrong—just as we judge Bundy's not turning himself into the police and Stangl's overseeing a death camp as wrong. And now we see Jones, like Bundy and Stangl, justifying his apparently wrong action to himself by pointing to the good consequences that will result. So we have three cases of appealing to consequences leading to agents performing wrong actions. Is there a problem with letting our decisions be guided by consequences? Or do our three case studies go wrong by appealing to irrelevant consequences, or by wrongly weighing the different consequences against each other? Do they give too much weight to their own interests or to the interests of their loved ones? How are we to go about answering such questions?

Thinking About Means, Ends, and Principles

While I am quite sure that none of us has had to face questions about whether to run a death camp, confess to serial rape and murder, or emancipate our slaves, we need to take cases like those of Stangl, Bundy, and Jones seriously because the issues raised by their situations are analogous to situations that we might very well have faced. Have you ever had to consider what career to choose, and worried that the attractive offer with a high salary might lead you to do things that won't sit well with your conscience? Have you ever lied to a friend and wondered whether you ought to confess having done so? Have you ever opted to increase your own luxuries, perhaps buying an even larger flat-screen TV, all the while knowing that the money could have been sent to a reputable charity verifiably doing good work? Have you provided your own child with all the latest technology, while knowing that you could have used that money to provide basic necessities to less well-off children? If we actually act on our duty of self-scrutiny, we will probably find choices and actions in our own lives that mirror those faced by our perhaps much more dramatic case studies. So we can all keep those cases in mind alongside those of Stangl, Bundy, and Jones.

The three examples of Stangl, Bundy, and Jones raise a lot of issues about how we ought to weigh the interests of ourselves and of our loved ones against the interests of strangers, what sorts of principles ought to guide our conduct and what to do if those principles conflict with one another, and how we determine which sorts of consequences, if any, are relevant to what we ought to do. All these issues are at the heart of the debate between two of the major types of moral theory: consequentialism and deontology. These theories offer very different approaches to moral deliberation, choice, and action, so understanding these two theories can provide us with a framework for understanding how and whether to critique the kinds of reasoning exhibited by our case studies—kinds of reasoning that we all engage in, albeit in less dramatic situations.

At the heart of the debate between these two approaches to moral thinking is a debate about the role of consequences in a determination of the right action. This debate plays a role in everyday moral discussions about issues such as torture, medical experimentation, and warfare, where a certain kind of criticism is often heard: "Inflicting torture on one or several in order to extract information that would prevent terrorist attacks?!" "Experimenting on human beings or on other animals in order to find a cure that will save thousands or even millions of lives?!" "Bombing civilians in order to end a war and thereby minimize future deaths of both combatants and noncombatants?!" Often, if someone advocates such measures for such reasons, they are accused of allowing the ends to justify the means.

But why is this supposed to be a criticism? The person to whom such a criticism is addressed might plausibly respond: "But means are adopted in order to achieve a certain goal or end! So in order to justify adopting certain means, what else could I point to except the ends at which I am aiming? And if the means will serve, in an efficient manner, to achieve my ends, haven't I thereby justified adopting those means?"

One appropriate response, of course, is to ask whether the end itself is justified. The Nazis justified moving from shooting people into open pits to gassing them in specially constructed installations so that (i) they could kill more people in less time, and (ii) they could kill with less "psychological stress" on those assigned to do the killing. If the end were justified, then it would justify adopting these efficient means with less negative side effects. But the end is not morally justified, and so it cannot justify the means taken to reach it. So an unjustified end cannot justify any means taken to reach it.

However, those who criticize torture, medical experimentation, and the bombing of civilians in justified warfare typically are not criticizing the goal of saving innocent lives for which these policies are intended to be implemented. Rather, they seem to be suggesting that no matter what one's goals, these sorts of means are not justified. But should we accept such a claim? If our end is justified, and the good of the end outweighs the bad of the means, then why reject the means as unjustified? Are there principles that we ought to use to guide our conduct that forbid certain kinds of actions, regardless of the consequences of performing such actions? Or is adhering to such principles simply a way of demonstrating an excessive concern with keeping our own hands clean? Or do our moral duties go beyond bringing about the best end result that we can produce? What, in any case, would constitute the best end result? Let's begin by considering a theory that takes *only* consequences as relevant to moral deliberation.

Consequentialism

Consequentialism is, simultaneously, both a widely accepted and widely reviled moral theory. Because one of my major concerns in this chapter is the role of certain nonmoral claims—namely, claims about the consequences or results of our actions—in moral reasoning, I am going to focus on consequentialism as a view that gives consequences the primary role in moral deliberation and then contrast it with a view that gives consequences a different role in moral deliberation. I hope to give my reader just a sense of the complexities involved in this debate; there are many versions of both theories that I will discuss and many other moral theories. While I myself am not a consequentialist, I think that the theory, in one form or another, has a great deal of plausibility and needs to be taken seriously by anyone interested in moral reasoning.

Let's begin by considering a hypothetical scenario requiring moral deliberation. Suppose I am a doctor in an emergency room when the victims of a multiple car accident are rushed in via ambulance. My hospital is a small one in a remote rural community, so our ER staff is minimal and there are very few medical personnel on call. Because of the number of critically ill accident victims, I have to make some choices. Suppose there is one victim so critically injured that it would take my entire staff to do what is necessary to save her life. However, the amount of time that those life-saving measures would take will cost us the lives of all other nine victims.

My other option is to spread my staff out, save the nine, and leave the one most seriously hurt to die. What ought I to do?

For most people, the answer is obvious: save the nine and leave the one to die. Why? Because more lives will thereby be saved, and more lives saved is, barring unusual circumstances, a better outcome. It is the apparent obviousness of the correct answer in this sort of case that can be used to motivate consequentialism:

> *Consequentialism*: The right action in circumstances C for agent S is that action which, out of all of the alternatives available to S in C, will produce the greatest net sum of intrinsic value in the long run.

The first important feature of consequentialism that we need to notice is that it makes reference to the notion of *intrinsic value* in its statement of the nature of right action. So before we consider the consequentialist account of right action, we need to address the concept of intrinsic value.

Intrinsic vs. Instrumental Value

Intrinsic value is to be contrasted with *instrumental value*:

> *Intrinsic value and instrumental value*: To say that X has *intrinsic* value is to say that X is valuable for its own sake, or as an end. To say that X has *instrumental* value is to say that X is a means to the production of something that has intrinsic value.

Consider a simple example: no one would consider undergoing a round of chemotherapy to be intrinsically good or valuable; no one would choose to have chemotherapy just for its own sake—that is, just for the sake of having chemotherapy. But, in certain circumstances, having chemotherapy is instrumentally valuable: if one has cancer and the cancer would be destroyed by chemotherapy, then the chemotherapy would be instrumentally valuable insofar as it would be productive of continued life that would contain some things—perhaps pleasure, loving interactions, intellectual and physical achievement—plausibly regarded as having intrinsic value, as worth having in and of themselves regardless of their consequences.[3]

The consequentialist needs to have some theory of intrinsic value if she is to determine whether any given action is the right action because, according to consequentialism, the right action produces the greatest net sum of intrinsic value (this sum is arrived at by subtracting intrinsic bad produced from intrinsic good produced). The basic idea is that, when choosing among actions, an agent ought to choose the one with the best consequences. (See the later discussion of alternative versions of the consequentialist principle of right action.)

Even if one is not a consequentialist, it is important to think about the relationships among our various ends: which are ultimate and which are means to those that are ultimate? Consider, for example, Albert Speer. He was extremely successful at finding means to achieving the goals of waging the war on behalf of the Third Reich, but it is not at all clear whether he evaluated the end of winning the war. Was that an ultimate end? If not, what was it a means to achieving? One possibility is that Speer, like Stangl, was primarily concerned with his own career advancement. But again, one needs to ask: is my "getting ahead" a good in and of itself, or is there something else I hope to achieve by being successful? For each of us, in the determination of life plans, we inevitably have to, or ought to, address the issue of what is good as an end and what is good only as a means. Many things we spend a great deal of time pursuing, such as money, are clearly only instrumentally good, so we need to have an idea of what the money is for if our pursuit of it is to be rational. So determination of what has intrinsic, as opposed to instrumental, value is vital for all of us, not just as moral thinkers but also as individual persons with life plans.

Figuring out what we and others take as ultimate ends can also be useful in determining the nature of our moral disagreement with someone or the nature of the mistake someone is making in moral deliberation. Consider the Nazi view that Jews ought to be eliminated. There are at least two possibilities with respect to the nature of our disagreement with the Nazis. First, it may be that the Nazis had some truly bizarre theory about what is worth pursuing as an end—perhaps they took purity of blood or "Aryan" civilization as good in and of itself. As a result, they would have seen destruction of the Jews as instrumental to preservation of intrinsic goodness. Or perhaps the Nazis had some more sensible theory about intrinsic value—perhaps they saw pleasure, the satisfaction of desire, or the use of talents as ultimate ends—but thought that the Jews were plotting to undermine society in such a way as to threaten the promotion of well-being, first in Germany and then in the world. In the first case, our disagreement with the Nazis would be with respect to a fundamental thesis about value, whereas in the second case, our disagreement with the Nazis would be with respect to a nonmoral thesis about the supposed conspiracies of the Jewish people. Thus, figuring out what the Nazis viewed as intrinsically good would help us to know how to respond to them and what sorts of evidence to produce to dissuade them from their project of genocide.

In what follows, I am not going to settle on one particular theory of intrinsic value in my discussion. However, I am going to delimit the range of theories about which I am talking by assuming that the well-being of sentient creatures (creatures capable of having mental experiences of some form), and only the well-being of such creatures, has intrinsic value. I am assuming, then, that a world without human beings, cats, pigs, Vulcans, Hobbits, and the like would have nothing intrinsically good or intrinsically bad. There are, however, competing accounts of what it is for such a creature to be well-off: Is a good life the pleasurable life, the life in which one's desires are satisfied, the life of intellectual accomplishment, the life in which one adheres to God's plan for one, or something else? I am leaving it to the reader to deliberate about this issue.[4]

Figuring out the Right Action

Once one has an account of what counts as good and what counts as bad consequences, it is time to determine which action is right. A very important feature of consequentialism is that it counts as relevant the effects of the action on all beings affected, not just on the agent or on the agent's loved ones or on members of the agent's culture or species or on any other such limited group of beings. The consequentialist is committed to the fundamental moral equality of all beings capable of living lives that can go well or ill, where what that comes to is that good is good, no matter whose life it occurs in. Any particular consequentialist's conception of intrinsic value will determine which beings are members of the moral community—that is, which beings have interests that need to be considered in doing calculations to determine the right action. For example, if one thinks that pleasure is intrinsically valuable and it is a fact that nonhuman animals such as cats and pigs can experience pleasure, then nonhuman animals will be members of the moral community and, as a result, the effects of our actions on them need to be factored in when we are determining which action is the right action. And for the utilitarian, it does not matter whether the agent cares about those she is affecting—even if the Nazi death camp commandants did not care whether Jews lived or died, the right action for them was still in part a function of the effects of their actions on the Jews transported to their camps.

This brings us to a good place to recognize that any plausible moral theory will have some kind of relativity built into it, but we need to see that there are different kinds of relativity. For the cultural relativist, the right action for an agent S is relative to—that is, determined by—the cultural norms of her society as measured by the attitudes of approval or disapproval of the members of that society. For the consequentialist, the right action for an agent S is relative to—that is, determined by—the alternatives available to her in her circumstances and to the outcomes of those actions in those circumstances. So neither the cultural relativist nor the consequentialist will say that some action type, such as killing an innocent person, is wrong absolutely—that is, wrong for everyone in all and any circumstances. For the cultural relativist, it depends upon the attitudes of those in the agent's culture toward killing that innocent, and for the consequentialist, it depends on the consequences of killing that innocent in those particular circumstances.

But, of course, it is a very different matter to suppose that right action is a function of cultural attitudes than it is to suppose that right action is a function of the consequences of the action in the particular circumstances in which the agent finds herself. The consequentialist denies that the rightness of an action is purely a function of the attitudes of some person or some group of persons; rather, she claims, the rightness of an action is a function of its consequences, and the consequences of an action are determined by the circumstances in which the action is performed. So even if everyone in my culture (maybe even including me!) disapproves of my performing action P, my doing P is still right if P is the alternative available to me with the best overall consequences.

Notice, however, that an important element of the circumstances in which an agent performs an action will be the culture of that agent and the culture of the various people affected, in one way or another, by the action. For example, the effects of a white woman having sexual relations with a black man would be very different in 1850s Alabama than in 2000s Chicago: in the former case, outrage, fear, and disgust would characterize the reactions of bystanders, and the white woman and especially the black man would likely experience terror and some form of torture. In contrast, while such a relationship might provoke some negative reactions in 2000s Chicago, they would be far less widespread, and the white woman and the black man will be far less likely to be terrorized or physically assaulted (although they still face a greater risk than does a non-mixed-race couple). Thus, facts about cultural attitudes play a large role in determining the consequences of our actions, because how others react to our actions is greatly influenced by cultural standards and expectations.

Before leaving the topic of relativity, I want to point out two important things that we need to keep in mind as we proceed. Consider the case of a mixed-race couple in a society that disapproves of such relationships. Of course, negative consequences will be the immediate result of such a relationship being made public. However, the consequentialist, we need to remember, is concerned with long-term consequences for everyone affected, not just with the immediate consequences for the principal players in the situation. So suppose that a society in which people do not disapprove of mixed-race relationships has far, far greater intrinsic value than one in which people display racist attitudes. Then it might very well be the case that, if we live in a racist society, the right actions or general policies are ones that move us toward a society in which race is regarded as morally irrelevant. Perhaps people need to be confronted with others defying racist standards in order for society as a whole to move away from its racist mores. Then it might very well be right for a mixed-race couple to have a relationship and to make it public, even if they and everyone around them suffers. The cultural relativist must deny this, because for the cultural relativist, the rightness or wrongness of an agent's actions is a function of the attitudes of those in her culture, not of the attitudes of hypothetical persons in some possible future mutation of her culture.

Let's hope you are beginning to see how complicated the process of figuring out the right action is if one accepts consequentialism: one must begin by identifying all the options available to one; one must then engage in a lot of nonmoral investigation to try to determine the consequences of each alternative, assign values to the consequences, and pick the action with the overall best consequences. Of course, as with any decision-making procedure, we need to find shortcuts that allow us to deliberate in a timely manner, and here we need to be careful: it is easy to adopt shortcuts that will give us the answer we want to get. Consider one way this can happen, one that we will discuss in more detail in chapter 6: we can decide to only consider a few alternatives, but we need to make sure that we are not doing this so as to eliminate those most costly to ourselves. Stangl, for example, seemed not to consider various forms of resistance at all, and this narrowing of alternatives allowed him to rationalize his actions to himself. We ourselves do this when we focus our attention on the consequences for those nearest to us, rationalizing this by supposing that we cannot really have any effect on, for example, the poor in Africa. This might be the case, but we can't assume it is, and we need to make sure that we are not making certain assumptions only because those assumptions work in our favor.

Alternative Consequentialist Principles and Probabilities

In this chapter, for the sake of not complicating the discussion too much, I have limited myself to discussing the version of consequentialism that is known as *actual consequence act consequentialism*. According to this version of consequentialism, the rightness of any particular action is determined by the actual consequences that it produces. One way in which consequentialists can reject this view is by rejecting the claim that an action's *actual* consequences determine its rightness or wrongness. So a consequentialist might say that the right action is the action that will *probably* produce the best consequences, or it is the action that the agent is *justified in believing will (or, will probably)* produce the best consequences, where these are only two of the possible alternatives. Notice that adoption of these views will require one to have some conception of how to determine what the probable consequences of an action are or how to determine what beliefs an agent is justified in holding.

However, it is important to see that knowledge of how to assess probabilities and determine which of our beliefs is justified is going to be relevant even for an actual consequence consequentialist. After all, in deliberating about what will actually result from our actions, we need to appeal to what is likely to occur. So any rational consequentialist will have to have some facility for determining the probabilities of various outcomes. Further, our assessment of likelihoods is another place where our self-conceptions can mislead us to weigh harms and/or benefits to ourselves as much more likely than harms and/or benefits to others about whom we are not concerned, thereby rationalizing to ourselves focusing on pursuit of our own interests.

Even if right action is determined by actual consequences and not by what the agent believed the consequences of her action would be, our responses to ourselves and to other agents need to be sensitive to what the agent was justified in believing. We may see no point in blaming or punishing an agent who performed a wrong action if all the evidence that was available to her supported her belief that that action would have the best consequences. Similarly, in trying to understand where we ourselves are going wrong morally, we need to be able to sort out our mistakes in moral thinking from our mistakes in nonmoral thinking, so we need to figure out where we went wrong in the process of performing the wrong action: Did we miscalculate the likelihood of various outcomes, did we let our self-interest cloud our assessment of potential outcomes, or did the world just end up going in a way that we could not have rationally predicted?

Another way in which consequentialists can deviate from actual consequence act consequentialism is by taking something other than the consequences (actual, probable, or justifiably believed to be probable or actual) of the particular action as determinative of that act's rightness or wrongness. So some consequentialists claim that the right action is the one that is in accordance with a rule such that, if that rule were generally followed, the greatest net sum of intrinsic value would be produced (*rule consequentialism*), or that the right action is the one that results from the kind of motivation such that agents with those kinds of motives are more likely to maximize net value in the long run than are agents who lack such motivations (*motive consequentialism*). To discuss the pros and cons of such views would take far more space, so I will not do that here. I would just like to point out the complexity of the field of moral philosophy even when it comes to considering the variants of one type of moral theory; recognizing such complexity can be a good antidote to placing too much confidence in hasty and/or badly thought-out moral commitments.

What's Wrong with Consequentialism?

Consequentialism has a straightforward attraction as a moral theory. After all, if some things are good and some things are bad, it almost seems obvious that what we ought to do is to bring about the greatest balance of good over bad that we can. But philosophers have rejected consequentialism for many and varied reasons. Here I will focus on only two of the features of consequentialist moral deliberation that have led to its rejection.

First, consequentialism is concerned with the total net sum of intrinsic value for all beings affected by an action, so in determining which action is the right action in a given set of circumstances, one needs to add up all good produced and then subtract the total of all bad produced. The final net sum does not differentiate between good and bad on the basis of the life in which it occurs. So the right action might be one that produces nothing but suffering for Richard and nothing but joy for Greg: the consequentialist not only allows but also requires that we balance benefits and burdens across different lives. In other words, the consequentialist allows that a burden imposed on one individual can be outweighed, or compensated for, by a benefit to some other, completely unrelated person. So maybe I should harvest the organs of a healthy person in order to save a greater number of lives. Many people find the suggestion that such a course of action could even possibly be the right action to be utterly outrageous and so reject consequentialism.

Second, any explicit consequentialist moral deliberation will involve beliefs about the consequences of our actions. Knowledge of consequences depends upon knowledge of causal connections, and such connections can be difficult to figure out. How can we be expected to consider all the possible consequences of all the possible actions that we could perform? Many consequentialists have turned, at this point, to so-called rules of thumb: we can formulate rules such as "Don't kill innocent people," which we have learned, by long experience, are such that following them most often has better consequences than violating them.[5] But the rules of thumb that the consequentialist will present to us look just look the rules that a deontologist will claim are fundamental. So let's consider such deontological views.

Deontological Rule-Based Theories

Consider again the case of the doctor in the rural emergency room I introduced earlier. Most people agree with the consequentialist that you ought to use your resources to save the nine less severely injured, thereby leaving the one most severely injured to die. But let's change the case, so that we have nine injured people, and one person with only minor cuts and bruises. I, as the doctor, need organs and blood not available from current supplies if I am to save the nine. I could acquire these organs and blood by killing the one and using her organs and blood to save the nine. What ought I to do?

If I am a consequentialist, then it seems that this case is precisely parallel to the earlier ER case: just as I ought to let one die to save nine, so I ought to kill one in order to save nine. For the consequentialist, it simply cannot make a difference whether I have to kill the one or merely let her die—all that matters is that it is nine lives versus one, and more value will be produced by saving the nine than by allowing the one to live. So I ought to kill the one. However, many people who agreed that I ought to save the nine and thereby let the one die will balk at allowing that I ought to kill the one in order to save the nine; in fact, many people will insist that it is morally impermissible for me to kill the one in order to save the nine, thereby rejecting consequentialism, because the consequentialist cannot accept that actively killing someone, as opposed to merely letting a person die, seems wrong.

But we don't have to consider such exotic examples in order to find cases in which consequentialism conflicts with the moral judgments that many people are inclined to make. Consider the following: Richard has made a promise to me to teach my class when I am out of town at a conference. On the morning of the class he gets a call from another friend, asking him if he wants to play a round of golf that afternoon. It promises to be a glorious autumn day, and its being October, Richard realizes that there will not be many more such perfect golfing days before the Iowa winter sets in. He also, let us suppose correctly, judges that my students will be happy to have an afternoon free to enjoy the weather for themselves instead of sitting in a classroom. If, in fact, more happiness will be produced by Richard's canceling the class and playing golf than by his teaching the class and thereby keeping his promise to me, then according to the consequentialist, Richard is not only morally permitted to break his promise but is actually morally required to do so.

What is significant here is that the promise itself is not of moral significance for the consequentialist: all that matters is what the consequences of keeping versus breaking the promise would be. Consequentialists often point out that people who consistently break promises will not be trusted in the future, and so there may be a loss in future happiness. But, of course, *Bundy* this may not be the case as well; suppose I am a particularly trusting person and Richard is charming enough to be able to talk his way out of hot water. Then, according to the consequentialist, consequences are on the side of breaking the promise. Thus, charming people with trusting, forgiving friends will more often be morally required to break promises than will people who are not charming and who have more demanding friends. This just does not seem right to many people; it seems that the fact

charming + forgiving

— promise to husband

that Richard has made a promise provides him a reason to keep the promise even if somewhat better consequences would result from his breaking it (and no matter how charming he may be).

Consequentialism seems to have similar difficulties in other cases. For example, suppose I have a small amount of an antivenin for the poison of a particular snake. On a camping trip, my best friend and two other campers have all been bitten by this snake. However, because my friend is a large person, he will need more of the antidote than either of the other two campers would need. If I give my friend the amount of antidote needed to save his life, there will not be enough left to save either of the other campers; however, if I divide the antidote and give half to each of the other campers, I can save both of their lives. Well, it's two lives against one life, and so the consequentialist seems to have to say that I am morally required to divide the antidote between the other two campers and let my best friend die. I will suffer greatly at his loss, especially given that I could have saved him, but my grief and guilt do not seem sufficient to outweigh the life of one of the other campers and all of the grief that would be suffered by that camper's friends and family. But many people are convinced that I have special obligations to my friends, and that even if it is two lives against one, the fact that the one is my friend may very well make it the case that I am morally required to save him even at the cost of worse overall consequences.

These cases suggest to some moral philosophers that what we are morally obligated to do is not solely a function of the consequences of the various alternatives available to us. The fact that it is my friend's life that is in peril and the fact that Richard has promised to teach my class both seem to be morally significant facts regardless of the consequences of saving my friend or of Richard's teaching my class instead of going to play golf. This is not to say that I ought to save my friend and that Richard ought to keep his promise *no matter what the consequences of doing so*. If

I could save one million people or my friend, it might very well be the case that I am morally required to let my friend die in order to save the million. Similarly, if Richard breaks his promise to me in order to rush to a dying friend's bedside for a last goodbye, it seems quite clear that he has done nothing morally wrong. The point, however, is that it is not solely the value of consequences that seems relevant to determining what we ought to do.

An early twentieth-century British moral philosopher, W. D. Ross, constructed his moral theory by taking these common moral judgments as his starting point.[6] He argued that we have various prima facie moral duties, by which he means that certain facts ground reasons for us to act, but that such reasons can be overridden by some other, stronger prima facie duty. Our strongest prima facie duty in any particular case is our all-things-considered duty. The basic idea is that there are lots of different morally relevant facts, including but not limited to the value of the consequences of various alternatives. These facts can generate or ground conflicting obligations, and the agent must try to figure out which of these conflicting obligations outweighs the others. Among the morally relevant facts are one's promises, one's special relationships (such as friendship) with the people affected, and the value of the consequences. Ross himself lists several other grounds of prima facie duties, but moral philosophers who accept the general structure of Ross's moral theory can disagree with him about which facts are actually morally relevant and, so, about which facts ground moral obligations.

The Rossian view is a version of what is known as *deontology* (derived from the ancient Greek word for "obligation," or "duty"). Deontologists reject the consequentialist claim that right action is a function of consequences and of nothing other than the consequences of action. But deontologists agree with consequentialists that the morally relevant facts are not solely a function of any person's or group of persons' attitudes toward those facts; in other words, deontology is not a version of cultural relativism. There are objective truths about which types of facts ground moral reasons—truths such as "One has a prima facie obligation to keep one's promises." These facts transcend culture or individual attitude, although, of course, the conventions for making a promise, for example, are a function of cultural tradition and social practice. But once a promise is made, however that is done in one's culture or society, one has a prima facie obligation to keep the promise.

Some deontologists reject the Rossian view because of the fact that the view allows there to be conflicting obligations and yet provides no procedure for determining which of these conflicting obligations is the one on which the agent ought to act. Ross himself simply said that one must use practical wisdom, which, of course, does not amount to much help, especially for those who might still be trying to acquire such wisdom. The most famous deontological view, that of Immanuel Kant, avoids this difficulty by having just one fundamental moral law from which all of our moral duties are derived.[7] Kant offered several formulations of this fundamental law, claiming that all of the formulations are equivalent to one another—that is, that they say the same thing but in different ways. It is quite difficult to see how these different statements could be equivalent to one another, and so I will ignore this aspect of Kant's view. Instead, I will present the two most famous versions of his moral law as two suggestions as to what the fundamental moral principle is.

The first suggestion is what is known as the *Universal Law Formula*. According to this principle, an agent is always to act in such a way that the rule motivating her conduct is one that she could will to be universal law. Take Kant's own example of a person considering whether to make a promise that she knows that she cannot keep, a promise that if her friend lends her some money today, she will pay her friend back within the week. Is she morally permitted to make such a promise in order to acquire the money from her friend?[8] She must, according to the Universal Law Formula, imagine a world in which everyone acts on the rule that is now motivating her conduct—namely, according to Kant, the rule that she will make a false promise in order to get what she needs. Then she is to ask herself, *Would I be able, by making a false promise, to achieve my goal (i.e., getting money from my friend) in a world in which everyone was motivated to act on my rule of conduct?* Kant claims that the answer to this question is no. If everyone made false promises to get what he or she wanted, then, Kant argues, no one would believe anyone's promises, and no one would ever lend money. Thus, because I cannot will my rule to be universal law (because by doing so I would be willing that my goal not be accomplished), I am not morally permitted to make a false promise to get money from my friend.[9]

Of course, a consequentialist will respond: "Why worry about what the consequences of my action would be in some hypothetical world which is such that my action is not likely to make that hypothetical world the real world?" I think that Kant is trying to give us a test for when we are making an exception for ourselves—that is, allowing ourselves to act in ways that we cannot allow everyone to act. In the case of the false promise, using the hypothetical universal law test, I can come to see that achieving my goal by acting on my rule of conduct depends upon everyone else's not acting on my rule of conduct; I am making an exception of myself, allowing myself a liberty that I am depending on others not to avail themselves of. But what justifies my holding others to standards to which I do not hold myself? If we are all morally equal, the answer must be: nothing. Thus, if an action does not pass the universal law test, then that action is morally forbidden.

So it seems that Kant's rules are meant to reflect a certain conception of moral agents as equal beings. This comes out in his

Ends in Themselves Formula, as well. This version of the moral law tells us that we are required to treat rational beings[10] (including ourselves) always as ends in themselves and never as mere means. What is an end in itself? Well, let's begin with the simpler notion—that of a mere means. Each agent has goals at which she aims. We attempt to determine how to reach these goals; in other words, we try to figure out the means to our ends. So our ends—what we aim at for its own sake—provide us with reason to act, to figure out how to achieve that end, and then to do what we need to do to achieve the end. What Kant seems to be saying with the Ends in Themselves Formula is that rational beings, like our ends, provide us with reason to act, and that these reasons do not stem from suitability for achieving something beyond themselves; rather, it is their nature itself that generates these reasons. Thus, to treat other people, like the lender in the false promise case, merely as a tool for achieving our end of getting money is to fail to respect that person's nature as a source of reasons.

A huge question is, of course, left hanging by all of this: What is involved in treating other people as their nature requires? What reasons for action are grounded by other people? Kant seems to take it as quite clear that killing an innocent, such as the person with only cuts and bruises in the ER, is never morally permissible, but why should we suppose that is right? A consequentialist might insist that we ought to kill one to save a greater number in the ER case because, after all, the greater number are also ends in themselves and seem to generate a greater number of whatever reasons are generated by the one.[11] Even other deontologists such as Ross might agree with the consequentialist: if enough lives are at stake, our prima facie obligation to promote value will override our prima facie obligation not to kill innocent people.

Without resolving this dispute, we can notice something that both deontology and consequentialism have in common: a commitment to the idea that we have reasons for action—what we typically call *moral reasons*—that are not identical with and can override our reasons of self-interest. These moral theories, then, acknowledge that what we ought to do may not be a matter of what is best for us as individuals. This is not necessarily to deny that we have competing reasons to promote our own good or that these latter reasons could outweigh our moral reasons. But it is to insist that practical deliberation does not stop with consideration of our own good. But how much sacrifice can morality require of us? As we return to our case studies, we will see that an appeal to self-interest is not uncommon. We must not, however, assess these appeals merely on the basis of our beliefs about how we might respond, given such pressures (real or imagined). Unless we think that we ourselves are morally perfect, we have to be ready to judge that an action is immoral even if we are forced to admit to ourselves that we might very well have committed it given certain circumstances. We must not fall into the trap of judging that an action cannot be evil because we can see ourselves performing it: that assumption begs too many questions about morality, evil, and human nature.

If I Hadn't Done It, Then Someone Else Would Have

We are now in a position to return to the reasoning exhibited by our case studies. What I hope to show by using these examples is how understanding different moral theories can help us to intervene in our own and others' moral deliberations by asking relevant questions, seeing why we are making certain judgments, and locating our disagreements with the conclusion reached by others. Further, we can see why certain phrases or slogans are best abandoned as misleading or obfuscating. In other words, the theoretical framework provided by these philosophical accounts of morality can play an important role in our duties of due care in moral deliberation and of moral self-scrutiny.

We will consider Stangl first. He presents his situation as one in which he is forced, out of fear for his own safety and that of his family, to take a job that was odious to him in every way, including morally. He justifies this action by arguing that if he had protested or refused the job, he would have put his own life and those of his wife and children at risk, and someone else would have taken over his job. Thus, the work at Treblinka would have gone on, and no good would have come of Stangl's sacrifice.

Sereny asks Stangl why he didn't stand on principle. To what principles is Sereny referring? She is probably not thinking about fundamental moral principles such as the consequentialist principle of right action or Kant's Categorical Imperative. Rather, she is probably thinking about a principle such as "It is wrong to kill people merely on the basis of their race or religion," or "It is wrong to kill innocent people." If we are consequentialists or Kantians, we need to decide if that principle is yielded in the circumstances at hand. If we are Rossians, we might take ourselves to have a prima facie duty not to kill innocent people, but we also need to consider any other prima facie duties that we have in the circumstances, one of which might very well be to take care of one's loved ones, particularly those who are dependent upon one, such as one's children. If we are deontologists, we have to ask whether there is an absolute prohibition on running a death camp (perhaps derived from an absolute prohibition on killing the innocent), whereas if we are consequentialists, there are no absolute prohibitions and we are left to compare the consequences of our various alternatives. So Sereny's contrast between those who stood on principle and those who didn't obscures important distinctions.

How should we understand Stangl's reasoning? Stangl is arguing that he chose the alternative with the best outcome for everyone affected: the Jews at Treblinka were going to die anyway, and as long as he took the job without rocking the boat too much, then he and his family would be safe. Notice that if this is actually the way Stangl was reasoning, then he could have responded to Sereny, "I did act on principle! I acted on the consequentialist principle, and thus attempted to maximize intrinsic value. In my case, the best that I could do was to produce a negative balance of value—but all of the other options had even worse results. What good would keeping my own hands clean have done? All it would have accomplished would have been the death of me and my family in addition to all the Jews dead at Treblinka—it would have been a pointless sacrifice."

Of course, the consequentialist, in applying her principle of right action, has to sincerely consider all alternatives available to her. But is Stangl really considering all the possible alternative courses of action open to him? He presents his situation as offering two alternatives: protest or keep doing his job. He has no definite ideas as to what form any kind of protest would take: if he does have any, he seems to imagine simply saying to his superiors, "No, I won't do this!" And he never indicates that he did any investigation in order to figure out how to use his position to, for example, provide information to resistance groups. One kind of subtle protest that Stangl could have engaged in would have been to do his job less zealously than whomever he imagined his replacement would be. Given the number of Jews who died at Treblinka, would his superiors have noticed if a couple fewer would have died? But Stangl himself insisted that whatever he did, he had to do to the best of his ability. So Stangl really did not think about the various alternatives available to him *even if* he kept his job.

Remember that the consequentialist insists that all are to count equally in consequentialist calculations. We can certainly wonder if Stangl really was giving anything like equal weight to the interests of the Jews and to the interests of himself and his family. The numbers of Jews killed at Treblinka were so high that it is difficult to see how any calculation could have had any result other than Stangl's finding some way to stop or slow down what was happening as being the right action. Even if Stangl were a deontologist committed to a prima facie duty to care for his loved ones, he would have to weigh that duty against his duty not to kill innocent people, which he had with respect to every person who entered the camp. Given the magnitude of the harm to the Jews and the number of prima facie duties not to kill, it seems clear that Stangl acted wrongly.

So it is not necessarily the structure of Stangl's reasoning— that is, its consequentialist nature—that is problematic. In this case, it seems that if Stangl was trying to justify his action on consequentialist grounds, he failed in his attempt to engage in consequentialist reasoning: (i) he did not seem to put much sincere effort into determining all the alternative actions open to him; (ii) he did not give anything approaching equal consideration to everyone affected by his decisions. It is difficult not to suspect that, in reality, Stangl was thinking only about himself and his family, not about the Jews dying under his watch.

Somebody might object to my attempts here to sort through Stangl's reasoning at all; doing so, it might be suggested, makes it seem as though Stangl might have been sincere and even justified in his thinking. I agree that we have to take whatever someone like Stangl says with many, many grains of salt. Is this really how he reasoned? Perhaps not, but it is the way he decided to present his reasoning in order to justify himself to Sereny, so it is still worth examining that reasoning. And unless we assume that certain actions are categorically forbidden, we have to allow at least the possibility of Stangl's having done the right thing. Further, we are interested here in seeing how people can go wrong in their moral thinking, so we need to examine instances of such thinking if we are to carry out that task.

Why Ruin My Entire Life?

Bundy presents himself as an optimist: although he recognized that he had "fucked up," he determined that he would modify his behavior. And so why turn himself in? Why ruin his entire life?

Even though Bundy was markedly different from us in many ways, he here demonstrates an all too common failing, and one that can have devastating moral results: Bundy (if he is being sincere, which is something we always need to question) demonstrates a complete and utter lack of self-knowledge. In determining the consequences of our courses of action, we often have to predict our own future actions, given what we do now. Bundy seems to suggest that he has learned his lesson and will give up killing. But would it have taken much in the way of self-knowledge for Bundy to know that he was unlikely to become a law-abiding citizen? And if he continued to kill, very, very bad consequences would result. There is absolutely no doubt that the best course of action, by far, was to turn himself in.

And while most of us do not pose the threat that a serial rapist and murderer does, we have to be wary of failing in our moral deliberations for the very same reason that Bundy does: we let our own self-interest and our favored conceptions of ourselves color our determinations of the consequences of the various alternatives available to us. Consequentialist reasoning requires the deliberator to try to be as impartial as possible, and one cannot be impartial unless one can openly acknowledge one's own nature and interests. For example, I know that I love to pass on juicy bits of gossip, and so I need to think before I insist to someone, "Oh, you can tell me, I won't tell anyone!" I can be sincere about being discreet in the moment, but when the temptation to reveal what I know is presented, I know I will have a difficult time resisting. So I have to put forth extra effort to be discreet when it really matters, or avoid coming to know that which cannot be shared with others. Acknowledging this weakness is important in my deliberations about engaging in conversation with others. Although indiscretion in sharing gossip is not on the level of serial rape and murder, it can have harmful consequences, and so openly recognizing and taking account of such moral flaws is an important element in moral deliberation.

Bundy, of course, seemed unable to completely understand the consequences of his actions, because of his apparent inability to empathize or sympathize. (See chapter 5.) It is quite clear that he is not considering all the consequences of his actions: there are friends and relatives who need to know what happened to their loved ones. But, as we saw in chapter 2, Bundy could not grasp why his victims would be missed, given how many people there are in the world. If one is unable to enter into the emotional lives of others, then one will be unable to assess the consequences of one's actions. While Bundy's inability was probably not corrigible, the same cannot be said for the rest of us. When our own interests are at stake, we may be so overwhelmed by thinking about our interests that we fail to put ourselves into the position of others affected by our actions, and thus fail to grasp the full implications of our actions. It takes consistent, determined effort to make sure that we are really considering the genuine interests of everyone affected by our actions.[12]

We also need to make a sincere and impartial attempt to assess the moral significance of the various consequences of our actions. For a consequentialist, this means that we need to do our best to calculate the value of those consequences. Bundy seemed to put little if any value on the well-being of other persons: he saw them as merely means to his own goals. Thus, he was completely unable to engage in any genuine consequentialist calculations. We differ from Bundy in being able to appreciate the value of others being well-off, but if we do not allow ourselves to engage fully with the impact of our actions on others, we will inevitably underestimate the benefits and/or burdens imposed on others—they will appear to pale in comparison to the benefits and/or burdens imposed on ourselves. In chapter 5, we will discuss more the importance of emotional engagement with the consequences of our actions for other people. So Bundy provides us with two more ways in which consequentialist reasoning can be undermined: (iii) he failed to understand himself; and (iv) he failed to understand the implications of his actions for others. The moral life demands that we acquire self-knowledge and put forth constant effort to understand the emotional lives of other people.

Notice that a deontologist may place just as much weight on an impartial understanding of the effects of one's actions as does the consequentialist. If one, for example, has duties to care for one's loved ones, one needs to know what will count as caring for them: What will promote their good, what will harm them? In order to balance my duty to promote the good of my loved ones against the good of strangers, I need to be able to determine how much my actions will benefit or harm others, because that will surely be relevant to the competing strengths of my duties. But Bundy, of course, didn't fully grasp the reality of others people's lives except insofar as they impacted him, so he simply could not appreciate any duties that he might have to other people.

Compromise as the Best Option

Finally, we can consider how Jones went wrong. Jones decided to become a minister to the slaves of Liberty County because, he claimed, by doing so he could benefit both the slaves and their owners: he would bring the slaves to God, thereby saving their souls, and he would also protect the interests of the owners and remain a member in good standing of the society in which he and his family had grown up.

At first glance, this might look like a paradigm of good consequentialist reasoning: Jones has taken into account the interests of all involved, white and black, free and enslaved, hasn't he? But, of course, even a hasty second glance reveals that he has not done so. Jones is doing precisely what Stangl did: he is viewing the entire situation through the lens of his own interests and the interests of his loved ones. If, as he himself said, slavery is an evil institution, then why should he be concerned to protect the white slaveholders of Liberty County? The interests that he is protecting are interests in causing harm to others in order to benefit oneself. Thus, in protecting the whites, he is protecting their ability to maintain an institution that caused great suffering to an extraordinary number of people.

Furthermore, Jones is not thinking about the long-term consequences of his actions. As I pointed out in my discussion of consequentialism, some actions that cause disruption and pain in the short term can lead to very good consequences in the long term. Jones fails to compare a society without slavery to one with slavery, and is only thinking about the immediate consequences—in particular, for himself—of bucking the system. In part, this seems to be the result of his unacknowledged prejudices about blacks and their relationships with whites. He sees the emotional lives of blacks as tied to those of whites in such a way that the former are disturbed if they cannot meet the needs of the latter. He also continues to view the system of slavery as beneficial for the slaves—in particular with respect to their religious salvation. But why couldn't he minister to the spiritual needs of free blacks?

I am going to return to Jones's reasoning in chapter 6. For now, we can note that Jones makes two very serious mistakes in his consequentialist reasoning: (v) he fails to think imaginatively about long-term consequences of various courses of action; and (vi) he makes his predictions about consequences based on un-examined prejudices and presuppositions. These false factual beliefs lead to false conclusions about the consequences of his actions.

I do want to point out here that Jones faced a kind of di-lemma that does not always have an easy answer, and it is re-lated to Stangl's decision whether to run a death camp. We will often think that "justice" makes certain requirements of us: an end to slavery, an end to genocide, and so on. But we can find ourselves in positions where there really is nothing we can do that will have the result of ending slavery or genocide. Ought we at that point to opt out, even if doing so accomplishes nothing, or ought we to participate and attempt to mitigate the negative consequences? Should we "stand on our principles" even if we could bring about better consequences by getting our own hands dirty? The messy reality of morally charged situations should not be covered up with slogans; it needs to be confronted, whether we are consequentialists or deontologists or hold some other theory.

Responsible Consequentialist Reasoning

So let's sum up the lessons that we have learned from Stangl, Bundy, and Jones with respect to how to engage in consequentialist reasoning:

- We need to consider all the alternative actions available to us. Of course, all that we can do in practice is to consider as many as we can imagine in the time allotted to us. However, we should keep in mind the human tendency to allow our minds to roam over only those options that have favorable outcomes for us.
- And this leads to the more general need to keep in mind how our deliberations can be affected by our biases, including our distorted images of ourselves. Before we get into moral crises, we have a responsibility to consider ways in which we have misconceptions about others and about ourselves.
- Self-knowledge is key to responsible consequentialist reasoning. An important consequence of our actions is our own future behavior, so we need to understand ourselves in order to understand which alternative has the best consequences.
- Knowing our own biases can help us to actually take into account the interests of everyone involved and to give them equal weight. Our partiality to ourselves can lead us to leave self-benefiting biases in place, so we need to be vigilant in ensuring that we are actually being impartial.
- In order to assess the interests of others, we need to cultivate empathy and be able to put ourselves in the positions of those affected by our actions. Understanding other people's

inner lives is crucial to seeing the full range of effects of our actions on others.

- We must remember to consider the long-term consequences of our actions. Sometimes the best alternative will not yield dividends for many years in the future.
- Finally, we need to get our facts straight. One cannot assess consequences if one has false beliefs about human beings and about causal relationships in the world.

I do not intend this to be an argument for consequentialism but, rather, a set of tools that allow us to consider consequentialist reasoning in its best light. Some of the most important ethical debates of our time depend on conflicts between consequentialists and deontologists, and we want to avoid eliminating a theory because of slogans or bad uses of that theory. Further, if one is a Rossian deontologist, consequences are going to be relevant, if we accept the plausible claim that one of our prima facie duties is to promote intrinsic value. Also, in order to figure out how to fulfill, for example, our duty to care for our loved ones, we need to understand how our actions will affect them and other people (in order to weigh our duties against one another). Good moral deliberators need to cultivate their abilities to think about consequences, and that is rarely an easy task.

even a true moral theory can be misapplied

5

The Feeling of Morality

Responding Morally

At the end of the previous chapter, I listed some things we need to keep in mind when we engage in consequentialist reasoning, or for that matter, any moral reasoning that takes consequences as relevant to the determination of what we ought to do. I argued that we need self-knowledge, including knowledge of our own biases and preconceptions, and that we need to be able to exercise empathy in putting ourselves in others' positions so that we can adequately take everyone's interests into account. Both of these activities require an understanding of and an ability to engage with our own emotions and with the emotions of other people. Our biases, for example, are in large part a result of our emotions—of what we love, what we hate, what we hope for, what we take pride or shame in. For example, consider Stangl's attempts to defend his activities at Treblinka—his self-pleadings are clearly, at least in part, the result of shame and self-love: he needs to be able to present himself as in some way justified if he is going to be able to continue to live with himself. Much the same can be said for Jones, whose love for his family and way of life corrupted his entire outlook on slavery. And both men obviously spent far too little time thinking about and engaging with the inner emotional lives of their victims.

It seems obvious, then, that if we are to fulfill our duties of due care in moral deliberation and of moral self-scrutiny, we need to understand our own emotions and be able to come to an understanding of the emotions of others. Our emotions are powerful forces in our mental lives, having effects on our beliefs and on how we reason. But they also have great import for how we actually engage with the world, because emotions are potent motivators of our actions. If you ask someone to explain why she did what she did, almost invariably she will point to some love, hate, fear, anger, shame, pride, pity, compassion, and the like in providing that explanation. Moral virtue has to do with our dispositions to think, feel, and act, so fulfilling our duty to cultivate moral virtue requires an understanding of the proper role of emotions in the moral life.

There is a tendency among some people, including some philosophers, to view feeling correctly as opposed to thinking correctly, as key to the moral life. And our case studies do seem to give some credence to such a view. It is difficult to avoid thinking that if men like Höss and Stangl hadn't repressed their natural emotional reactions to the grisly business in which they were employed, then they never could have overseen the brutal death, torture, and enslavement of millions of their fellow human beings. Similarly, if Jones had seriously attempted to engage with the moral life of his slaves, surely he would have seen that they felt sorrow, loss, and grief just as he and his family did. Those inclined to argue in this way would likely be drawn to the idea that moral education should focus primarily on what has become known as "emotional intelligence" rather than on the deliberative and reflective skills inculcated by the study of moral philosophy.[1]

The history of moral philosophy reveals that philosophers themselves have given emotions widely divergent roles to play in the moral life. Some moral philosophers have denigrated emotions as psychological wildcards apt to lead us astray. Kant famously (some would say, infamously) argued that even love and sympathy are inadequate as motivation to moral actions, because they can as easily lead us to act immorally as they can lead us to do what duty demands of us. Consider, for example, the many "ordinary" Germans who averted their eyes from the horrors perpetrated by the Nazis in order to protect and promote the interests of their own families; in such cases, it seems, love can blind people to their wider moral duties. In recent years, some feminist and virtue ethicists have valorized emotions as constituting the most important part of the moral life insofar as being apt to experience the right emotions is an important and essential part of what it is to be a virtuous agent. Some neuroscientists and their allies among the so-called experimental ethicists claim to have empirical scientific data that links emotions and moral judgments in such a way as to provide evidence for the view that our moral judgments are nothing more than judgments about our attitudes and/or emotions.[2] According to such a view, there is nothing to morality over and above how each individual feels about various matters. Some historically prominent consequentialists can, perhaps, be understood as having taken a moderate road: both John Stuart Mill and Jeremy Bentham saw emotions as crucial motivators for good consequentialist moral agents, and so they saw the training of children to feel appropriately as an essential task of society. Mill, for example, stressed that we must educate children to identify with the well-being of all, so that the well-being of others naturally enters into their assessment of the outcomes of their actions.

In this chapter, the position I will defend comes closest to the one I have attributed to Mill. While there is a great deal of truth to the claim that repression of emotions can cause or lay the groundwork for immorality, "being in touch with our feelings," even if we have somehow been raised to "feel appropriately," is hardly sufficient preparation for recognizing and responding to moral crises. The reflective analytical stance inculcated by philosophical study is crucial for good moral agency, given the complexity of both our own emotional lives and the moral situations we face in our daily lives, as well as in circumstances of larger moral import. Moral deliberation of a philosophical nature cannot be avoided, and so we need to educate the young in at least the rudiments of moral philosophy.

That being said, I certainly do not intend to disparage or downplay the centrality of emotions to the *human* moral life.[3] In fact, it is precisely *because* of their centrality that philosophical deliberation needs to be brought into play. However we understand emotions, it is clear that they can motivate us to action and that competing emotions can pull in opposing directions. Theory can help us to sort through such situations. Further, I will argue, intellectual deliberation requires emotion for its integration into agency, but only deliberation can guide that integration in an appropriate and meaningful way.

In what follows, then, I will employ our case studies in order to explore the connections between moral reasoning and emotional response. Several questions about such connections are particularly pertinent. First, do these responses (to use as generic and noncommittal a term as possible for that group of human experiences) have any role to play in the acquisition and maintenance of moral knowledge? Is it possible or likely for someone like Bundy, who seemed not to have these types of responses, to have true or even justified moral beliefs? Is it possible for someone like Bundy to have moral beliefs at all? Others, like Jones and Jefferson, certainly seemed capable of such responses and seemed, at one point in their lives, to have justified true moral beliefs. Was their loss of that knowledge related to or caused by a shift in their emotional or sympathetic responses? Must we feel appropriately if we are to sustain our understanding of the nature of moral demands?

Second, are emotions and the like crucial motivators to moral action? Are they, contrary to what Kant held, praiseworthy forms of moral motivation, or are they, as Kant claimed, dangerous responses that the moral agent must cordon off from her moral deliberations? I will argue that matters are not so simple that we can give a yes or no answer to these questions. Our emotions will inevitably, it seems, play a role in motivating our moral actions just as they play a role in motivating our nonmoral actions. The interplay between judgment and emotion is difficult to parse, both as a theoretical matter and as an empirical matter. Once again, here we will see why self-scrutiny is so important, so that we can attempt to discern how our emotions are impacting our deliberations and our choices.

Third, if emotions and related responses are important for both moral knowledge and moral motivation, are we going to be forced to significantly reduce the scope of moral responsibility? Many people are inclined to think that how we feel is not something we can control and thus not something for which we can be held responsible. But then, if we are not responsible for our emotions, or for our lack thereof, how can we be responsible for the beliefs and actions that result from such emotions? I will suggest that we can in fact train our emotions and we can educate ourselves and others to come to respond in appropriate ways. We will see that some of the perpetrators of the Holocaust seem to have trained themselves to feel *inappropriately*. The acquisition of moral knowledge and of appropriate affective responses is a complicated give and take, with each influencing the other; prying them apart, although conceptually or theoretically possible, is not so easy in practice—that is, in the reality of human moral lives.

Before we can take on any of these three tasks, however, we need to have some understanding of the nature of emotions, sympathy, and empathy. So how are we to understand the nature of these responses?

Feelings and Beliefs

The best way to begin our attempt to understand the nature of the emotions and related responses is to examine ourselves as we undergo or experience such responses. I think that a particular episode from Stangl's narrative of his time as commandant of the Treblinka death camp easily evokes in readers several emotional responses, and so we can use that episode to not only have those responses at hand to examine but also to use our own responses to highlight what seems to be going wrong in the case of Stangl. Recall that Blau, one of the worker Jews in the camp, had come upon his elderly father arriving in one of the transports to the camp. Stangl insists that such an elderly man cannot be allowed to live, but he does give Blau permission to take his father for a last meal and then to be shot rather than gassed. When Blau returns, Stangl interprets Blau's speech and behavior as grateful and accepts thanks for what he regards as his kind action.

If one engages with this story as one reads, one inevitably experiences various emotive responses: compassion and pity for Blau and his father and, upon reflection, for all the victims of Treblinka, despair and sorrow as one imagines the last moments of father and son, rage and anger at Stangl's obtuseness and self-righteousness, and hatred of Nazis like Stangl who could treat other human beings in such a way. And what is peculiarly striking about Stangl's relation of this episode is his apparent lack of any of the emotions that we experience for Blau and his father: Stangl's feelings and thoughts seem to remain with Stangl and with what he perceives as his kindness and rewarding interactions with the prisoners in his death camp. (His lack of any real concern for Blau is further attested by his response to Sereny that he does not know what eventually happened to Blau.) The context in which he describes Blau's second visit to him suggests that he believes the tears in Blau's eyes are tears of gratitude for what he, Stangl, has allowed Blau to do for his father. We, however, know better: those tears are tears of grief, despair, loss, and hopelessness. The fact that Stangl misinterprets those tears is extraordinarily revealing about the inner life of a man who oversaw and organized the death of roughly one million of his fellow human beings.

After Stangl relates this episode to Gitta Sereny, she finds herself overcome, "wrestling with the most intense *malaise*" she had experienced during her talks with him.[4] She leaves the prison and requires time to move beyond both the story that Stangl had just related and the manner in and purposes for which he had related the story—he was trying to put himself in a good light by recounting this horrid episode that is so emblematic of one of the darkest periods in human history. Our responses as readers are likely very similar to those of Sereny: without doubt, our reactions to this story are *painful* to endure. We feel bad—and, it seems, sorrow, anger, grief, and so on are all ways in which we feel bad. These unpleasant feelings are what Sereny is dealing with when she leaves the prison, and what caused me to need to put down the book and take a few deep breaths the first time I read of Blau's predicament.

For many of us,[5] this is a hallmark of emotional experiences: they are, at least quite often, either painful or pleasant. It is often and for many of us pleasant, enjoyable, and nice to experience love, gratitude, pride, and affection; and it is unpleasant, painful, and not at all nice to experience ha-tred,[6] shame, guilt, grief, and sorrow. These experiences that we label emotions, then, seem to be different from many of our experiences of making judgments or holding beliefs. Merely judging that Blau accompanied his father for a last meal before the old man was shot to death is not, it seems, either painful or pleasant; after all, Stangl shared that judgment with us and did not seem to experience any pain as a result. And if one has rethought the episode of Blau and his father, as I have done, for the purpose of making certain philosophical points, one can, in such contexts, make judgments about that episode without experiencing pain. This is why I stressed the importance of my reader's *engaging with* the story; such engagement seems to be required for the calling forth of the painful or pleasant emotional experiences that can accompany certain judgments or beliefs.

It does seem to be an important feature of emotions that they are, again, at least often and for many of us, either painful or pleasant experiences.[7] Emotions *feel* a certain way, and it seems that distinct emotions have distinct feels. I experience different feelings when I am angry than when I am proud or grieving. Emotions share this aspect of feeling a certain way with bodily sensations. In the case of the latter, a headache feels different from a stubbed toe, stomach cramps feel different from a pulled muscle in the back, and fatigue feels different from sinus pain. Nonetheless, emotions are not bodily sensations; we do not lo-cate our pride or grief in a specific part of the body. However, bodily sensations are often associated with emotions: anxiety is correlated with that butterflies-in-the-stomach sensation, anger is correlated with that warmth and tension we describe as our blood boiling, and sorrow is correlated with fatigue and achiness. I have used the term "correlation" in order to avoid making any claims about the direction of causation here: Do emotions cause bodily changes, do bodily changes cause emotions, or do emotions and bodily changes have common causes? Whatever the causal relations here, it is important that we sometimes are brought to awareness of our emotions via an awareness of bodily sensations. For example, I have often been forced to acknowledge my anxiety because of insistent stomach upset. Bodily sensations are not infallible guides to our emotional feelings, but they are important bits of evidence that we do well not to ignore.

So one possibility, then, is that emotions are just the psychic analogues of headaches and muscle cramps—that is, they are painful or pleasant sensations that are felt as having a "location" in the psyche rather than in the body. But there are at least three reasons why this account seems, at best, incomplete. First, consider the example of anger. It is true that when I first learn of the perfidy of a friend, I will feel that distinctive sensation or some subset of the family of sensations that we think of as anger sensations. But if my friend does not apologize and make amends, I will continue to describe myself as angry; in fact, it is not uncommon for someone to say of herself that she has been angry with a friend for years and that the anger will not be resolved until the friend acknowledges and apologizes for her betrayal. But do I feel any distinctive sensations continuously over the course of the years that I am angry with my friend? It seems not. So how can we accommodate the idea that emotions are feelings with the apparent truth that we can be angry or proud for long periods of time during which we do not continuously experience any such feelings?

Second, there are cases in which we might very well reject the attribution of an emotion no matter what distinctive sensations were being felt. To use an example inspired by Hume, consider the case of pride. Suppose I report feeling proud of the clock in my neighbor's condo. We would first speculate that I made the clock, someone significantly related to me made the clock, or that I gave my neighbor the clock. But if I am in no way related to that clock, it seems at the very least odd for me to be proud of the clock. To make the case even stranger, suppose I judge the clock to be of terrible quality and quite ugly. Hume argued that the claim that some person S is proud of some P (be it an object, person, event, action, etc.) entails that S judges herself specially related to P in some way and that S judges P to be good or to exhibit some good quality. The relationship between S and that of which she is proud, P, may be quite close: P is S's creation, for example, or quite distant: S is from Chicago, and P is the Cubs' winning the World Series. And the good qualities that S attributes to P might be quite minimal, such as a parent's pride in her child's very straight white teeth. Nonetheless, it just seems incompatible with pride that S judges the object of her pride to be unrelated to her and worthless or even bad: Does it really make sense for me to say that I am proud of Hitler's absurd and ugly mustache, no matter what the peculiar sensations I feel upon contemplating that horrid bit of hair?

Third, emotions, like beliefs and judgments, seem to be intentional states. In other words, emotions have objects—they are *about* something. When I believe that Stangl was cruel, the object of my belief is Stangl's cruelty—that is what my belief is *about*. Similarly, when I am angry with Stangl for being cruel, the object of my anger is Stangl –my anger is directed at Stangl in virtue of his cruelty. But bodily sensations do not seem to have objects in this way. When I stub my toe, I feel a painful sensation that I locate as being in my toe, but it is at the very least odd to say that my pain is about my toe's having been stubbed.[8] The pain directs my attention to my toe, and is certainly the causal result of my having stubbed my toe; however, that pain seems to lack content—it is just a simple sensation that feels a certain way. But the same does not seem to be true of my sorrow at the death of Blau's elderly father—the sorrow is about that death, the death is the object of my sorrow.

The nature of emotions remains contested by philosophers because of emotions' apparent connections to both feelings and beliefs. Philosophers have offered varying accounts of the emotions, ranging from identifying emotions with certain types of judgments to identifying emotions with bodily sensations or changes. In between, on this range, are various hybrid views that attempt to understand both sensations (either bodily or psychic) and judgments as either constituents of or necessary conditions for the experience of emotions. Instead of trying to adjudicate these disputes directly, I want to look at the ways in which a lack of appropriate emotion plays a role in the motivations, actions, and experiences of some of our case studies. Maybe we can come to understand emotions and their role in moral thought and motivation by seeing what is missing in cases of evil actions and evil motivations. However, in what follows, the ways in which emotions are tied, somehow, to both our feelings and our beliefs, will be shown to be of crucial significance to the nature of moral deliberation and of moral agency. All that I am going to assume, then, is that emotions have characteristic ties to both belief and sensation without assuming any particular understanding of the nature of those ties.

Before moving on, however, I want to say something about sympathy and empathy, both of which are connected to one's emotions. These terms can be used in different ways, so it is important to be clear how I will be using them. Empathy is the ability to put yourself in the position of another person (or animal, perhaps) and, as a result, experience the emotions (perhaps to a lesser degree) of that other. So, for example, I empathize with Blau when I take up his perspective, and I feel grief and hopelessness about his inability to save his father. I can also empathize with Stangl when I put myself in his position of just having been appointed to Treblinka, and I feel fear about the consequences of not accepting the appointment. Sympathy, however, involves caring about another person's (or animal's) plight. So, as a result of my empathy for Blau, I sympathize with him: I care about his bad situation, wish that he hadn't suffered as he did. Notice that Stangl didn't empathize or sympathize with Blau. His response to Blau's apparent thanks reveals that he is either unable or unwilling to take up Blau's perspective and feel what Blau is feeling. Perhaps as a result of that lack of empathy, Stangl fails to sympathize with Blau: because he fails to see how deeply Blau is suffering, he does not have sufficient concern for Blau's plight; this is revealed by his smug self-congratulatory attitude.

Insofar as sympathy is a kind of care or concern, it can motivate us to act to relieve the sufferings of the one with whom we feel sympathy. So sympathy can be dangerous to our self-interest—it can lead us to care about the situations of others making it more difficult to perpetuate our involvement in their oppression or to deny that we are acting wrongly. If empathy can cause sympathy, blocking empathy may be a way to insulate ourselves from having to face the immorality of our own actions. And one often effective way to block empathy is to judge that the other is too dissimilar to us for us to be able to take up her perspective. This may be legitimate when it comes to, say, our failure to empathize with bats—creatures who are very differently constituted from us and whose mental lives probably are also very different.[9] It is clearly not legitimate, however, in the cases of Jones and Jefferson's failure to empathize with their slaves: either consciously or unconsciously, they avoided full engagement with the perspective of their slaves and thus, as a result, were able to dampen their sympathy with the plight of the enslaved. Similarly, in his encounter with Blau, Stangl was avoiding putting himself in Blau's position because, if he had done so, it would at the least have been much more difficult for him to see this episode as showing him in a favorable light.

Sentimentality and the "Virtue" of Hardness

During the period of the Third Reich in Germany, especially in the war years, men and women committed acts that, in their cruelty, depravity, brutality, and horror, remain unsurpassed in human history. As one reads the words of those who ordered these atrocities and of those who carried them out, it is striking how a great number of these people moved from what we might think of as "natural" reactions of outrage and revulsion, to acceptance of and even pride in their work. The Nazis themselves constantly spoke of this process as one involving suppression of "sentiment" and the development of a peculiarly SS virtue—"hardness."

One cannot read the words of the men who planned and executed the Final Solution without being struck by their constant warning against "sentimentality" being directed toward their Jewish (and other) victims. Consider the following remarks by Josef Goebbels:

> Jewry is thus now enduring a fate that is hard but is more than deserved. Sympathy or even regret is wholly out of place.
>
> [Reporting on a speech of Hitler's] This question must be viewed without any sentimentality. We are here not to express sympathy for the Jews, but only to express sympathy for our own German people.
>
> We cannot allow any false sentimentality; One cannot allow any sentimentality in these matters.
>
> The Jews are evacuated in large numbers and sent to the East. This is taking place on a rather large scale. There the Jewish question is handled in the right place without sentimentality.[10]

In the last quotation, Goebbels is speaking about the clearing of the Warsaw ghetto and the transport of its inhabitants to

Treblinka. Why is there this obsession by Goebbels and Hitler with "sentimentality"? In order to answer this question, we need to examine what the men under their orders were actually doing. Before Jews were murdered in assembly-line fashion in camps such as Auschwitz and Treblinka (beginning in the late autumn to winter of 1941 and going at full force by late spring of 1942), they were shot in mass executions by *Einsatzgruppen* (special task forces) and police battalions on the Eastern Front. As the regular German armed forces (the Wehrmacht as opposed to the SS and the Waffen-SS) invaded the Soviet Union in Operation Barbarossa (commenced in June 1941), it was closely followed by these special units, whose job was to clear the occupied territories of "partisans," intellectuals, communist political officials, and, of course, Jews. These mass executions were accomplished via the shooting of usually naked or partially naked men, women, and children into large open pits. One commander on the Eastern Front, Friedrich Jeckeln, found a new, cruel, but in his view more efficient way of going about his task:

> He called the method of mass killing he invented *Sardinenpackung*. As Meier describes, it involved forcing victims to lie together face down and side by side and killing them with *Genickschussen* [a shot in the neck at the point where spinal cord and skull meet; see page 7 of Rhodes, *Masters of Death*], then forcing the next group of victims to lie down on top of the torn, bleeding corpses of the victims who preceded them to form another layer, ignoring the victims' terror and horror in the interest of efficiently filling up the killing pit.[11]

Rhodes describes another mass killing (of 400 Jews), in which the "victims had been positioned facing them [the executioners] at the edge of the pit, and when the young soldiers fired they had been sprayed with their victims' blood and brains."[12] In some cases, "mothers with infants were told to hold their babies over their heads; one man then shot the mother while the other shot the child."[13] All the while, cries of terror could be heard from those victims still awaiting their turn at the killing pits.[14]

Initially, quite unsurprisingly, the men involved in these shootings were shaken, to say the least. The leaders of the SS and of the police battalions recognized that these men were suffering from what they themselves described as "psychological and *moral* stress."[15] One battalion commander, Paul Blobel, when questioned at his postwar trial in Nuremberg, claimed that "our men who took part in these executions suffered more from nervous exhaustion than those who had to be shot. . . . Our men had to be cared for . . . [because they] experienced a lot, psychologically."[16] Likewise, Ohlendorf complained about the mass killings, not on behalf of the victims, but because he "deplored the inhuman burden which was being imposed on the men in killing all these civilians."[17]

There is, without a doubt, an extraordinary tension between what is being acknowledged by these Nazis on the surface and what is implied by their descriptions of the effects of participation in mass killings on their men. The phrase "moral stress" is quite revealing—it is not a term one would use for labor that was merely disgusting and physically exhausting, such as cleaning sewers or toilets. The members of the *Einsatzgruppen* were suffering in a way that those forced to clean outhouses would not, and their suffering was due to the fact that they were being forced to kill men, women, and children, none of whom had been convicted of any crime other than that of being Jewish. Most likely, the "moral stress" referred to was some jumbled and confused experience of compassion, guilt, shame, pity, and outrage. The killers were probably also experiencing a deep cognitive tension: the vast majority of them had been raised by

parents and religious teachers to believe that killing the innocent is wrong and also that one ought to obey one's superiors
and to act to defend one's country. But now those superiors were
commanding them to kill apparently innocent people (some were
infants, after all) and being told that doing so was somehow necessary for the defense of their country. Thus, these killers were
assailed by an overwhelming mix of emotions, conflicting moral
beliefs, and a barrage of visual and auditory sensations (people
screaming and crying, bits of brains splattered through the air,
deep pools of blood forming, massive piles of dead and naked
bodies growing by the minute, overwhelming stench) unlike any
before experienced.

If the massive killing operations were to continue in anything resembling an efficient manner, the killers had to be "cared
for." And so social evenings were organized. These evenings were
to involve comradeship, traditional German music, food and
drink, perhaps amateur theatricals. What they were not to include was discussion of and reflection upon the day's events.
Diversion in the form of German culture and comradeship with
fellow Germans was called for. The hope was that eventually the
killers would cease to experience "moral stress"—that is, that
they would become "hard." Reinhard Heydrich, Himmler's right-
hand man, said "we must be hard as granite,"[18] and one former
Auschwitz guard, talking about men who had served on firing
squads, said "Those people lose all feeling."[19]

Now hardness could be a matter of blocking the conver-
sion of one's emotions into actions, either by developing or
cultivating countervailing motivations strong enough to outweigh the emotions involved in one's "moral stress" or by deeply
suppressing the emotions, or it could be a matter of eliminating
those emotions altogether, as the former Auschwitz guard
suggested. Most likely, different killers developed different kinds
of "hardness." The evenings of German culture and comradeship

could work to develop sufficient solidarity so that one's loyalty to the group and unwillingness to diverge from the norm took priority over feelings of pity and compassion and over motivations resulting from competing moral beliefs. Or such evenings could work to reinforce the idea that Germanization was the most important goal, and that the German people were entitled to *Lebensraum* (living space). If the Jews stood in the way of achieving these goals, then the Jews had to go, in fact deserved to die—it was either them or the German people.[20]

We can now see that Rudolph Höss, the commandant of Auschwitz, in his memoirs, was presenting himself as the ideal "hard" SS man. He says that even those such as Eichmann "who had a reputation for being truly hard" wondered at how he could carry out his tasks. His response to such queries was "that only iron determination could carry out Hitler's orders and this could only be achieved by stifling all human emotion."[21] He went on:

> I had to bury all my human inhibitions as deeply as possible. In fact, I have to confess openly that after such conversations with Eichmann *these human emotions seemed almost like treason* against the Führer. There was no escaping this conflict as far as I was concerned. I had to continue to carry out the process of destruction. I had to experience the mass murder and to coldly watch it without any regard for *the doubts which uprooted my deepest inner feelings.* I had to watch it all with cold indifference.[22]

Höss understood his overriding duty to be to obey orders. Thus, he said, "I was not permitted to let anything come in conflict with these orders. I had to be like steel—colder, harder, and even more merciless toward the misery of the prisoners. . . . I could not allow feelings to overcome me. I could not allow any emotion to stand in the way."[23]

If we are to take Höss at his word, then he, like the killers on the Eastern Front, did experience emotions such as pity and compassion for the victims that he saw herded into the gas chambers at Auschwitz. However, he made apparently successful attempts to suppress or eliminate these emotions so that he could obey orders and act as a model SS officer for the men and women under his command. What is particularly interesting about Höss's commentary is his linking of his feelings with his thoughts: he regarded his emotions as being like treason, and his feelings were tied to his doubts, supposedly with respect to the moral permissibility of what he was doing. For these reasons, he could not allow himself to examine his emotions, for fear that they would more fully reveal his misgivings about what was happening under his command.

Suppressing Emotion, Suppressing Morality

There is little doubt that for many of the perpetrators of the genocide in the Third Reich, their willingness and even enthusiasm for this grisly project was related to how they dealt with their emotions. One possible response to this story of Nazi atrocities is to decide that we need to let our sympathetic responses—that is, those that respond to others in a caring way, such as compassion and pity, guide us as moral agents. Surely, it might be said, if Höss and many of the men on the Eastern Front had listened to, cultivated, and acted upon their sympathies, then the atrocities could never have reached the level they did.[24] While there is certainly some truth in this response, it also takes too narrow a view of matters, because sympathetic feelings can conflict not only with actions dictated by a bad morality but also with actions dictated by a good morality.

For what I have reported about events during the Nazi regime is only a part of the story. We cannot ignore that Goebbels contrasts "sympathy for the Jews" with "sympathy for our own German people." Given that at least some number of Germans believed Hitler's and Goebbels's propaganda about the Jews, they probably believed, at least to some extent, that their actions in concentration camps and on the Eastern Front benefited their friends and families back in Germany. And wherever they went in Eastern Europe, they were greeted by anti-Semitic locals, those more than willing to encourage and take part in their grisly genocidal work. Daniel Jonah Goldhagen, in his admittedly controversial *Hitler's Willing Executioners: Ordinary Germans and the Holocaust*, makes a case that those soldiers who did not opt out of the work of the killing squads—and they were offered the opportunity to do so without threat of reprisal—had at least some serious anti-Semitic beliefs which provided emotional responses that pulled against whatever sympathy they had for their Jewish victims.[25] What was happening inside of these perpetrators was not merely a conflict between sympathetic emotions and cold rational Nazi or more generally nationalistic principles; there were also conflicting principles, conflicting emotions, and resultant intense confusion about how to deal with both external and internal or psychological events. We can never understand the members of the *Einsatzgruppen* if we simply project ourselves, with all our own moral and nonmoral beliefs, into their physical, external circumstances.

I have argued that emotions have an important if not essential connection to beliefs or judgments. But the beliefs that give content to our emotions are often vague and inchoate. Shame or guilt, for example, does not seem to require that one make the very determinate judgment that she has done something wrong, either prima facie or all-things-considered. Rather, such emotions seem to require nothing more than a sort of moral unease on the part of the agent, a worry that *maybe* she is acting wrongly in some respect or a concern that she is in a situation calling for moral judgment and/or action to which she may prove inadequate in some way. Similarly, sympathetic emotional responses such as compassion seem to involve some sort of belief that someone is suffering.

But even given all this, we need to see that even if emotions are not infallible or even particularly reliable moral guides, they can serve an important, and often crucial, signaling function. Guilt alerts me to examine my situation—it seems that if I experience guilt, I at least believe some sort of moral decision/action/factor may very well be in the offing. Of course, there could be any number of such factors: perhaps I believe that the consequences of my action are very bad, that I am violating some important moral rule, or that I or some other relevant person(s) disapproves of the action.[26] Then I need to examine whether my belief holds up in the light of an examination of the relevant evidence, assessing the weight and significance of anything I may have uncovered.

In cases such as those we examined in the last section, we might, as a result of trying to determine why we are experiencing counterbalancing motivational pulls (e.g., a motive to shoot, and a motive not to shoot), discover moral beliefs that yield conflicting answers (e.g., "Obey authority," and "Do not shoot innocent people"). Again, how we deal with such conflict will depend on how we view the status of such rules: Are they rules of thumb derived from a consequentialist moral principle? Are they derived from the Categorical Imperative? Or are they both foundational moral rules that need somehow to be weighed against one another in the current situation? But obviously, before we can begin to deal with the conflict in our beliefs and the resulting motivational conflict, we need to get clear in our own minds what exactly the source of the conflict is. Then we need to have some theory on hand with which to deliberate concerning the status of the rules uncovered.

In the second instance, emotions can provide data about other persons, or at least about our beliefs about other persons. We respond with compassion and pity only when we are picking up on what we take to be evidence of another's suffering in some way. So we need to pay attention to these emotions in order to determine what is giving rise to our belief that someone is suffering. Human beings, of course, pick up on even subtle cues of body language, facial expression, and tone of voice to infer what others are feeling. And we use these to initiate an argument from analogy: that person is showing cue X; when I show cue X, I am feeling Y; thus, that person is probably feeling Y. Because morality is, to at least a large extent, other-regarding, we need to be attentive to cues about the effects of our actions on the people around us. If the cues put forth by others trigger our emotions, then we need to be alert to what our emotions are telling us about those others. There is no doubt that we do not always register all our evidence at the conscious cognitive level, so if we ignore emotional responses, we may fail to attend to some of the evidence available to us. What we do after we assess the evidence again depends on our theory. We need to address questions such as: Is all suffering bad? Is some suffering deserved? And, if so, is deserved suffering bad? If suffering can be deserved, what can make a moral agent deserve to suffer? Is there a limit to how much suffering an individual can deserve?

At the beginning of this chapter, I mentioned that some moral theorists think that moral judgments are really just judgments about our own attitudes and/or emotions, and that some have suggested that psychological research shows a serious correlation between emotional capacity and moral capacity, thereby providing evidence for such moral theories.[27] But this sort of move is far too quick. There are many ways in which emotional attentiveness and sensitivity can play a role in moral deliberation other than emotions being the subject matter of our moral judgments.

Consider, for example, the ways in which emotional responsiveness would be crucial for a consequentialist who found herself faced with the task of the killing squads. For the consequentialist, rightness is a function of the consequences of action: right action is that which produces, on balance, the most happiness or well-being. Human beings are, as Hume pointed out, constituted so that we are keyed into one another's emotional responses, not only in the sense of being able to judge how others are feeling but also in the sense of having our own emotions triggered by those of others. So our own emotions, when we are in the presence of other human beings, are often mirror reflections of those being experienced by those around us. If we often pick up on subtle cues from others before these facts are registered at the conscious level, then our own emotions may be our first indication that others are, for example, suffering in some way. Thus, it becomes critical to be able to identify our emotions and to attempt to figure out what has triggered these responses. Given our capacity to feel what others are feeling, we ought to know to look to those around us when we are seeking the cause of our own emotions. Our own emotions, then, if we are consequentialists, may be our first cues to look for negative or positive affects in those people affected by our actions. But, again, moral deliberation cannot stop here. Our sympathy is usually triggered first by features of persons in our immediate environment and/or by persons about whom we care personally. Allowing ourselves to deliberate about further effects of our actions forces our emotions to range more widely. Jones sympathized with his wife's worries about household disruptions owing to disobedient and runaway slaves, but he failed to let his sympathy come into play in his interactions with and deliberations about those disobedient and runaway slaves.

Now it may be thought that none of this could possibly be relevant to the members of the killing squads, because the cues they had that the people around them were suffering were hardly subtle: screams of terror, desperate pleas for life, faces and bodies contorted in pain and fear. Surely these cues would be registered at the conscious level and so a judgment about suffering need not be made via a detour into vicarious emotions. And it is absolutely right that you or I, as we are now, with our backgrounds and beliefs, would have no trouble cognitively assessing the situation immediately and directly. But what we respond to directly in this way depends to a great extent on our previous experiences, our cultural background, our education, and our background beliefs. An example relevant to an ongoing moral debate within our own culture can help to illustrate the point here.

How do people respond to the slaughter of nonhuman animals being killed for the production of meat, or to the separation of mothers of other species from their young? Here again, the cues indicating pain and suffering are not subtle: eyes rolling in fear, shrieks and yelps of various forms, attempts to break free or to harm the threat, bodies writhing in pain. And yet many people insist that nonhuman animals do not suffer in the way that human beings would under similar conditions. They make these claims even though they are often assailed by compassion and pity when actually confronted with vivid images of animals being slaughtered or torn from their young. But when we are upset by such scenes, what do we do? We turn off the TV and seek out some diversion—perhaps we even divert ourselves by playing with our own pet cat or dog. And later we settle down to a delicious meal of pork or beef. The analogy with the killers on the Eastern Front, I hope, is all too close.

What is happening in us when we respond in these ways? We are overwhelmed with feelings of compassion, pity, and outrage when we view animals being slaughtered or torn from family members. But we have also been raised in a culture that takes meat for granted as part of our diet, and regards farm animals (as opposed to domestic pets) as having little, if any, moral standing. Most of us have a vested interest in continuing to have meat in our diets—we love steak and barbecued ribs and hamburgers and bratwurst. And, after all, we tell ourselves, we must not anthropomorphize animals. All our emotional responses, we insist, are merely the result of projecting ourselves into the situation of the animals, and that is an illegitimate move to make.

But the appeal to the illegitimacy of anthropomorphizing is purely question begging, of course. It is only illegitimate to project our own feelings and reactions onto other beings in cases in which those beings lack those feelings and reactions. When all the cues point to nonhuman animals such as pigs and cows feeling as we would in their circumstances, why do we insist on reinterpreting our evidence? In some subcultures, such as the 4-H clubs of America, something akin to "hardness" is encouraged and developed when young people devote time and energy to nurturing young animals and then sell those animals at county and state fairs. Rather than having these young people sort through their conflicting reactions, they are uncompromisingly socialized into the practices of their subculture, which is always particularly dangerous when self-interest is on the side of such socialization.

In such cases children learn mechanisms for suppressing, eliminating, or cordoning off from the sources of motivation, their "sentimentality" with respect to farm animals. Furthermore, they are discouraged from examining their emotions in the context of their beliefs, both moral and nonmoral. And, of course, getting into such habits with respect to one category of being is highly likely to affect interactions with and responsiveness to other beings. This sort of case provides a very eerie parallel to the process undergone by members of the killing squads on the Eastern Front.

Thus, our emotions provide important data for moral reasoning, and so we need to learn how to examine our emotions if we are to carry out our duty of moral self-scrutiny. Emotions can alert us to features of our environment that we may not be picking up on in a direct cognitive manner. They can also alert us to conflict in our beliefs and/or attitudes. Practice in noticing, identifying, and contextualizing our emotional responses is one of the first steps to getting clear on the nature of the moral situation in which we find ourselves. It is, however, as I have tried to show, just the first step in a process that must involve appeal to theory in order to decide and act in a morally responsible manner. Given our natures, we need to be aware of and responsive to our emotions, but we cannot let them be our unreflective guides in action.

Feeling Moral Concepts?

It is now time to consider the ways in which emotions play an important role in grasping moral concepts. Ted Bundy provides us with a stark way of posing the questions at issue. Before moving to a discussion of Bundy, I want to issue a cautionary note. Ted Bundy is understood by both the lay public and professional psychiatrists and psychologists to be a psychopath or sociopath. (The distinction between these concepts, if any, is not important for our purposes here.) There is growing evidence that those who exhibit the cluster of traits associated with psychopathy differ from the rest of the population with respect to brain structure and/or brain development, and that it is this abnormality in brain structure and/or development that accounts for the psychopath's deficiencies with respect to emotions.[28] If this research is correct, then you and I differ from Ted Bundy in a different way from that in which we differ from our examples of Nazis and slaveholders: the latter found themselves in situations very different from those that you and I have faced in our lifetimes, but Bundy differs from us in the biological basis of his mental life. There is an important sense, then, in which we can identify with, for example, Jones and Stangl, but not with Bundy: we can project ourselves into Nazi Germany or the antebellum American South, but how could we project ourselves into the position of someone with a different brain structure?

Further, Bundy is not your ordinary, run-of-the-mill psychopath: only a small proportion of psychopaths are killers, and even a smaller proportion (I am surmising) are necrophiliacs. So the content of the desires that drove Bundy are, at one level, very different from those that drove, for example, Jefferson: Bundy wanted to rape and murder and have sex with the corpses of his victims, while Jefferson wanted to live a life of material comfort with the leisure to pursue intellectual activities that would cement his reputation with his peers. Jefferson's desires, clearly, are ones we can all identify with while Bundy's are repugnant and horrifying. But on another level, Bundy is not so different from Jefferson: both derive pleasure from certain activities, and satisfaction of those desires requires imposing a sizable burden on other people. So seeing how both these men reason about their situations reveals much about the way they understand themselves and their relationships to other people.

And much of the way we understand ourselves and our relationships to other people involves, in one way or another, the evocation or employment of emotions, sympathy, and empathy. We assume that Jefferson and Jones had ordinary capacities for emotions, sympathy, and empathy, but it is clear that Bundy did not. So Bundy can provide us fascinating information about how deficiencies in emotions and the like can impact the way that we think about moral issues. But why, we might wonder, would that be at all relevant to those of us who do not have those kinds of deficiencies? It is relevant because if we have certain capacities or abilities, we do not always exercise them—one may be able to run a 7-minute mile, but choose not to go running. Sometimes a failure to exercise our capacities can cause them to diminish or even to disappear; I used to be able to run a 7-minute mile, but I have not run in years, and I am quite sure that my aging joints and lack of practice would prevent me from doing so today. People often suppress their emotional responses, and doing so can lead to a diminution in or even loss of emotional capacity. I think, then, that seeing how lack of emotional capacity impacted Bundy's moral capacities can both be theoretically informative and provide us incentive to deal appropriately with our own emotions.

Let's begin by considering Bundy's views about guilt:

> I've learned to live absolutely and completely and totally in the *here and now*. I don't worry, think or concern myself with the past, or, for that matter, with the future, except only to the extent necessary. . . . Well, whatever I've done in the past, you know—the emotions of omissions or commissions— *doesn't* bother me. . . . I guess I am in the enviable position of not having to deal with guilt. There's just no reason for it.[29]

When and why do most of us feel guilt? The obvious answer seems to be: when and because we believe we may have acted wrongly or we are facing a moral situation to which we are not adequate. The intensity of our guilt seems to be a reflection of just how wrongly we believe ourselves to have acted or how serious the moral crisis we face is: a wee bit of guilt for a minor moral misdemeanor or moral decision, a whole heck of a lot of guilt for a major moral transgression or a looming potential moral disaster.

Bundy treats guilt as an entirely gratuitous bad feeling that follows certain actions that we would do well to eliminate. The analogy for Bundy seems to be something like the following: just as we would regard as foolish a person who took a hammer to her toes after performing certain actions, so someone is foolish who allows herself to feel guilt after breaking the moral rules. Guilt, for Bundy, is a way that we punish ourselves, and according to him, there is no function to imposing such negative feelings upon ourselves.

But guilt, of course, is not some sort of self-imposed punishment. It is quite true that guilt, as an emotion, is usually an unpleasant experience we would prefer not to have. But it is also perhaps the best illustration of Hume's claim that we refuse to call certain bad feelings by the name of a certain emotion unless the person having the bad feelings also has certain beliefs, no matter how inchoate or vague. It would be bizarre for me to insist that I feel guilty about having given some money to charity while also insisting that I believe that I was morally required to do it, that it was a morally commendable action, that I was never taught that it was wrong, that I am not aware of anyone who would regard it as wrong, and that I am convinced I have not thereby ignored any competing moral considerations. If, however, I find myself in such a situation and my guilt is persistent, I certainly do well to give further thought to my predicament; perhaps I will uncover unacknowledged beliefs that I ought to be doing even more for charity given my privileged life and that my lifestyle plays a role in perpetuating the poverty these charities are attempting to alleviate. Alternatively, maybe my "guilt" really is just bizarre. But given the possibility of uncovering further beliefs that I am, for whatever reason not dealing with, I do well to examine my guilt and attempt to put it into context. At the very least, my guilt seems to be an indication that I have some sort of unease about a moral dimension of my situation that I am overlooking on the conscious level.

So guilt can play a crucial role in sorting out moral conflicts that we face. But it seems that the very experience of guilt—as guilt and not just as some bad psychic sensations—requires the possession of moral concepts. Bundy's equation of guilt with a "social control mechanism" suggests that he really only understands guilt as a bad feeling that could functionally be replaced with a hammer to the toes or a whack on the nose with a newspaper, as some people apply to dogs whose behavior they wish to alter. So if Bundy lacked moral concepts, then in fact he could not really feel guilt. And, I will suggest, we have some reason to think that Bundy lacked moral concepts and, thus, lacked moral beliefs.

I am going to use the literature on psychopaths not only to help illuminate the ways in which Bundy went awry morally but also to show how those ways of going morally awry are not necessarily unique to some sector of the population with a discernible "disorder." In this chapter, our concern is to see how close "ordinary" bad people can come to "psychopathic" bad people, and how that similarity can illuminate the significant role of the emotions in moral deliberation. Merely because Bundy and others like him can correctly be labeled "psychopathic" while you and I cannot does not mean we can assume that Bundy is of interest only as an anomaly. We will see that we in fact have much to learn from men like Bundy that can help us to see the nature of the moral life, even if we are unable to fully empathize with psychopaths. I believe that psychopaths, unlike bats, can provide us with insight into our own potential moral missteps.

It is telling that early nineteenth-century discussions of those we now call "psychopaths" or "sociopaths" diagnosed such individuals as suffering from "moral insanity," a condition involving defects of the "moral sense."[30] Benjamin Rush, the early

American physician and penal theorist, discussed what he called "moral depravity," and various British legal acts referred to the "moral imbecile" and the "moral defective."[31] Clearly, the early diagnoses and categorizations were guided by a view of such offenders as having certain disabilities with respect to moral reasoning and/or moral motivation and were, thus, not normatively neutral. And the psychopath's moral deficiencies continue to play an important role in how theorists understand their condition. Carl Elliott and Grant Gillett point out that psychopaths seem quite capable of grasping how other people apply moral terms, but that they fail to internalize the norms that employ those terms:

> [A]lthough the psychopath clearly knows what moral norms are operative in society, he does not seem to have endorsed such moral norms for himself. He appears to realize what moral rules and values govern the lives of others, and he is not blind to the fact that others expect him to abide by such rules and values as well. . . . But he [the psychopath] does not seem to internalize moral norms and values. Though he may profess to hold certain values, these professed values have little relationship to the way he lives his life.[32]

The notion of the internalization of rules or norms is an important one. In his well-known discussions of the nature of law, H. L. A. Hart made a distinction between the internal perspective on rules and the external perspective on rules.[33] Those who take the internal perspective on a rule or system of rules regard the rules as binding on them, in the sense that, whether or not sanctions will follow a breach of the rules, others would be justified in imposing such sanctions. The notion of justification is the notion of the possession of good reasons for action, and so internalization of rules involves understanding those rules as tied to reasons for action. One does not merely predict that bad consequences will follow a breach of the rules; one understands that such bad consequences are the appropriate response to any breach of the rules.

Those who take an external perspective on a rule or a system of rules understand the rule as nothing more than a statement of a correlation between certain actions and certain sanctions: if I or someone else does X, then it is likely that others (if they find out that I did X) will impose some unpleasant treatment on me. Thus, the rule is just like a prediction of natural events—for example, if one holds a golf club aloft during an electrical storm, it is likely that one will get struck by lightning and be electrocuted. There is no reference to justification or reasons: in both cases, that involving human response and that involving a natural consequence, the statement of the rule is nothing more than a prediction of what will (or is likely) to happen.[34]

This description of the external perspective on rules fits Bundy perfectly. Recall, first, that Bundy claimed to feel remorse. However, remorse for Bundy was not a moral emotion but, rather, simply a fear resulting from recognition that he had done something that exposed him to danger: "he was full of remorse and remonstrating with himself for the suicidal, uh, nature of that activity," "the course of conduct that he had engaged in was . . . [f]raught with danger, badly thought out," and "guilt and remorse were most prevalent . . . during that period when the individual was uncertain about the results of the police investigation." Bundy recognized that he would be punished if he were caught, and he feared that punishment. But there is no acknowledgment that he had done something wrong—something for which he would *deserve* or *merit* punishment.

Second, we saw that Bundy saw one breach of the rules as just the same as any other breach of the rules: he equated stealing textbooks with raping and killing young women. Everyone, he says, has "gaps" in his or her conscience. But for many of us, there is a more or less conscious deliberation about which rules are such that our reasons to obey them outweigh our reasons of self-interest and which are not. We attempt to justify our breaches of the rules by asking, "Whom could it hurt?" Now, there is no doubt that we often deceive ourselves into thinking that no one is hurt, either directly or indirectly, by our breach of the rules, but our very deception shows that we think some justification for breaking the rules is called for. Given his external perspective on the rules, Bundy does no connect them to reasons or justification for punishment because he does not see any reason independent of the punishment for acting in accordance with the rules.

In spite of their differences from Bundy, we saw very similar phenomena in the cases of the death camp commandants Stangl and Höss. Both men had a deep commitment to doing their jobs and seemed to understand duty largely (perhaps entirely in the case of Höss) in terms of complying with the norms of their positions and with the demands of their superiors. Stangl insisted that he "would be carrying out this *assignment* [of running Treblinka] as a police officer under his [his superior's] command." His main concern was the handling of the valuables stolen from the Jews being killed: because corruption had been dominating this handling, he as a police officer had a "legitimate" interest in overseeing it and in eliminating the corruption. His obsession with rules reached darkly comic proportions when he was determined to ferret out and punish the officer or soldier who promised water to a Jew in exchange for the latter's gold watch, but never got the water to the Jew. He insisted, "What's right is right, isn't it? . . . Once a complaint is made it has to be investigated." As I pointed out in chapter 2, the watch (along with all his other possessions) would have been stolen from the Jew before he was herded naked to the gas chambers—but Stangl, in this situation, understands his duty in terms of the rules, which disallow the taking of the watch by the officer but allow the taking of it in the undressing barracks before death. And the Jew whose watch was the object of so much concern is entirely ignored by Stangl: he is unable to tell Sereny what the man's fate was. Höss's understanding of duty was, if anything, even starker than that of Stangl, saying "I saw only my work, my duty," clearly equating doing his job with doing his duty. He insisted that, as a soldier, he had to obey orders: "I had received an order; I had to carry it out. I could not allow myself to form an opinion as to whether this mass extermination of the Jews was necessary or not." Höss regarded the orders of Himmler and of Hitler as "sacred" and not to be questioned. His understanding of what he ought to do was simple: do what I am told by my superiors in the name of either Himmler or Hitler.

The "moral universe" of the psychopath "seems characterized by rules set by some authority where harm to others or concern for them is not at all salient."[35] Psychopaths notoriously have difficulty distinguishing between moral rules and non-moral, or conventional rules, where an instance of the former is "Don't kill innocent people" and an instance of the latter is "Drive on the right-hand side of the road." Stangl and Höss most likely could distinguish between these two types of rules, but they failed to think about that distinction and about its significance: they failed to seriously consider what justified the moral rules and why they have a kind of importance that conventional rules lack. This failure resulted in their moral thinking being exhausted by the rules that, even if they had internalized them, lacked the sort of depth that would have allowed them to consider when and why the rules had exceptions or were outweighed by other rules.

How might we explain this understanding of morality as a system of rules without any understanding of the foundation of or justification for the rules? One possibility, of course, is the lack of empathy or sympathy, a phenomenon that we find in the cases of Bundy, Stangl, and Höss. Bundy attempted to justify the killing of his victims by saying, "there are *so* many people. This person will never be missed." This remark suggests that Bundy failed to individuate his victims and, thus, failed to appreciate them as having individual mental lives with a significance unrelated to his own need to dominate. He describes them as "problems," "threats," and "symbols," thereby objectifying them. The most telling indication of his obliviousness to the significance of the mental lives of other people is his equation of harm with physical harm or bodily damage: he claims that on one occasion he set out not to harm a young woman but only to rape her. It seems that he did not understand rape as a harm. Did he fail to grasp the harm he had done because he objectified his victims? This could explain his mindset: if he could not see external bodily damage, then there was no harm, because he failed to consider the inner lives of those he raped and killed. Bundy certainly understood that certain actions could elicit negative responses from others, but he seems to have had no understanding of the pain that he caused or of that pain as the ultimate basis for moral proscriptions. Or, if Bundy did see his victims as experiencing pain, that fact was relevant for his deliberations only insofar as it complicated his plans or enhanced his sense of control and domination.

Both Stangl and Höss admitted to engaging in emotional distancing from their victims. Höss claimed that compassion for the Jews "would be unworthy of an SS officer," who needed to be "hard" to carry out his orders, the carrying out of which constituted his duty. Höss wanted to stifle any feelings of pity or compassion because he understood such feelings as hindrances to doing his duty and, thus, as potentially traitorous. So Höss's conception of duty required him to shut off any tendency to empathize with his victims; he thereby in fact shut himself off from the very content of morality that, on any plausible conception, has something to do with human suffering and well-being.

Stangl was notorious for overseeing the killing operations while wearing white riding clothes, but he never thought about how that incongruous apparel would appear to those being run to their deaths. And, of course, why would he do this, given that he thought of the Jews as "cargo"? The story about Blau and his father that I mentioned at the beginning of this chapter is an excellent example of Stangl's inability to get into the mind of the inmates: Stangl treats Blau as a mirror for his own self-conception as a benevolent man doing his best in a bad situation, rather than conceptualizing Blau in his full humanity as a person with a family, life projects, and a full-blown inner life involving loves, fears, hopes, and hatreds.

While Stangl's white riding clothes stuck in the minds of the few survivors of Treblinka, they were unaware of Stangl's own explanation for his purchase of those clothes. He says that he was attacked by sandflies and the clothes he wore to Poland had to be burned. He recounts how uncomfortable the sandflies attack was, obviously trying to get Sereny's sympathy for his plight. But did he not stop to think about those work-Jews with whom he claimed to have friendly relations? They might just as easily be attacked by the flies, but they had no one to get them new clothes and nowhere to have a nice hot bath. They had to work and stand at attention regardless of whatever insects they had to contend with. But the plight of the work-Jews doesn't seem to have even occurred to Stangl.

We can use these examples to understand a distinction often made in the literature on psychopaths between knowing what moral norms require and appreciating those moral norms.[36] Take a moral norm about avoiding causing pain or suffering to others. One may know that the system of rules known as "morality" disallows conduct with such consequences. Bundy, for example, stresses that he tried to avoid causing pain to his victims, but it is unclear whether he had much, if any, sense of the inner lives of his victims, leading us to wonder whether he was simply mouthing words. He wanted to avoid conduct that had negative consequences for himself, but with no or little grasp of the mental lives of other people, he was unable to understand what the moral norms were forbidding or why they were forbidding them. His inability to empathize meant that he could not put himself into the shoes of his victims: whatever was happening inside their heads was conceptualized by Bundy only through the lens of his own sexual needs—needs that required, for their gratification, dominance and control over others. Bundy, then, was locked into an external perspective on the moral rules.

The accounts of Stangl and of Höss, in contrast, suggest that they were not locked into such a perspective. Rather, they molded themselves psychologically to resemble those such as Bundy that we think of as psychopaths. Höss admits to being raised with a conception of duty that involved, fundamentally, deference to superiors in various human hierarchies. Whenever he began to feel emotions such as compassion or pity—emotions that could have functioned as stimuli to empathetic engagement and reflection on the foundations of moral strictures—he simply shut them down and moved his focus to conforming to the ideal of an SS man. Stangl also admits to having to distance himself from the victims of Treblinka, reconceptualizing them as "cargo." Stangl's unwillingness (or inability?) to deal adequately with hypotheticals (recall that he never put himself in the position of relatives of those killed in the euthanasia program or of those who actually had to work in the death complex itself) facilitated his imaginative and emotional deficits.

An important difference between a man like Stangl and a man like Bundy may lie in their differing capacities. It seems plausible to suppose that Stangl had the capacity for sympathetic emotions—he had, for example, an apparently loving relationship with his wife—while Bundy may not even have had that capacity. So while Bundy may not have been able to grasp moral concepts and was thus unable to grasp the underlying foundations or grounds of moral principles, it seems more likely that Stangl simply didn't exercise his capacity for thinking about those grounds. Stangl's moral thinking was shallow: he simply did not consider the justifications for various rules and principles, and, even if he had been forced to, he would probably have been willing to content himself with some sort of canned understanding that he had heard repeated by others. Most likely, he needed to divert his thought from considering the underlying grounds of his principles so that he could continue to keep his emotions at bay and thus keep them from interfering with the motivations that he was determined to act upon.

While Stangl may have done this in an extremely all-encompassing way, it seems that many of us do this on a daily basis with respect to at least some moral principles. If we were to really reflect in a robust way upon our commitment to not cause immense suffering for some trivial gratification for ourselves, repulsion and guilt might surface as we smell the ribs on the barbecue at a friend's party. But then those emotions might disrupt our motivations to eat the ribs and to play a certain role at the party, so we simply do not reflect on the animals who now are nothing more than meat to us. We might have to adopt more radical tactics if we were forced to take jobs in a slaughterhouse, where we would be confronted on a daily basis with the ways in which those animals are converted into meat. But our ordinary meat-eating practices, at least for many of us, seem to require us to step aside from any sort of depth or appreciation in our thinking about our fundamental moral commitments.

Being willing and able to engage in this kind of distancing is dangerous, because an engagement with the feelings, thoughts, and experiences of both ourselves and other persons is fundamental to an understanding of moral rules that involves an internal perspective on those rules. For the consequentialist, the rightness or wrongness of an action is a function of the value of its consequences relative to available alternative actions, and the relevant consequences involve the suffering or well-being of human or other sentient creatures. For the Kantian, morality is fundamentally about having and showing respect for other rational beings, where the justification for the demand for respect appeals to the nature of those beings as capable of formulating and pursuing life plans—plans that can be frustrated or brought to fruition, thereby causing either pain or satisfaction. If one is a cultural relativist, one must understand the attitudes of other people to grasp the nature of the moral restrictions and demands that are placed upon one.

Thus, if one is to have what Elliott calls a "conceptually rich understanding of morality,"[37] one must have a robust grasp of the nature of the emotional, and more generally, of the inner lives of other beings (and of oneself), because those lives are what provide the foundational justification for moral demands. Bundy seemed unable to understand other people as having inner lives; this inability is often pointed to as a feature of psychopaths. And, if those who are characterized as psychopaths really lack this ability, then they would, it seems, have at least lessened responsibility for their moral and, thus, their criminal offenses.[38] But our only evidence for their inability to empathize is their failure to do so, and we have seen that both Stangl and Höss also failed on this score, but we have no evidence that they could not have avoided that failure. The evidence that we have underdetermines a choice between a person's being unable to empathize and a person's simply failing to do so for one reason or another.[39]

Empathy and sympathy, then, seem intimately tied to our capacity to take the internal perspective on the system of moral norms, no matter which conception of morality we adopt. The psychopath may simply represent someone who is able to avoid such empathy and/or sympathy easily and with little or no internal conflict, whereas others such as Stangl, Höss, and many of the members of the death squads on the Eastern Front in World War II had to work to reach a point at which their empathy/sympathy was suppressed to a sufficient extent to allow them to carry out their grisly work. Keeping alive our emotional sensibilities, then, seems key to maintaining our internal perspective on the system of moral norms. I am not suggesting that emotional sensitivity guarantees correct moral decisions and actions, only that it appears to be an important prerequisite for us, as human beings, to maintain the appropriate sort of commitment to the moral life. It is precisely *because of* their connection to our grasping of moral principles that moral emotions have such great ethical significance—we simply cannot ignore the role of theory and principles in the moral life.

Taking Action

Consider the following well-known passage from David Hume's *A Treatise of Human Nature*:

> Philosophy is commonly divided into *speculative* and *practical*; and as morality is always comprehended under the latter division, 'tis supposed to influence our passions and actions, and to go beyond the calm and indolent judgments of the understanding. And this is confirmed by common experience, which informs us, that men are often govern'd by their duties, and are deter'd from some actions by the opinion of injustice, and impell'd to others by that of

obligation . . . . [M]orals, therefore, have an influence on the actions and affections.[40]

Hume is pointing out the complicated connections between our emotions ("passions" and "affections"), our moral judgments, and our actions—complicated connections that I have been trying to unravel in this chapter. Certainly Hume is right that our moral judgments influence how we feel and act, but we have seen that how we feel also influences which moral judgments we make and, in fact, whether we make moral judgments at all. There is no doubt, then, that knowing how to examine our emotions and how to allow those emotions to influence judgment and action is crucial to being prepared for the moral life.

Our studies of Bundy, Höss, and Stangl provide us with robust examples of these connections. Walter Glannon, in his discussion of the moral defects of psychopaths, makes the following claim: "a person who adheres to a principle *as a moral principle* is thereby disposed to experience certain emotions and to have certain attitudes in certain situations."[41] One way of understanding what it would be to accept a moral principle *as a moral principle* is to understand it as involving a grasp of the underlying justification of the principle and thereby being led to take the internal perspective on the principle as a rule governing behavior. If one engages with that underlying justification, one will do it via empathetic identification with the inner lives of other beings (something that Hume thinks we are naturally constituted to do). Such empathetic identification involves our imaginatively entering into the feelings and emotions of others, thereby coming to share those feelings and emotions. This kind of empathy will often cause us to feel sympathy for others—that is, to care about their plight. And once we care about someone, we have a motivation to act to prevent his suffering or to promote her well-being.

But what happens all too often is that we get lazy or self-centered, and so we do not engage with moral norms in the most robust way—as, I argued here, happens in the case of our meat-eating practices. In such cases, the connection between our acceptance of those norms and our motivational springs can become severed, or at least sharply attenuated. All of this suggests why we need to constantly emotionally reengage with the facts that provide the foundation for morality; if we fail to do so, we could find ourselves, like Stangl and the killers on the Eastern Front, slipping from the internal perspective to the external perspective on morality. Taking moral concerns for granted, then, can lead us to lose our robust appreciation of morality and its norms. Perhaps there are beings who could have such an engagement in a cool, purely intellectual way, but we are not generally those kinds of beings. And, given our own failures of engagement with respect to nonhuman animals, we might become concerned about our own capacities to take the sort of road that Stangl took—the road to complicity with unimaginable atrocity.

Answering Our Questions?

In the opening section of this chapter I posed some questions, suggesting some issues that were to be explored: (1) What are the connections between emotions and acquisition and maintenance of moral concepts and moral beliefs? (2) What role do or ought our emotions to play in the motivation of moral actions?, and (3) If emotions are important for acquiring and acting on moral beliefs, can we be held responsible for performing the right or the wrong action?

We have already addressed both (1) and (2). We have seen that being able to think about the underlying justification of moral rules is crucial to our maintaining a robust sense of the moral rules, and being able to think clearly about that underlying justification both employs and calls forth empathetic and sympathetic responses. We thus come to care about how our actions affect other people, and caring motivates us to action. But we have also noted that our emotions as motivation need to be guided and structured by our theoretical reflections, because emotions can lead us to ignore the larger picture. Further, what emotions are evoked in us is a function of our theoretical beliefs—as the case of nonhuman animals shows—and we do not want our motivations to be determined by false or unjustified beliefs.

But many people believe that we are not responsible for our emotions, and, thus, cannot be responsible for our deliberations and actions to the extent that those deliberations and actions are influenced by our emotions (question 3). But I hope that the discussions in this chapter have revealed that, although we may not be able to control at any particular moment how we emotionally respond right then and there, we can have an effect on our emotions through deliberation and empathetic engagement. Both Stangl and Höss suppressed their emotions and, over time, they had to work less and less at that suppression. By refusing to empathize with their slaves, Jefferson and Jones were able to maintain false beliefs about the nature of black people. Reflection on and revision of our beliefs—say, about the nature of Jews, blacks, or nonhuman animals—can lead us to empathize and thus feel, for example, compassion, where we previously did not empathize and so had no sympathetic responses.

We can also engage in various activities that keep our powers of empathetic engagement strong and lively; art and literature provide insight into unfamiliar lives, allowing us to get a glimpse into the heads of people very different from ourselves. I will return in chapter 7 to ways in which the study of art, literature, history, and the like complement and extend philosophical reflection.

So our emotions play important roles in our acquisition of moral knowledge and moral concepts and in the actions we take. Given that we can affect our own emotional lives, we have a duty to scrutinize both the emotions we do feel and, in certain circumstances, the emotions we are not feeling. Our emotions will play a role in our moral deliberations, and if we are to exercise due care in those deliberations, we need to understand our own emotions and those of people and other animals around us.

6

Moral Evasion

Albert Speer was a man at the very top of the Nazi hierarchy: he was Minister of Armaments and, most important, he had Hitler's ear. There is absolutely no doubt that Speer was intelligent and extraordinarily capable. And yet Speer insisted that he did not know about the Final Solution, an enterprise that dominated the activities of the Third Reich during his time as a minister. How could anyone take Speer seriously when he insisted that he did not know what was happening to the Jews of Europe?[1]

It says much about human nature and about our understanding of that nature that we *can* take Speer seriously—whether or not we ultimately believe him—when he denies that he had knowledge of the Holocaust as it was occurring. We also take Thomas Jefferson, dogged champion of liberty and human rights, seriously when he insists to Edward Coles that the morally right course of action was to passively accept the status quo of slavery, rather than strive to eradicate it. (The case of Jefferson is very complicated, as we will see later in this chapter.) Somehow people can remain ignorant of what is, either metaphorically or literally, right under their noses. People can also, it seems, sincerely hold beliefs that are undermined by most or even all of the evidence available to them and even acknowledged by them.

Philosophers describe many of these cases as instances of self-deception or of wishful thinking. Human beings seem capable of believing what they want to believe and avoiding belief in what they do not want to believe. It may be that such a capacity is important to our survival in a world that often frustrates us and denies to us what we cherish most. But in the moral context, this capacity can lead to apathy, inertia, and heinous acts that most of us want to deny we are capable of even considering performing. So, understanding the ways we can evade knowledge is a crucial part of being responsible moral agents. Only by understanding these ways of evasion can we hope to be able to avoid engaging in them.

But the very names that are commonly given to the most worrisome forms of evasion—"self-deception," "wishful thinking"—indicate that understanding how evasion occurs is not enough to prevent it. After all, if I can deceive myself, then how can I uncover my own evasion? And might I not deceive myself into believing that I am being open and honest with myself when that is the last thing that I am being? These are serious worries about the elusive nature of self-knowledge; however, the difficulty of the task is no excuse for failing to do our utmost to understand our beliefs and to evaluate our own rationality in order to engage in moral self-scrutiny.

Forms of Evasion

Philosophers have spent a great deal of time and effort trying to analyze the concept of self-deception, thereby distinguishing it from concepts in its neighborhood, such as wishful thinking. Which of the many ways that human beings evade knowledge is properly considered self-deception, which is properly considered wishful thinking, and other questions of this kind will not be my focus in this chapter. I use the philosophical discussions of these issues to illuminate what is happening in our case studies, and I use our case studies to inform an understanding of the ways in which people can avoid or suppress knowledge of morally relevant facts. One thing that the philosophical literature can do for us is to provide some helpful distinctions, and those distinctions provide our starting place in this section.

Let's return to Jefferson for a moment. Jefferson attempted to defend his continuing to hold slaves by claiming that they would be unable to take care of themselves. He had, in his response to Edward Coles, said that the black population "are by their habits rendered as incapable as children of taking care of themselves, and are extinguished promptly wherever industry is necessary for raising young. In the mean time they are pests in society by their idleness, and the depredations to which this leads them." The man who wrote these words had trained artisans, cooks, and managers to perform virtually all the tasks necessary to keep Monticello functioning profitably, and had, during his term as president, employed many free blacks at the White House.[2] His household at Monticello was run by slaves, including Jefferson's mistress and at least one of his sons. How could a clearly intelligent and perceptive man claim that blacks were incapable of prudent work and effort when he himself relied on such efforts for his and his (white) family's needs and comfort?

One possibility, of course, is that Jefferson is lying to Coles in an effort to cover his own immorality. But is it possible that Jefferson believed the claim that blacks are capable of prudent care of self and families through industry and labor, while simultaneously believing the denial of that very claim—that is, that blacks are *not* capable of prudent care of self and families through industry and labor? We need to note that claiming both that Jefferson believed the first claim and that Jefferson believed its denial does not commit us to the claim that Jefferson believed that blacks are capable of taking care of themselves and that blacks are not capable of taking care of themselves. To believe the conjunction of the two beliefs would involve putting the two beliefs together, and many philosophers who understand self-deception as involving the holding of contradictory beliefs insist that the self-deceived employ various tactics to avoid putting the two beliefs together and thereby avoid having to confront their inconsistency.

But how can a person keep contradictory beliefs from confronting one another in her psychic space? One popular response involves appealing to some sort of compartmentalization. As an analogy, consider the ways in which we attend to objects in our field of vision. Right now, I am sitting in a coffee shop, typing on my laptop. The coffee shop is full of people doing various things: having conversations, drinking coffee or tea, eating pastries, operating espresso machines and cash registers, and so on. I can, however, block these people out as I focus on what I am typing. Just now, however, as I typed that last sentence, my focus shifted and I looked around me, attending to the activities of the other people in the coffee shop. Our focus can shift, leading us to attend to different objects and events, and we can narrow our focus, thereby failing to attend to what is happening in our immediate vicinity.[3]

Advocates of compartmentalization argue that our minds are like our fields of vision and our immediate physical vicinity: we can narrow our mental focus, thereby taking account of some select portion of our beliefs, emotions, and/or other mental states, or we can range further afield, searching out our own hidden assumptions, buried memories, and unpleasant recognitions. While our mental focus is on one belief or set of beliefs, we will not be attending to our myriad other beliefs, intentions, and desires. Jefferson, then, might, while confronted with the evidence of his slaves' capability and humanity, refrain from thinking about natural rights and human beings' duties to one another in virtue of those natural rights. Similarly, in thinking about moral philosophy, he would keep his thoughts off his black slaves. There is certainly evidence of the latter; for example, in his lengthy correspondence with his old friend John Adams near the end of both of their lives, the topic of slavery was assiduously avoided as they debated and contemplated the past and the future of the new republic.

Those who have advocated the contradictory-beliefs approach to self-deception have often accepted a thesis known as *intentionalism*, according to which self-deception is an action undertaken intentionally. How could one maintain a strict segregation of beliefs, intentionalists argue, unless one is aiming at such segregation? Unless one is actively engaged in the project of keeping some of one's beliefs from colliding with one another, it seems implausible to imagine them simply staying quietly in their respective corners of the mind.

There is an important distinction between culpable ignorance and nonculpable ignorance. Consider an example of culpable ignorance: a student is shocked to learn that the mid-term exam was administered on Wednesday, a day that she skipped class in order to sleep late. The student asks me if she can take the exam on another day, explaining that she was unaware we were having an exam on Wednesday. I will deny her request, and tell her that her failure to know about the exam was her own fault: the exam date was noted on the syllabus, and I reminded students in lecture, several times, that an exam was upcoming on the specified date. In this case, the student's ignorance is clearly culpable: she had available to her sufficient evidence for concluding that the exam was on Wednesday, and she ought to have examined that evidence.

In other cases, however, one's ignorance is not culpable—that is, one is not to blame for one's lack of knowledge. Suppose I have recently had my car thoroughly checked by my mechanic, who assured me that everything was in fine condition. This morning, however, the distraught student who missed the exam decided to take her revenge on me by tampering with my brakes and with the system that would have alerted me to a problem with my brakes. On my way to my office, I attempt to brake to avoid hitting a dog that has run into the street, but my brakes do not work, and I run over and kill the dog. I was unaware of my brakes' having been cut, and I had no reason to recheck them so quickly after my mechanic had done so. Thus, my ignorance of the state of my brakes is not culpable, and, thus, it seems, I am not morally to blame for the death of the dog, given that my killing of the dog was due, in part, to a lack of knowledge for which I cannot be held blameworthy.

So a crucial issue when discussing ways in which people evade knowledge is whether their resulting lack of knowledge is culpable. Some philosophers have suggested that evasions of knowledge such as those involved in self-deception are culpable only if intentionalism is true: we must be aiming to avoid knowledge or we cannot be regarded as blameworthy for successful evasion. This, I think, is clearly false, and we will see why when we examine our cases in the following sections. It turns out that all too often we avoid knowledge through lack of attention or sheer thoughtlessness; we may not be intending to avoid knowledge, but as moral agents we are nonetheless culpable for doing so. We can be as culpable for what we fail to do, for example, for failing to think through the consequences of our actions, as for what we do—or as some intentionalists would say, for deceiving ourselves via an intended compartmentalization of our beliefs.

Those who reject the idea that self-deception involves contradictory beliefs instead understand the standard examples as involving some form of motivated irrationality. One's irrationality is motivated when it is at least partially the result of one's desire regarding the subject matter of the irrational belief. We are all familiar with the charge of rationalization—that is, "a person's explaining away what he would normally regard as adequate evidence for a certain proposition."[4] Rationalization is a form of motivated irrationality that involves explaining away certain evidence because it fails to support or even undermines what one wants to be true. Consider as an example the ways in which slaveholders would respond to their slaves' expressions of grief when a family member was sold and sent away. Slaveholders would insist that their slaves did not experience the separation as deeply as a white person would, and that the expressions of sorrow were merely histrionics aimed at achieving from their masters, whom they knew to be soft-hearted, some extra privileges or benefits. This convoluted explanation of behavior, the natural and simple explanation of which was that the agent was suffering deep sorrow and grief, allowed slaveholders to preserve their favored self-image as kind and benevolent by appealing to the view that the slaves themselves understood their masters as kind and benevolent.

Rationalization can often involve what psychologists call a "self-schema"—"a collection of beliefs an individual has about his own personality and character."[5] Slaveholders' self-schemas often involved the belief that they were benevolent and wise father figures for their slaves. Because slaveholders had a vested interest in continuing to think of themselves in this way, their self-schemas influenced how they interpreted data and even what data they took note of. As Patten notes, self-schemas function similarly to stereotypes in the ways they influence our taking account of and weighing data. If we have a stereotype, we are more likely to find cases that confirm the stereotype than if we did not possess it, and we are similarly less likely to notice cases that disconfirm the stereotype.[6]

Kurt Bach, in his article "An Analysis of Self-Deception," discusses two other ways, besides rationalization, in which one can continue to hold a belief that one wants to hold even under conditions in which, but for one's desire that the belief be true, one would be led to reject the belief. One can engage in evasion, which involves "turning one's attention away from some touchy subject."[7] One can justify this shift of focus by convincing oneself that the topic is really just not worth thinking about.[8] One thought that seems particularly prevalent among those engaged in evasion is, *But what could I do?* By convincing ourselves that even if some practice is wrong, we are helpless to change the situation, we come to believe that expending further intellectual effort is futile. In such a case, even if we do not form the belief that we are acting in a morally justified way, we avoid forming the belief that we are acting in a morally unjustified way.

Another technique discussed by Bach is what he calls "jamming."[9] If one does not want to accept a certain claim, one can, whenever that claim occurs to one, immediately begin thinking about the denial of that claim and mentally marshal whatever evidence one can in favor of its denial. Most likely Jefferson engaged in a form of jamming when Coles's unwelcome missive arrived. Jefferson probably began immediately thinking of objections to Coles's proposal before he even seriously considered its merits. He also had to avoid thinking about Coles's moral courage, because such thoughts would have highlighted his—Jefferson's—moral weakness and cowardice.

In what follows, I will, in attempting to paint a robust picture of the ways of moral evasion, make no use of the case of Ted Bundy. I believe it a very revealing fact about Bundy that he had no need for evasion of any sort. The need to evade moral knowledge presupposes a capacity for such knowledge. If I am right that Bundy lacked moral concepts, then he had no need to evade moral knowledge—he simply was not even capable of forming moral beliefs. Bundy's only concern was to evade others' knowing his real nature; thus, his use of moral concepts is purely imitative of others and part of his attempts to manipulate the world. Further, Bundy felt no guilt or shame about his own actions, so he had no motivation to deceive himself about his true nature. As we will see, for Speer, Stangl, Jones, and Jefferson, evasion allowed each man to maintain a self-schema that involved a conception of himself as a good man, or, at the least, to be able to continue doing his job without being disturbed by pesky pangs of conscience.

Some would probably be inclined to take this as a sign that Bundy was truly evil, while our other case studies are "ordinary" people led astray by culture or circumstance. This, however, is too simple: if capacity for moral knowledge is a prerequisite for moral agency, then Bundy was not a moral agent. If not, then he was no more evil than is a tiger or a bear that attacks human beings. Vicious characters and heinous actions are more often than not the result of evasion on the part of those who lack the courage or the desire to confront the truth about themselves and about the world. Vigilance, then, and courage in the face of the results of that vigilance, may be our best moral hope.

Evading Reflection, Evading Responsibility

Although he does not use the same words, Stangl himself admits to Gitta Sereny that he compartmentalized his thoughts in order to continue with his horrific assignments at Sobibor and Treblinka. However, it is clear that he was not aware of the full range of ways in which he did this. Many of the ways in which Stangl evaded the full moral force of his own judgments—or, at least, his own reported judgments—of what was being done in the death camps were probably ingrained habits. He certainly did not acknowledge them as ways of evading a full moral confrontation. These habits of thought are obviously not in any way particular to Nazis, and we will see in the next chapter how the study of moral philosophy can help us to avoid developing such habits.

Perhaps the most significant way in which Stangl evaded a confrontation with the true nature of what he was doing is by failing to consider hypotheticals and thereby failing to engage his imagination. When Sereny asked him if he had ever wondered how he *would* feel if one of his loved ones were killed in one of the prewar euthanasia institutes, he replied that relatives of staff were exempt from such treatment. Similarly, when he was asked how he *would* have responded if he had been assigned to actually work the gas chambers at Treblinka, he replied that that task was carried out by two Russians.[10] As I pointed out in chapter 2, Stangl is not really responding to what Sereny had asked him: she already knows that none of his loved ones were "euthanized" and that he himself was not charged with herding people into gas chambers and dropping in the Zyclon B pellets. She wants Stangl to consider a possible, not actual, situation, and Stangl simply refuses or is unable to do it.

Why is this failure of Stangl's so significant? By refusing to consider counterfactual situations, Stangl avoids confronting the full effects of his actions. Some of the worst suffering caused by the prewar euthanasia actions were those of family members whose loved ones were simply taken away and killed. When they were told that their family members had died of natural causes, many had to suspect that this was not the case, especially given that no bodies were returned to them. Stangl, in his wartime position as commandant of Treblinka, was able to avoid the places in the camp that disturbed him the most: the gas chambers and the undressing barracks. As he says, he avoided the undressing barracks and the gas chambers to help psychologically distance himself from any meaningful contemplation of the mass suffering that he oversaw. But imaginative projection into the place of those who had to work the gas chambers, the Russians to whom he alludes, would have forced the psychic confrontation that he was working so hard to avoid.

Stangl's inability or unwillingness to contemplate the full range of alternative actions open to him is related to his handicap with respect to hypotheticals. He claims to have continually applied for a transfer, but given that he was not granted one, what was he to do, he asks? If he had openly protested, he claims, he would have been killed and someone else assigned to his post—so why sacrifice himself in such a futile manner? It is difficult to know precisely what Stangl is imagining as open protest, because there would have been so many ways to engage in "protest": he could present his objections to his superiors, he could send letters and documentation to underground resistance movements, he could attempt to get documentation to Allied forces or leaders, he could try to help some prisoners to escape, he could blow up the camp, and so on. Arguably, the consequences of these different options varied, as did their degrees of risk to Stangl himself. But he himself provides no evidence of having seriously deliberated about the various options available to him, and we have every reason to think that he would have done so if he could, given his obvious attempts to make himself appear as sympathetic as possible to Sereny.

As we saw in chapter 2, Stangl (like Höss) had a very rule-bound conception of duty and obligation. When a Jew complained that an officer had reneged on a promise to provide water in return for the Jew's gold watch, Stangl, with righteous indignation (according to his report of the incident), insisted that the officer be called out on the matter. Of course, in short order the Jew would be divested of the gold watch, along with all his other belongings, before being herded naked into the gas chambers. But, Stangl insisted, "that [reneging on the promise] wasn't right, was it?"[11] And yet Stangl claims not to know what happened to the Jew who complained, although it seems reasonable to infer that he died later on the day that the incident occurred.

Stangl appealed to rules again when he related the story of Blau and Blau's father (discussed in detail at the beginning of chapter 5): he says that he insisted to Blau that there is no way that an old man could be saved. So Stangl convinces himself that he did all that he could for Blau and his father in the circumstances, because the rules would allow no more. But Stangl had the power to protect Blau's father from death, if he had so chosen—the fact of the matter is that he did not choose to do so, but an appeal to the rules allows him to evade his full responsibility for the death of Blau's father and for Blau's resultant suffering. In this case, as in the previous one, when asked, Stangl claims not to know what eventually became of Blau. (See the discussion in chapter 5.)

Stangl narrowed his understanding of his own responsibility for the deaths at Treblinka by, over and over again, focusing on the rules. He combined this strategy with a rigid focus on "doing his job properly," while ignoring the wider context of that job. Thus, Stangl insisted to his superior that in accepting command of Treblinka, "I would be carrying out this *assignment* as a police officer under his command."[12] He was able to understand his task as a proper one for a police officer because there had been corruption in regard to the handling of the valuables stolen from the murdered Jews; thus, preventing such corruption was a "legitimate police activity," and his "specific assignment from the start had been the responsibility for these effects."[13] There is no clear acknowledgment of the wrongful nature of the way in which the "effects" had been obtained in the first place.

Thus, Stangl presents to us a model of several of the modes of thought that can allow us to divert our attention from morally troubling facts and maintain a self-schema satisfactory to

ourselves. We can think of his forms of evasion as all being ways
of narrowing the scope of his thinking:

- *Failure to entertain hypotheticals*: Stangl refused to consider
  hypothetical situations. By so refusing, he blocked himself
  from experiencing empathetic engagement with those affected by his actions. He was able in this way to avoid facing
  the full effects of his own actions.
- *Failure to allow his deliberations to range freely over
  alternatives*: Stangl limited his thought about what the
  options were with respect to protesting what was happening
  at Treblinka, thereby convincing himself that there was no
  option with better consequences than staying put and in
  command.
- *Using rule-bound forms of evaluation*: Stangl conceived of morality in terms of the application of rules without consideration for the context in which the rules were being applied
  or for the underlying justification of the rules. In this way
  he was able to think of himself as a morally upright man
  without having to confront the true nature or foundations
  of moral demands and their complexity.
- *Narrowing range of individual responsibility*: Stangl understood himself in terms of his job, and thereby limited his
  own responsibility to what came within the purview of his
  job. His appeal to rules also aided him in limiting his own
  responsibility—insofar as he followed the rules, he could
  not be to blame for any horrific consequences.

In all these ways, Stangl succeeded in straitjacketing his thought.
To return to the analogy with the field of vision I used in the previous section, we can say that Stangl put on intellectual blinders.
These blinders were so effective that he came to forget that he
had put them on in the first place. In his conversations with

Sereny, one can begin to see his hazy recognition of the artificial restriction of his thought, but he is never able to remove the blinders or to find a way to see around them. Having narrowed his thought so effectively, Stangl simply finds himself unable to let it range more widely so late in the game.

Once we have diagnosed Stangl's cognitive failures, we can better understand many facts related by Sereny. Remember as a paradigmatic example Stangl's attire at the mass killings—his pristine white riding clothes. The nature of his attire is jarring when one sees photographs of him at Treblinka, and survivors of the camp routinely commented on its bizarre nature. Stangl seems mystified by Sereny's questions about it. He begins his response to her queries with the following description:

> "When I came to Poland," he said, "I had very few clothes: one complete uniform, a coat, an extra pair of trousers and shoes, and an indoor jacket—that's all.[14] I remember, during the very first week I was there, I was walking from the forester's hut— my quarters—to one of the construction sites and suddenly I began to itch all over. I thought I was going crazy—it was awful; I couldn't even reach everywhere at once to scratch. [A friend informed him that it was sandflies.] . . . I remember just handing all the stuff to somebody out of the door, and they boiled and disinfected everything."

This recounting of his response to the sandflies is part of his explanation of how his clothes fell apart, necessitating his having new ones made—and he just happened to find some nice white linen being made in a nearby town. Given the heat and the fact that riding was the "best mode of transport," white linen riding clothes seemed, to Stangl, quite appropriate. Thus, he totally misses the real import of Sereny's question about how he could wear such clothing in a death camp. Stangl simply did not think about the wider effects and implications of his actions—heat and mode of transport made white linen riding clothes a natural choice, end of the story and end of Stangl's thinking on the matter. Stangl's narrow focus and lack of empathy go hand in hand here, as they do in his broader view of his role in the Final Solution (see chapter 5).

There are various questions, arising from a study of the philosophical literature on self-deception and motivated irrationality, that are important to consider as we reflect on Stangl. First, for all his modes of evading acknowledgment of the full moral import and of the nature of the consequences of his actions, did Stangl at some level, conscious or unconscious, recognize these features of his situation? In other words, were his modes of evasion successful only at keeping his conscious thought away from troubling subjects, nevertheless allowing thoughts about those subjects to congregate and fester in some other sector of his mind, away from conscious awareness? These are psychological questions, and all we can do, from the perspective of moral philosophy, is try to decide if one or other of the options really, in the end, makes no sense. Using the tools of moral philosophy, we can also examine the moral implications of the various options.

Interesting as these questions may be, let us leave aside issues about the structure of Stangl's psychic space and return to an issue addressed in chapter 5: our own apparently conflicting attitudes toward nonhuman animals. Notice how the forms of evasion Stangl used are common to those of us who live in a society that devotes attention and care to domestic pets and yet brutally confines and slaughters animals raised as food:

- *Failure to entertain hypotheticals*: We simply do not think about what it would be like to work in a slaughterhouse, for example. This is parallel to Stangl's refusal to consider how he would have reacted to being assigned to working in the gas chambers. Furthermore, we refuse to consider situations in which we had pigs and sheep as pets and we ate cats and dogs, particularly kittens and puppies (because they are tender just as calves and lambs are). There is little doubt that we would then have very different attitudes toward the species than we now have; this should make us question, at the very least, our current differential attitudes toward kittens and toward calves.

- *Failure to allow deliberations to range freely over alternatives*: People often respond to moral concerns about factory farming and/or livestock farming more generally by pointing to how hard it is to be a vegan and how little effect their actions would have, just as Stangl pointed out that his refusal to be in charge at Treblinka would have had little effect with dire consequences for himself. But, of course, there are many alternatives to simply becoming a vegan: one can try to limit one's use of animal products; one can try to engage others in debate on the issue; one can donate money and/or time to the ASPCA, HSUS, or PETA; one can encourage small steps, such as humane treatment of livestock animals; one can arrange field trips to slaughterhouses, and so on. Finding one difficult and less than fruitful option in no way justifies our acceptance of the status quo.

- *Using rule-bound forms of evaluation*: The way in which this happens with respect to our treatment of nonhuman animals is somewhat subtle. We all have a list of paradigmatic moral rules—Do not kill innocent people, Do not steal, Do not rape, and so on—rules that, most often, involve our not interfering with other people in specified ways. One way we use these rules is in defense of our moral character when we feel threatened, as many of us do when confronted with any discussion of livestock farming. "Hey," I might say, "I don't kill, I don't steal, so don't get on my case about eating meat!" Also, if we have such rules at hand, we run through them, check that we behave in accord with them, and end our examination of our moral characters there, failing to consider whether there might be unconsidered rules or unconsidered implications of familiar rules.

- *Narrowing range of individual responsibility*: We insist that we are not the ones torturing animals or making money from such torture. But, we need to ask: How are we aiding and abetting those who do engage in and profit from such torture?

I know perfectly well that well-meaning people who openly discuss our treatment of nonhuman animals can still disagree about the morality of livestock farming. My point here is that most of us do not openly discuss and deliberate about these issues, and we use the same forms of evasion as Stangl did in order to avoid such open deliberation with others and with ourselves.

So while we are aware of morally questionable practices—we know that they are occurring—we do not let ourselves reflect too deeply on them. Of course, as we saw in chapter 5, this blocks emotional response, and this blocks our motivational sources. Like Stangl, we are not ignorant of what is happening, but it registers with us in a superficial way, obscuring the full moral import of the events.

Choosing Not to Know

Stangl, then, represents a form of evasion that involves knowing what is happening but refusing to engage in the sort of deliberation that would allow that knowledge to play a role in shaping emotions and motivation. Stangl also refused to confront his knowledge with his imaginative capacities, thereby shutting himself off from a full moral appreciation of the events occurring around him. This, in turn, helped him to maintain his emotional distance from his own knowledge. Let us call Stangl's form of evasion *refusal to engage*: he could not avoid a certain level of knowledge, but in an important sense, he kept his distance from his own knowledge.

Albert Speer represents a different form of evasion. I am reluctant to call it "motivated ignorance" because motivated ignorance involves one's coming to believe something because one wants it to be true or one's refusing to believe something because one wants it to be false.[15] For example, if we were to say that Speer's ignorance of the slaughter of the Jews of Europe was motivated, we would be saying that Speer did not believe that the Jews of Europe were being slaughtered because he did not want it to be the case that they were being slaughtered. We would, then, be saying that Speer had some desires with respect to the subject matter of the relevant belief—namely, the slaughter of the Jews of Europe. But did Speer really care one way or another about what was happening to the Jews of Europe? Or did Speer only care about himself, his career, his projects, and his power? I am inclined to believe that Speer's range of concern was very narrow: like Stangl, he focused on his job without putting that job in its broader context. But, I will suggest, while he was indifferent about the fate of the Jews, he was not indifferent as to what his beliefs were with respect to their fate: it was his own mental states that really concerned Albert Speer, not the state of the external world. Speer did not want to believe anything that would distract him from his task. Thus, Speer's form of evasion is best understood as a kind of *belief avoidance*.

Speer himself seems to acknowledge precisely what he was doing throughout his years as a minister in the Third Reich, in his report of his meeting with his friend Karl Hanke, who warned Speer to stay away from a camp that was most likely Auschwitz.

Speer says that he "did not want to know what was happening there": "from fear of discovering something which might have made me turn from my course, I had closed my eyes."[16] He quite clearly states that he did not want to have any beliefs that might come in the way of his projects—projects the completion of which were the cornerstone of his power and prestige. Whatever doubts or suspicions started to nibble at his conscious mind were simply pushed aside and not allowed to grow any larger.

We might wonder how someone really could simply shut down such doubts and suspicions. It seems that, in Speer's case, his ability to avoid coming to have beliefs about the fate of the Jews was closely connected to the abilities that made him so good at what he did. Many successful people have amazing powers of concentration and focus, and they let their lives be taken over by their ambitions—in popular psychological terms, they are "workaholics."[17] Thus, for Speer and for people like him, the universe narrows to the people, events, and projects that can either hinder or promote the agent's success. Given that, for Speer, his power and prestige originated in Hitler's preference for and promotion of him, he could not allow doubts about Hitler's aims to invade his conscious mind.[18] As he said when asked about Hitler's having Rohm murdered, "I suspect all I would have thought, if I thought at all, was that as Hitler was doing it, it had to be right."[19]

Just how successful Speer's focus on his work was becomes apparent in his relation of his encounter with Russian POWs working at the Krupp factories in Essen. Here he notices that the Russians are being treated badly because, as he notes, their "rations were so minimal that they couldn't work properly."[20] Speer's mind was focused on successful completion of his projects regarding war production, and data were registered, it seems, only to the extent that they were relevant to his task. Our background values can shape our focus so that we notice only what is deemed important. For Speer, only what was work-related was important, so that acted as a filter on the data that registered with his conscious mind.[21]

Speer's difficulty lay in his inability to think in the sense not of seeking means to ends or of tackling a complex organizational problem but, rather, in reflecting, synthesizing, assessing, allowing emotions and imagination to range freely, and questioning the value of chosen pursuits. People need to be trained to think in this deeper, more wide-ranging way, but our success-oriented culture simply does not encourage it. We all feel the need to "get ahead," to make sure that we set ourselves apart from the competition. And social media sites such as Facebook encourage us to present our lives to other people in the most attractive and jealousy-inducing manner possible, so we spend time crafting our life narratives with an eye to how we appear to others. We spend so much time thinking about whether to adopt carb-free or sugar-free diets in order to live as long as possible and be as thin as possible that we have little time left to think about the people who never have sufficient food to eat. We find ourselves in culturally shaped lives with predetermined goals, consumed by superficial minutia. Where is there any room left for broad and deep thinking about intrinsic value and ultimate ends?

Developing habits of thought that roam broadly and deeply is particularly important for those of us who have jobs in large organizations—as most of us in the modern world do. It is very easy to simply do one's job within the scope laid out by one's superiors, without questioning how that job fits into the larger picture. If we do not ask certain questions, we, like Speer, will fail to form beliefs about what is happening around us and what we are in fact contributing to. This is true, also, of our failure to find out how we can contribute to addressing worldwide problems such as hunger. For most of us, our projects are egoistic, just as were those of Speer: we pursue *our* careers, take care of *our* families, spend time with *our* friends, devote time and resources to *our* hobbies and homes, and so on. Is it any wonder, then, that people tune out, either literally or metaphorically, when commercials about starving children appear on TV? Equally unsurprising are the unopened mailings from Doctors Without Borders, the Humane Society, Habitat for Humanity, the Red Cross, the ASPCA, and on and on. We, like Speer, simply do not register data that are not relevant to our current projects, and we avoid taking opportunities to learn more—in particular, we avoid learning more about ways in which, however small, we can help those in need. If we were to have all of the data, both about those in need and about the ways we could help, we might be confronted with a belief that we have a moral duty to use resources to help others rather than to contribute to our current projects.

The fact that we are attempting to avoid forming beliefs about matters which might force us to rethink our priorities helps to explain why many of us get very defensive when we discuss issues such as our duty to help the needy or the morality of using animals as sources of food. We are, most likely, upset by being forced to think about what we have successfully been avoiding forming beliefs about. And making matters worse, it is not difficult to avoid thought about unpleasant topics: we can fill our minds up with plenty of other topics.[22] Technology is proving to be a great boon to this endeavor. People now constantly have their eyes glued to their cellphones. Phone-based activities like Twitter or taking and sharing selfies make trivialities time-consuming: by the time we report the minute details of our days to our friends via phone, "tweet," or Facebook post, we have little time left for reflection that delves below the surface minutiae of life. Celebrity culture also aids in avoidance of thought about important issues: we can spend our time analyzing Taylor

) conversatn' ?

Swift's sex life, Kim Kardashian's body and clothes, and Brad and Angie's divorce instead of examining how we are spending our own lives. There is an unceasing supply of trivial news for us to consume, keeping us diverted and distracted from what ought to matter the most to us.

Because it is so very easy to avoid thought, we need to be taught to develop habits of reflection and of information seeking. Speer was right in the midst of perhaps the worst moral catastrophe in human history and managed to avoid thinking about it one way or another. How much easier is it for those of us fortunate enough to live lives of relative ease and comfort in a stable nation such as the United States or Canada, free from civil wars and military coups?

So far, then, we have examined two modes of evading moral knowledge— *refusal to engage* and *belief avoidance*—exemplified by, respectively, Franz Stangl and Albert Speer. For our final form of evasion, we turn to an American slaveholder, Charles Colcock Jones, who engaged in what I will call *wishful compromise*.

From Desire to Reality

Jones was born into a wealthy slaveholding family in Georgia. His extended family were leading figures in Liberty County and neighboring regions, and that family was integral to his sense of self and of his place in the world. All his strongest affections and connections were to his family and to his region. The only commitment of his that vied in strength with his familial one was that to his religion.

That latter commitment led him to choose a career in the ministry and, as a result, led him to study in northern schools, where he encountered both teachers and classmates strongly opposed to slavery. At this youthful stage in life, Jones did not engage in either of the evasive tactics we have seen adopted by Stangl and Speer: he did not avoid forming beliefs about slavery and he did not refuse to engage with his beliefs. Rather, he gave every evidence of thinking deeply about slavery and of reaching the conclusion that slavery was a great moral wrong. In letters to his cousin and future wife, Mary, Jones begins with the premise that the souls of blacks and of whites are the same, and that, as a result, blacks and whites are moral equals. Jones concludes that slavery "is unjust, contrary to nature and religion."[23] Furthermore, he acknowledged that all his privileges and opportunities were due to the labor of slaves: "How often do I think . . . of the number of hands employed to furnish me with those conveniences of life of which they are in consequence denied—how many intellects, how many souls perhaps, withered and blasted forever for this very purpose."[24] Here Jones is admitting that he enjoyed many good things in life at the cost of other human lives. But he himself seems to admit that he could well do without these things, because they are "conveniences," not necessities.

But this is clearly an untenable and unstable cognitive position to be in. Jones is claiming that slavery is a terrible evil, not a minor moral peccadillo, and he is admitting to be highly complicit in and to be gaining profit from this evil. Something has to give here, and neither of the two starkest options is attractive to Jones: he certainly does not want to alienate his family and his way of life by emancipating his slaves and starting over in the North, but neither can he simply return to his familial way of life and pretend as though he has no moral objections to that way of life. The latter option would force him to see himself as a moral hypocrite, hardly a "self-schema" with which a "man of God" could live. He has to find a middle way if he is to preserve his self-image without having to sacrifice his family, his wealth, and his status.

Immediately, Jones begins to ask himself: "Could I do more for the ultimate good of the slave population by holding or emancipating what I own?"[25] He decides to try to find some strategy that would be in "the best interests of the coloured population" and would also be acceptable to white neighbors and friends.[26] He decides that by ministering to the souls of the black population, he can lead them to God, thereby justifying their continuation in bondage. This strategy allows Jones to reconcile his actions with his conscience and to remain ensconced in his comfortable home, with family, status, and wealth all intact.

Now, I do not want to be taken as claiming that the sort of strategy Jones adopts is always morally objectionable. In fact, I believe that sometimes "standing on principle" is itself the wrong course of action, particularly in circumstances where no good consequences, and plenty of bad consequences, will be the result of doing so. For example, some people will pride themselves on being honest, even when doing so results in deeply hurt feelings and no counterbalancing good consequences. If we are consequentialists, we need to choose that action which, in the long run, will have the best consequences for everyone affected—and, what is important to remember, we need to think about the consequences in the *actual* world, with people and social circumstances being what they are, not in some *ideal* world. That is not to say that we ought not to think about changing the world—*of course* we should think about trying to change the world for the better. Rather, it is a reminder that we have to try to change the world starting from where we are right now, and our starting position may make some less than perfect outcomes the best that we can do.

Or, suppose that we are not consequentialists but, rather, deontologists who believe that we have various competing prima facie duties, the strongest of which will be our all-things-considered duty in any particular circumstance. So Jones is quite right to think about not only his obligations to his slaves—obligations of justice and of benevolence—but also of his obligations to his loved ones and neighbors—obligations of special attachment and of contract. Moral philosopher W. D. Ross rejected the idea that there is some prioritizing of duties that we can apply in all situations such that, for example, justice always wins out over special attachment or vice versa. Our circumstances determine the strength of our various duties, and so the strengths of duties of various types can differ from one set of circumstances to another. Moral deliberation and action that is guided by one or two moral principles as having absolute priority is rightly considered to be fanaticism and can lead to terrorism, pointless self-sacrifice, and plenty of hurt feelings— not a minor matter that we can ever ignore.

But there are always dangers when one finds oneself in a situation in which self-interest is as heavily at stake as Jones's was in his deliberations concerning how to deal with his slave "inheritance." As Jones himself wrote to Mary, the human heart "is deceitful above all things,"[27] and human beings' reasoning processes are heavily influenced by their desires, hopes, and emotions. Psychological studies have revealed that our merely thinking about some possibility will result in our taking that possibility to be more likely than we otherwise would have. Also, we are more likely to come up with theories or hypotheses that are attractive to us in terms of our desires, and, given that our taking note of and evaluating evidence is biased by our hypotheses, it turns out that desire plays a large role in determining the theories that we come to accept.[28] Not surprisingly, then, psychological studies back up commonsense beliefs that our desired picture of the world can influence the way that we actually perceive the world.

So consider what happened when Jones opted for a compromise that he had convinced himself was better than the extreme option of emancipating his slaves. Jones had to minister to the slaves in a way that actually secured the "approbation of the whites,"[29] while also providing benefit to the slave population. This was no easy task, and perhaps not one that could be successfully carried out: Jones himself did not manage to actually benefit the slaves. As we saw in chapter 2, Jones's sermons to the slaves were chockfull of admonishments to obey their masters, to keep the Sabbath (when doing so would most likely undermine any independent initiative on the part of the slaves), and to keep marriage sacred (when whites did not respect slave marriages as valid). Jones also urged slaves not to make their masters angry and thereby lead masters away from virtue.[30] What, then, was the upshot of Jones's sermons? He was basically preaching to the slaves that they ought to behave in ways that maintained the slave system, and he did so by claiming that the system was legitimate, in the sense of generating actual moral duties on the part of slaves to obey their masters. He also put the burden of white virtue squarely on the shoulders of black slaves, by implying that white abuse of their slaves could be traced back to provoking behavior on the part of the slaves.

We might have predicted that if a man who viewed slavery as immoral immersed himself in the world of slaves and planters to the extent that Jones did that he would see the abuses and cruelty of the system. But Jones was determined to placate his white neighbors *and* his conscience, and his sermons show us the lens through which he decided to view the world. We have to wonder whether his antislavery stance was ever one with emotional and motivational resonance for him; he seems to have arrived at a theoretical position and then been more concerned with finding a way to maintain his lifestyle without having to think of himself as a bad man, than with the actual welfare of the slaves. This is shown to be the case in a devastating way by Jones's sale of Jane and several members of her family: the actual fate of the slaves seemed to be of less concern than Jones's being able to convince himself that he had tried to do the best that he could.[31] He cared more about upsetting his wife's "domestic arrangements"[32] than about splitting apart families in the slave quarters.

I think two important lessons can be learned from Jones's wishful compromise—that is, from his convincing himself that an option acceptable to him also happened to be the morally best option. First, we need to try to make sure, as best we can, that we are emotionally and motivationally committed to our moral principles. If it is really the case that we are primarily concerned with maintaining a self-schema involving our own virtue, then any middle path poses the danger of our too easily convincing ourselves we have done the best we could under the circumstances. We also have great motivation to reconceive the situation so as to convince ourselves that the evil with which we were concerned is not so bad or is actually justified after all, as when Jones claims that "the salvation of one soul will more than outweigh all the pain and woe of their capture and transportation, and subsequent residence among us."[33] Our moral concern needs to be with other people, not with our own goodness, or we can too easily be led to "compromises" that turn out to be nothing more than complicity with evil under another name.[34]

Second, while our emotions are extremely important to the moral endeavor, as we saw in chapter 5, they also need careful monitoring. We have various moral claims upon us—various morally relevant factors—among which are the close, intimate, loving ties we have to friends and family members. Love and affection are valuable and powerful motivations to benefit those about whom we care. Thus, we need to cultivate strong emotions about other people more generally in order to counterbalance our more intimate emotional responses. Trying to balance the legitimate claims of those we love with more impartial duties of benevolence is tricky, but we do not want to be acting to ensure that a loved one has the maidservant she wants even if it means breaking up the family of the maidservant.

"I am governed solely by views to their happiness"

These are the words that Thomas Jefferson spoke to Monticello's plantation manager about his slaves.[35] Did he actually believe that that was true? One possibility is that Jefferson was a master of compartmentalization, that he had one portion of his mind for the whipping of small boys at work in his nail shop, the separation of families, and the turning of people into currency, and a different portion of his mind for his cherished self-schema as a benevolent man doing the best anyone could under difficult circumstances, and yet another portion for his Lockean theorizing about natural rights. Another view is that Jefferson was, as he got older, guided more and more by his own concerns and those of his family, so that eventually he just didn't care enough about his slaves to be particularly bothered by how he treated them.

Henry Weincek, in his *Master of the Mountain: Thomas Jefferson and His Slaves*, offers a portrait of Jefferson according to which Jefferson simply changed over time from a fiery radical and believer in the natural rights of all who was willing to put his words into action to a complacent egotist who was willing to use people to secure the good life for himself. Weincek dates the shift in Jefferson to about the early 1790s, when Jefferson wrote "I allow nothing for losses by death, but, on the contrary, shall presently take credit four per cent. per annum, for [my slaves'] increase over and above keeping up their own numbers." He advocates slaves as the way to build an investment portfolio, because slaves "besides a present support bring a silent profit of from 5. to 10. per cent in this country by the increase in their value."[36] So Jefferson was conceptualizing slaves as wealth and realizing just how wealthy his slaves did and could make him and his family.

But how can one take satisfaction in wealth that one derives from participation in the exploitation of other human beings? I think that Weincek explains it very well: "Jefferson and his family could not conceive of themselves doing anything that was evil. So they redefined evil."[37] Jefferson, I think, presents a highly cautionary tale of the dangers of rationalization: one can come to believe one's own lies. Selfishness corrupted Jefferson just as it corrupted Jones, and both, as a result, became supporters of a terribly evil institution.

But acting in our own self-interest and being selfish aren't the same thing. We all act to take care of ourselves; we all act to promote our own interests. We become selfish when we consider our own interests to the exclusion of those of others or, even if we consider those others, we do so to too little of an extent. But how do we determine where a legitimate concern for self becomes selfish absorption? How do we keep ourselves from rationalizing away our moral duties? These are questions for the final chapter.

The Moral of Mr. Jefferson's Story

All the case studies I have used in this book have shown us people who have made quite egregious moral errors—genocide, slavery, and mass murder are certainly among the most heinous of moral crimes. And, apart from Bundy, who is always our outlier, they did so under great cultural, social, and legal pressures. We often thank our moral luck that we were not born in Nazi Germany or in the antebellum American South, because (at least if you are like me) we wonder if we would have had the fortitude and courage to engage in clear-headed moral deliberation and then to act on our considered moral convictions. In such situations, what we think of as ordinary failings (in my own case, laziness) can lead to, at best, complicity in horrendous evil. My laziness now leads me to miss deadlines in my work and not to read the newspaper often enough, but in Nazi Germany, would it have kept me from putting sufficient energy into seeing behind the Nazi propaganda and thus to failing to see the horror of the regime?

But the more important question is: Am I now failing to see moral crimes right in front of me and thus failing to exercise moral virtue? Can I assume that my character flaws are harmless because I am not in Nazi Germany or the antebellum South? We must not facilely assume that we have fulfilled our duties of moral self-scrutiny and due care in moral deliberation but, rather, need to be vigilant. We cannot assume that our behavior is such that future persons will not look back upon us and think, *How could they have gone so wrong?!*

It is very difficult for us to challenge our self-schemas as virtuous people, and that is one of the reasons why I included—most likely to some people's astonishment—Thomas Jefferson as one of my case studies. It can be just as difficult for us to face the undermining of our conceptions of our heroes as it is to face the undermining of our self-conceptions—I think that Douglas Wilson's attempt to exonerate Jefferson (see chapter 3) is a good example of such difficulty. But if we challenge the schoolbook presentation of Jefferson, we might begin to wonder what we can challenge in our presentations of ourselves. So in returning to Jefferson and how the various impediments to moral deliberation I presented in chapter 1 tripped him up, perhaps we can be more open to seeing the impediments that block our own paths.

Thomas Jefferson and Us

With respect to the issue of slavery, I would argue that Thomas Jefferson failed in both his duty of moral self-scrutiny and his duty of due care in moral deliberation (to say nothing of his duty to develop moral virtue). And his errors can come to seem glaringly obvious to us—so glaringly obvious that it is hard not to wonder how such an intelligent man could have gone so wrong, particularly given his early commitment to ideals of liberty for all, *including* blacks, and his constant exposure to abolitionists and their ideals. How could a man with so much potential to live a virtuous life and to make a significant difference for so many people go so rotten, morally speaking?

As with any person, the case of Thomas Jefferson is complicated, but we can identify certain elements of his character and of his situation that contributed to his moral failure on the issue of slavery. And as we do so, we will find it difficult not to see the analogies between his situation and our own with respect to nonhuman animals.[1] Thinking about how someone like Jefferson, whom many of us grew up admiring and whose name is attached to schools and streets in almost every town in the United States, went so wrong can help us to see that we might need to do some moral examination of ourselves, of our culture, of our particular situations, and of our thinking (or lack thereof), where we might have previously thought none was needed. So let's consider how the obstacles to good moral deliberation impeded Jefferson and may very well be impeding us, here and now.

Cultural Norms and Pressures

There are many different ways in which the norms of our culture influence our thinking, choices, and actions. Thomas Jefferson and Edward Coles were both born in a culture that endorsed, for a variety of reasons, holding persons of African descent in bondage. Both Coles and Jefferson (along with Charles Colcock Jones), during their youth, became convinced that slavery was an evil that ought to be eradicated. But Coles stuck to the course of emancipation and abolition while Jefferson became firmly enmeshed in the plantation system, dependent on slaves for his wealth and position and urging others to invest in slaves and to refrain from emancipation. What went wrong in the case of Jefferson?

I think that Jefferson presents a stark example of how we can use widely accepted cultural norms to foster evasion of our own moral failure. Culture shapes what we value, what we desire, and how we want to see ourselves (and as a result, how we do in fact see ourselves). Jefferson was clearly shaped by southern plantation culture and by his other life experiences to want a certain lifestyle and to pass that lifestyle on to his children and grandchildren. He was a proud (and perhaps even arrogant) man, who needed to have others revere and honor him—not surprising in a culture based on honor such as the antebellum South.[2] But he also needed to preserve, both in his own mind and in the mind of others, the image of himself as the fiery revolutionary who was forced to moral compromise by excising his condemnation of the slave trade from the Declaration of Independence.

Jefferson took advantage of his society's endorsement of the source of his wealth—slave labor—and continued to live in the manner to which he was accustomed, if not even more extravagantly. He paid his grocery bill by the labor of young boys forced to make nails, young boys whose whipping he authorized if they did not work up to his standards. He gave away slaves, thereby breaking up families, in order to provide gifts for his children and grandchildren. And he kept a teenage slave girl in his bed by holding her (and, thereby, most likely his own) children's well-being as hostage. He recognized how profitable slave increase was, and he convinced himself, at least on some level, that the inferiority of blacks justified their enslavement and even that they owed him work in order to compensate him for their purchase price and upkeep![3]

Jefferson's self-interest propelled him from antislavery revolutionary to complacent plantation owner and slave master. He took advantage of his society's endorsement of an evil institution in order to benefit himself, and he took advantage of a prevailing racial ideology to preserve his self-schema as a man who would never do evil. He convinced himself, even in the face of Edward Coles's challenge to him, that he could not hope to end slavery, and so he sighed to himself as he hefted the "burden" of his slaves—a "burden" that paid his bills and allowed him to live in style. And then he seemed to cease thinking about the slavery issue altogether except as a business proposition and investment strategy.

Unless we are cultural relativists, we cannot simply view as right any actions endorsed by our cultures. (We need to make sure that we do not uncritically adopt cultural relativism as a mode of evasion: we do not want to self-servingly assume that if everyone else approves of it, then it is thereby morally right.) And Jefferson himself was no cultural relativist; his commitment to natural rights and liberties was not a relativist view.[4] According to Jefferson, persons had these rights and liberties in virtue of their being persons and not in virtue of cultural attitudes or legal rules. But he found a way to excuse his own wrongdoing by viewing himself as trapped by the culture in which he lived, and then he transformed that excuse into a justification by latching onto and promoting his own society's racial ideology. Jefferson's culture provided a way for him to maintain a certain self-schema while promoting his own interests by participating in a morally odious institution.

To what extent do we do the same when it comes to nonhuman animals? Most of us will claim to abhor cruelty to animals and are outraged when we here of the abuse of cats or dogs. We would never confine an animal in a space so small that it cannot even stand up or continuously breed an animal while never allowing it to have direct contact with its young. And yet such things are done on a daily basis over and over again to millions of animals, and we do nothing to stop it. In fact, most of us take advantage of this treatment of animals by eating steak, fried chicken, pork chops, and bacon, and by wearing leather shoes and boots. And we do not let our eating habits affect our images of ourselves as good people. How do we accomplish this feat?

As with Jefferson, we find ourselves immersed in a particular culture. It is a culture that takes for granted meat as food and

even incorporates meat into some of its significant rituals: turkey at Thanksgiving, hot dogs on the Fourth of July and at baseball games, and, depending on your religion, ham on Easter Sunday or brisket on the Sabbath. At these rituals one can be viewed as a "party pooper" or as "holier than thou" if one refuses the proffered hot dog or turkey leg. I have seen tee-shirts that say "Real Women Eat Meat." We laugh at bumper stickers that take the acronym for People for the Ethical Treatment of Animals (PETA) and reinterpret it as standing for People for the Eating of Tasty Animals. And, of course, as a result of being raised eating meat, many of us like it—nothing like a good bratwurst or rack of barbecued ribs.

So, like Jefferson's self-interest did with slavery, our self-interest propels us to acquiesce in our society's meat-eating practices. But we bemoan the treatment of animals in factory farms (when we cannot avoid thinking about it altogether), as the young Jefferson bemoaned slavery. So we make excuses for ourselves: we have to participate in those rituals, we were raised this way, everyone does it, and then we move to justification, adopting commonly held views about how we ought not to an-thropomorphize animals, how we need animal protein to be healthy, and how various people's economic well-being depends on the livestock industry. With these beliefs in hand, regardless of their truth or whether we are justified in holding them, we put the animals out of mind and order the burger and fries.

In the case of our treatment of nonhuman animals, it is not clear that adopting cultural relativism would provide us with jus-tification. It's not at all clear to me whether people in our cul-ture approve of the way we treat animals or whether they simply choose not to think about it. Consider the popularity of the film *Babe*, in which we cannot bear the thought of the cute little pig getting eaten. How many of us saw that movie and not long after ate some bacon without a second thought? How many of us urge criminal penalties for those who abuse domestic animals but still help to support factory farming by purchasing its products? Our culture is deeply schizophrenic when it comes to animals, and we will return to that fact when we discuss moral evasion later on.

Regardless of our commitment or lack thereof to cultural relativism, the case of nonhuman animals vividly illustrates how our self-interest can conspire with cultural practices and pressures to keep us enmeshed in practices whose horrors we either ignore or feebly rationalize. And because so many of the people around us have no interest in challenging society's meat-eating norms and, in fact, disparage those who do, we seldom face challenges to our participation in the practices resulting from those norms. But will people in two hundred years ask the same sorts of questions about us and nonhuman animals that we now ask about Jefferson and his slaves? Will they wonder how we could have our burgers and our leather bags while millions of beings suffered every day all around us?

How can the study of moral philosophy help us to overcome the impediments to good moral thinking that culture creates for us? The place from which we must begin our philosophizing is that of our current moral beliefs. So we must examine ourselves in order to figure out what we actually do believe, for example, about the moral status and appropriate treatment of nonhuman animals. Whatever beliefs we uncover, our next step is to see whether they are consistent with one another and with the beliefs that we accept, for example, about the moral status and appropriate treatment of various categories of human beings. Engaging in this activity drives us to formulate more general principles or theories about the nature of morality and of its demands upon us, such as cultural relativism, consequentialism, or some form of deontology.

As we engage in the activity of (i) checking for consistency, we will, if we are sincere in our endeavors, notice that we seem to condemn certain kinds of treatment of dogs but do not criticize ourselves for benefiting from even worse treatment of pigs. Is this an inconsistency in our beliefs, or are we merely ignoring, motivated by self-interest, the terrible treatment of pigs that lies behind our morning bacon? Well, at this point, we can begin to think about why we condemn similar treatment of dogs; this moves us toward (ii) theorizing about the nature of morality and its demands upon us. We need to think about which features of dogs make them morally significant—their intelligence? Their capacity to experience pain and pleasure? Their social nature and ability to bond with other dogs and with human beings? Then, of course, we need to ask: Do pigs have those features, and if so, do they have them to the same degree as dogs do? This, of course, is one place at which we need to examine some of our nonmoral beliefs—namely, beliefs about the capabilities and mental lives of dogs and pigs, and because these are difficult issues, we need to be wary of cooking the books, as it were. We do not want to allow ourselves to search out all and only that data that will get us the answers that we want.

The process of philosophical deliberation, then, is not going to be easy or straightforward. But once we force ourselves to (i) check for consistency and (ii) theorize about the nature of morality and its demands upon us, we are forced to confront cultural practices and norms that we might otherwise have taken for granted—they, like our other beliefs or claims that we take to justify our beliefs, must be brought out into the open and examined. *not how Jones did it*

Ends and Means

Jefferson claimed that in his actions, he was "governed solely by views to their [his slaves'] happiness."[5] Of course, we are surely justified in doubting that Jefferson's actions regarding the running of his plantation were guided to any significant extent by the happiness of his slaves; to whatever extent he did think about the happiness of his slaves, that consideration seemed to be easily outweighed by consideration of his own and his family's interests. But supposing that Jefferson had sincerely tried to promote the happiness of his slaves, what did he need to consider?

First, it seems quite clear that what it is for a being to be happy or, at least, which conditions are likely to result in that being's happiness, must be in some way a function of that being's nature: what makes my cat happy is surely quite different from what makes me happy, which again is quite different from what makes a toddler happy.[6] So if Jefferson were to aim at his slaves' well-being, he needed to have some conception of his slaves' nature, and as we know, his own beliefs on that topic were apparently the result of motivated irrationality on his part. He needed to justify continuing to hold slaves, and so he was motivated to seek out and maintain a conception of blacks that would provide a justification for doing so. As a result, he held and propagated a view about the incapacity of blacks that was contradicted by evidence right under his nose: his slaves performed skilled tasks that kept his plantation running, and his White House staff was partially composed of free blacks making their way in a highly hostile environment. Further, he never seemed to make any allowances for the fact that blacks were denied the kinds of educational opportunities to which he and others of his class had access.[7] For a man of science, these were the kinds of errors in observation and reasoning that most likely resulted from a need to protect his self-schema from threats.

Second, what any of us can hope to achieve or to be is always a function not only of our own capacities and the extent to which those capacities are developed but also of our outward circumstances. There are certainly circumstances that no matter what we do or have the potential to do, will hold us back.

Sometimes we have to settle for something less than complete happiness because that is the best that circumstances allow us. Jefferson insisted that his time and place were not such as to allow blacks whatever happiness freedom would provide, both because of the inabilities of blacks themselves and also because of the attitudes of whites. Thus, he claimed, in his response to Edward Coles, the best he could do for his slaves was to take care of them as their master until southern opinion and the blacks themselves advanced sufficiently to allow him to emancipate his slaves in a responsible manner.

In assessing Jefferson's claim, we encounter two difficulties that are familiar to anyone engaged in moral deliberation: How can we determine which of our actions will, or are likely to, bring about the best consequences, given the situation in which we find ourselves? And, are there some actions that ought to be taken (or not taken) regardless of the actual or likely consequences of those actions? To address the first question, we need to acquire various kinds of nonmoral knowledge and some facility in using that knowledge to determine what the causal effects of our actions will be. To address the second question, we need to be prepared to consider whether the rightness or wrongness of our actions is a function only of the consequences of our actions, or whether we have certain duties that are the result of some facts about the world other than what our actions will produce. In considering both of these issues, Jefferson's own self-interest clouded his thinking: his response to Coles clearly indicates his unwillingness to consider the likely effects of various courses of action, and he seemed to leave aside his own theorizing about justice and rights when it came to his own slaves. He quite clearly also not only put too much weight on the interests of himself and his family but also construed those interests in an extravagant way—that is, as requiring inordinate domestic help and luxuries of other sorts.[8]

To be fair to Jefferson, we have to concede that thinking about consequences and probabilities is extremely complicated, especially when we are trying to determine the effects of our actions involving a practice deeply entrenched in our culture. When we think about how we ought to respond to practices such as factory farming, we have to think about what we are capable of doing, given the world as we now find it. But doing this requires that we do our best to impartially consider our various moral and nonmoral beliefs.

Just as Jefferson had to think about the natures of his slaves in an objective way—that is, in a way not colored by his own self-interest—so we need to think about the nature of pigs and cows in an objective way. We have to consider what it would be for such animals to be happy and how much suffering we are causing through practices such as factory farming. We then have to weigh that suffering against the happiness gained by eating meat. But we also need to think about other effects of livestock farming on a vast scale—effects on the environment, on our total food supply and the nature of that food supply, and so on. We have to explore the extent to which we actually need animal protein in our diets and whether we can only supply that need via factory farming.

Even if we decide that factory farming is morally wrong, we have to think about what we can do that will have some impact on its demise. Should I become a vegetarian or a vegan? Would my ceasing to eat meat or use other animal products have any effect? Ought I to focus on supporting groups such as the ASPCA or PETA? Will my doing so matter if the amount of money I donate is less than what I spend on animal products, thereby supporting factory farming? How can I effectively change other people's attitudes? The complexity of these questions leaves plenty of room for us to rationalize and to engage in motivated irrationality, especially given the sorts of cultural pressures and norms that exist in our society regarding meat eating.

→ 10% decrease?

Our deliberations get even more complicated if we find ourselves in situations in which our duties conflict. When I decided to stop eating meat, my grandmother, to whom I was very close, was still alive, and I would have dinner at her home at least once a week. She conceived of a meal as necessarily involving meat, and she took great pleasure in cooking for me. She just couldn't be brought to see why I didn't want to eat meat, and looked crushed when I rejected her pork chops. I decided that I would eat the meat that my grandmother prepared for me, because I thought that no good consequences would come from not doing so, and that I had a special obligation to my beloved grandmother to promote her happiness and to sustain our close, loving relationship. Did I do the right thing? I believe I did, but I continue to wonder whether I, like Jefferson, put too much weight on the feelings of my loved one and also just wanted to avoid conflict with someone about whom I cared deeply. Alternatively, what would sticking to my guns have accomplished in this case other than hurt feelings?

The issue of ends and means reveals just how complex moral thinking is and, thus, why we always need to be open to opposing views and to reevaluating our own. As we engage in philosophical thinking, we must (iii) identify which claims we are using as premises in our argument. Once we do that, we can ask whether we have good reasons for accepting those claims and, if we decide that we do not, figure out how to evaluate the claim in as objective a manner as possible. We can also assess whether we are drawing on moral claims that are consistent with each other. It is easy to let ourselves have whatever premises seem to support our conclusion, but we cannot draw upon conflicting moral theories without inconsistency. If we understand the foundations of various moral theories, we can make sure that our arguments rely only on one or, at least, only on those that are consistent with one another.

Once we have identified our premises, we need to try to (iv) sort out the moral from the nonmoral claims. Many of our moral arguments will draw on complicated claims from, for example, economics, biology, cognitive science, technology, or agriculture. To assess these claims, we need to draw on the expertise of economists, scientists, engineers, farmers, and the like. But these experts often disagree among themselves, and so we need to learn how to weigh the claims of these experts against one another and make our best judgment based on all the evidence available to us.[9] This task is greatly complicated by the internet, social media, and news outlets, because various of these sites purport to a form of expertise only in order to push an agenda. But at least if we have identified the places at which we need to rely on experts in various fields, we can flag those as ones where we need to remain open-minded and ready to reevaluate our considered opinions.

The case of Thomas Jefferson illustrates the danger of deciding which moral conclusion we want to reach and then devising nonmoral theories that will support that moral conclusion. He wanted to reach the conclusion that he was justified in living off of his slaves, and so he tailored his theory of the nature of blacks to help him reach that conclusion. Many of us do the same with our meat-eating practices: we want to justify them and so we search for theories about nonhuman animals, human biology, or economics that will help us reach our favored conclusion and allow us to enjoy our BLTs. Thinking about the structure of our arguments can help us to see when we are doing this, and, let's hope, help us to avoid doing it.

Emotional Engagement and Emotional Detachment

As one reads about the ways in which Jefferson had small boys whipped or tore families apart, we are inevitably moved to feel sorrow and compassion for the slaves involved. By putting our-selves in their positions, we can try to imagine the grief, fear, and hatred that those slaves must have felt. As a result of this exer-cise in empathy, we sympathize with their plight: we care about their misfortunes, and this concern plays a role in our resulting judgments about the immorality of the actions of Thomas Jefferson.

Did Jefferson feel or even acknowledge the grief of his slaves? If so, how could he have failed to sympathize with their plight and, as a result of that sympathy, have championed the actions of Edward Coles? If not, how could he have avoided doing so, when thoughts about the running of his planta-tion were so often in his mind, and as he strolled about that plantation or lived in his beautiful home, he was constantly confronted by those he held in bondage? These are, of course, the same questions that arose in our discussions of Jones, Stangl, Höss, and the members of the killing squads on the Eastern Front.

Just as the questions are similar in the various cases, so are the answers to those questions. Just as Stangl avoided the undressing barracks, so Jefferson structured the spaces on his mountain to avoid the worst confrontations with the realities of slavery. As one ascended the mountain on which Monticello occupied the summit, the conditions of the slaves became better: lowest down were the unskilled laborers and field hands; next came the skilled artisans living higher up on the mountain; highest up were the house slaves who had the best conditions.[10] But it wasn't just physical separation that worked to block em-pathetic and sympathetic reactions: just as Höss called upon the orders of Himmler, and the members of the killing squads drew upon the views promulgated in the evenings of fellowship organ-ized by their officers, so Jefferson drew upon his views about the alleged inferiority of blacks and the agreement of members of his culture; this was one reason why Coles had to be dealt with so peremptorily and put out of mind.

Jefferson employed none of these strategies when he interacted with his family members.[11] Thus, the needs and interests of his daughter and grandchildren were made lively and vivid, while the needs and interests of his slaves were less so, particularly as their location on the mountain was lower. Thus, in Jefferson's deliberations, it was harder for the good of his slaves to be seen as pressing, even if he had been able to correctly perceive what was good for them. When he considered the consequences of his actions, his emotional engagement with some and his detachment from others kept him from seeing how out of balance the scales really were.

It is all too clear how we create both the physical and the psychological distance from farm animals that allows us to remain emotionally detached from them. Most of us do not have jobs that involve transporting, raising, or killing animals bred for meat, and we avoid the spaces in which these tasks are performed. Our meat comes prepackaged so that it no longer resembles the animal from which it came by the time we purchase and then cook it.[12] This physical distance is then reinforced by admonitions not to anthropomorphize farm animals.

And, of course, our emotional attachment to ourselves, our loved ones, and our domestic pets allows us to put the emphasis on consequences other than those for the farm animals. If anyone treated our domestic pets in the way that farm animals are treated, we would feel rage, grief, compassion, and, most significantly, moral outrage, as we do when we read about puppy mills. Who can pet her cat while that animal relaxes on her lap and not feel pleasure as the cat purrs and, as a result, sympathize with that cat? Who can hold her cat and not feel horror and outrage at the thought of someone harming her? We can avoid these feelings for other animals because we are not forced to engage with them by physical proximity.

As mentioned in chapter 1, one of the philosopher's most important tools is (v) the use of thought experiments: these are imaginary scenarios designed to isolate morally significant features of situations in order to help us to see familiar scenarios in a new light. They are hypotheticals that begin with "Suppose . . ." or "What if. . . ." We saw that Stangl seemed unable or unwilling to actually consider hypotheticals, and this seemed to help him to avoid empathy and sympathy with, for example, the victims of the euthanasia institute and their families. So we can construct thought experiments involving having dogs and cats treated as pigs and cows are, and having those cats and dogs then killed for meat and skin. Or we could ask ourselves: If we could synthesize a meat-like substance indistinguishable from the genuine article, and do so without harming any animals, would we choose to do so? Similarly, Jefferson could have considered hypotheticals in which his daughter was taken away from him to serve someone else and it was unlikely that he would ever see her again. Or he could have tried to imagine how his capacities would be viewed by others if he had not been educated and given other opportunities.

Here is where art and literature can greatly supplement this philosophical endeavor and also provide training in how to engage in that endeavor. The very best fiction takes us into other people's lives—lives very different from our own. By engaging with the detailed perspective of fictional characters, we can hone our capacities for empathy. When those characters are quite different from ourselves, we are forced to see past our preconceptions. It is not surprising, then, that propaganda has always relied so heavily on caricature: racist portrayals of dumb and lazy blacks, Nazi portrayals of evil Jews. These caricatures do not call for deeper examination in the way that

research ?

genuine first-person narratives or thoughtfully constructed fiction does.

Philosophy can, however, provide us useful tools for our engagement with art and literature. After all, skillful authors can get us to sympathize even with odious characters. They can channel our attention in ways that suit their purpose. Novels and films like *Gone with the Wind* have had huge impacts in promoting and perpetuating unjust social institutions, because readers and viewers are brought to sympathize with, in this case, the white slaveholders and to push blacks out of focus except when they are needed on stage for comic relief or as villains. We saw in chapter 5 that while emotions are important for maintaining an engagement with the foundations of morality, they cannot be relied upon, in the absence of a theoretical framework, to guide us to do our duty. So philosophical thinking is needed for (vi) putting our emotional engagement into context.

Know Thyself

How did Thomas Jefferson live with himself? How could an intelligent defender of natural rights and liberty hold people in bondage? How could he enjoy his lifestyle knowing that it was funded by the labor of slaves, including the labor of children? How could he have sex with a woman whom he knew was extremely constrained in her choices and was not a free agent able to consent in any meaningful sense?

Human beings are always complicated, and the task of understanding them is further complicated by cultural and temporal distance. But we can certainly speculate about which forms of moral evasion Jefferson availed himself of in order to maintain his psychic peace. Like the other slaveholder whom we have discussed, Charles Colcock Jones, Jefferson seemed to be a master of wishful compromise. His response to Edward Coles relied on the claim that he, Jefferson, was doing what was best for his slaves, while Coles was engaged in a pie-in-the-sky fantasy, hoping to achieve what neither blacks nor whites were ready to achieve. Sure, Jefferson seemed to say, it was not ideal, but it was hopeless to fight public opinion and, in any case, blacks would not survive outside of the institution of slavery. Whether or not Jefferson fully believed his own attempted justification of his actions, his narrative provided him with a response to the Edward Coles of the world.

Jefferson's claims about the supposed inferiority of persons of African descent also aided his refusal to engage. When we conceive of someone as very different from ourselves, we can keep ourselves from empathizing with them, and this aids in preventing sympathy. By assuming that blacks were quite different from him, Jefferson felt no need to put himself in their position. He could stroll around his plantation and feel no more for his black slaves than you or I would feel for a horse strapped to a carriage or oxen pulling a loaded farm cart. He could write about giving a slave to his daughter, thereby breaking up a family, with very little more feeling than I would have about giving a serving platter to a friend, thereby breaking up my grandmother's wedding china.

It is quite clear how evasion is at work in our ability to eat meat and enjoy other animal products while, at some level, abhorring cruelty to animals. Just as Jefferson's views about blacks aided his refusal to engage, so our hasty dismissal of any kind of anthropomorphizing of animals helps us to refrain from empathizing and thus from sympathizing with animals. In this case, we are, however, quite schizophrenic: if actually confronted with images of pigs or cows suffering in factory farms, we naturally empathize and sympathize. For this reason, many of us avoid forming beliefs about factory farms by trying to avoid any further information about or images of such institutions.

I know from first-hand experience how prevalent wishful compromise is in the case of our treatment of nonhuman animals. A whole host of unexamined and unjustified beliefs play a role in our "justification" of supporting factory farming: we need the protein, we don't want to put all of those people out of work, and so on. In my own case, while I have given up meat and leather, I continue to use other animal products, often pushing aside my doubts by telling myself that I do more good with my monthly contributions to animal welfare organizations. But at bottom, I know that I just can't bring myself to give up cheese and milk chocolate. Am I justified in weighing in my own self-interest in this way? How much am I obligated to do to help animals? How effective is my refusal to eat meat? I fear that I do not give the position I have reached enough reexamination. I am lucky enough to have friends who are vegans, and I need to make sure that I do not respond to them on the issue of nonhuman animals in the way that Thomas Jefferson responded to Edward Coles on the issue of slavery.

I believe that, at bottom, philosophy's greatest contribution to the moral life is its promotion of self-knowledge. We must fulfill our duty of self-scrutiny if we are to have any chance of actually taking due care in moral deliberation. We need to figure out what we really believe and what we have justification for believing if we are going to make any progress in reaching moral truth. The kind of intense reflection encouraged by the philosophical endeavor forces us to confront our beliefs, even the ones we have been trying to hide from ourselves. It forces us to form beliefs on issues about which we have been trying to avoid forming beliefs. Of course, this is only true if one approaches philosophy with sincerity and open-mindedness. Any form of moral evasion makes our tasks of moral self-scrutiny and due care in moral deliberation extremely difficult. But if we sincerely want to carry out those tasks, and we are convinced that philosophy can aid us in doing so, we are that much closer to being unable to hide from ourselves.

Who Are They to Me?

In the example I gave from my own life—that involving my grandmother and her pork chops—I said that, in my deliberations I considered not only the well-being of nonhuman animals but also my special ties of love and commitment to my grandmother as providing me with reasons to act. In almost all our case studies, we saw the men pointing to their concern for their families as at least part of their reason for running a death camp or selling slaves away from their families. In the cases of Stangl, Jones, and Jefferson, I think that probably many of you are inclined to agree with me that the moral crimes are too great to be justified (or even excused) by an appeal to the well-being of a few family members. And certainly we think that considerations of self-interest cannot exonerate these Nazis and slaveholders: one cannot justify human bondage or genocide by an appeal to a desire for domestic help or to advance one's career.

But when, if at all, can we justifiably plead our own interests or the interests of our loved ones as reasons not to aid others? We all receive in the mail requests for donations from the ASPCA, UNICEF, Doctors Without Borders, Habitat for Humanity, and the like. Most of these mailings, I would wager, end up in the recycling bin without any sort of acknowledgment, let alone a donation. Yesterday, I bought a pistachio frappe at my favorite coffee shop that cost me $5.50. Earlier in the week, I took my mother out for dinner and the bill for two people totaled around $50. These were extravagances, even if you and I might not categorize them as such—they are luxuries that most people in the world will never be able to afford. How can I justify treating myself and my mother in this way while there are millions of people in the world who are hungry and who lack basic sanitary and medical needs? How can I justify the degree of privilege that I have while so many people are in danger of starvation or are displaced and homeless due to war? What are my moral responsibilities to strangers, be they human or nonhuman animals? These are questions that every responsible moral deliberator must confront.[13]

Different moral theories provide us with different answers. Consider the relationship between moral demands and one's own interests. Consequentialists claim that we are allowed, even required, to count our own good as we determine which actions have the best consequences, but we are not allowed, they say, to give any additional weight to our own good merely because it is our own. For Kant and certain other deontologists, we are allowed to pursue our own interests only to the extent that we can do so without violating or failing to fulfill any of our impartial duties. Some philosophers in recent years have insisted that morality itself grants us "permissions" to promote our own good—permissions that exempt us from, for example, what they see as the excessive or overly demanding requirements of a moral theory such as consequentialism.[14] Philosophers such as Hobbes have insisted that what we call moral demands are really derived from self-interest—that is, that once we see the true nature of morality, we see that it is a system of rules we ought to follow out of rational self-interest. Another possibility is that our own desires and concerns give us reasons to act that compete with our moral reasons, where sometimes the former win out and sometimes the latter win out.[15]

For many of us, to pursue our own interests involves taking care of those we love or like: friends, family, and so on. But many philosophers insist that morality not only allows but also demands that we take special care of our intimates, that we have special obligations to them that we do not have to strangers or to mere acquaintances. (Consequentialists, even, often claim that we can best promote overall well-being by focusing our efforts on those we know best.[16]) Some who defend special obligations limit them to those to whom we have very close personal ties, such as parents, children, friends, and lovers, whereas others claim that our special obligations extend to colleagues, neighbors, and fellow citizens.[17]

As I said at the beginning of this section, these kinds of reasons—of self-interest and special obligations to loved ones—have recurred in our discussions of our case studies. Jefferson and Jones loved their families, and their own lives were deeply embedded within the communities formed by those families and by their neighbors and others of their class. They were also used to a certain way of life, one involving servants, a secure home with like-minded neighbors, and the respect of their peers. (Just as we are used to lives involving frappes and dinners out.) Höss and Stangl each had much of their own interests bound up with their careers—careers that demanded terrible things of them. Like Jefferson and Jones, they also had people about whom they cared, and Stangl explicitly expresses his concern for his wife and children for whose safety he says he feared.[18] We cannot help but think that if these men were actually trying to balance all of their reasons, they did not do a good job of it; surely, we think, they placed far too much weight on their own interests and those of their loved ones.

But are we doing the same? It is much easier for us in the Western democracies (at least those of us in the middle and upper classes) to put out of our minds the immense amount of terrible suffering in the world. Even though we now have so much more information available to us from multiple sources about conditions around the world, we are also in a much better position to ignore that information. When we connect to the internet, we can check out the celebrity gossip sites instead of respectable news sources or charitable organizations. And, of course, when we compare our own economic situations to those of celebrities, we do not look privileged at all. Here moral evasion is comfortably at home, helping us to justify a new car or the latest flat-screen television when the money could instead help starving people or refugees who have been forced from their homes by war.

But, you might be wondering, how much does morality demand of us? Already, you might, with good reason, be thinking, *It seems that moral deliberation itself, complicated as it is, is going to eat up a lot of time. Do we have to forgo small luxuries for ourselves and our loved ones? Are we acting immorally by enjoying our lives even if others are unable to do so? Is it wrong to ensure a good life for our children, even if we could give them less in order to aid children who are far, far worse off? Am I acting immorally when I buy myself books when I could instead get them from the library and send the money to a charity? In the end, who are all of these other people to me?*

Our case studies are interesting because they lead us to judge as immoral, perhaps even evil, men like our Nazis and slaveholders who put their own good and the good of their loved ones above moral concerns for all persons. Again, we need to ask: Are we doing the same? You, like I, will probably start looking for reasons why our situations are very different; one common response is, *I*, unlike Jones or Höss, am not enslaving, starving, or killing someone. This is true: we are bystanders, like those in Nazi Germany who refused to aid those being persecuted. But don't we judge such people as doing wrong as well? I am certainly not raising these questions in order to answer them; as I said, the weighing of reasons is one of the most difficult parts of moral deliberation. And when our own self-interest is involved, as we know from our case studies, evasion is all too likely to occur. This is another reason why I think that these kinds of case studies are so valuable: on issues such as so-called charity,[19] we can ask whether we are allowing ourselves excuses or justifications that we deny to Jefferson and others.

Conscience and Virtue

Ted Bundy said that we all have "gaps" in our consciences. As we saw, Bundy's gaps were so large that they were more adequately described as canyons. In fact, most of us would say that Bundy lacked a moral conscience, and such lack has long been taken to be one of the defining features of psychopathy. But what is it to have a conscience? Is it some sort of guide to moral conduct with which we are born? People often say that one ought to follow one's conscience, that one's conscience will lead one to the right action. What do they mean?

It may be that some believe we do, in fact, have an innate sense that can reveal right and wrong action to us.[20] But given how complicated moral deliberation is and how it often depends to a great extent on premises about complex nonmoral matters— economics, medicine, biology, agriculture, and so on—it really does not seem plausible that we have an inborn barometer of moral rightness and wrongness. It is true that most of us are born with some capacities that psychopaths lack: the capacity to empathize with others, the capacity to feel such emotions as pity and compassion, the capacity to care about the good of other persons for their own sakes rather than merely instrumentally. These capacities, as we have seen, play an important role in our ability to acquire moral concepts and to understand the under-lying foundations of moral rules. But even once we employ our capacities and have those concepts and an understanding of the justification of moral rules, we still need to employ a broad range of intellectual capacities if we are to arrive at justified moral beliefs.

So we do not want to allow ourselves to be lazy moral deliberators by claiming that we are simply following the deliverances of our conscience, where what that means is that we rest content with whatever moral beliefs we find ourselves convinced of at some particular time. But what we might mean when we talk about following our consciences is actually what it means to exercise moral virtue. As our case studies and our discussions of animal welfare issues and charity show, morality can make demands of us that put not only our interests but also our very lives at stake. Even if we fulfill our duties of moral self-scrutiny and of due care in moral deliberation, all we have is a justified (and we hope true) moral belief about what the right action is in our particular situation. But a moral belief about the nature of right action is a belief about how we ought to act, and so the next step is actually doing what we ought to do. If someone attempts to divert us to act contrary to our best judgment or we find ourselves tempted to promote our own interests by doing what we know to be wrong, we might find ourselves thinking *But I have to follow my conscience*, where what we mean is that we have to act on the moral conclusions that we have reached after doing our best to sincerely figure out the moral truth.

And here I think we have reached an important feature of the moral life: we each have to be our own moral philosopher; we each have to exercise the capacities we have, both affective and cognitive, in order to engage in sincere moral deliberation. Once we do that, while we have to continue to be open-minded, to engage with those who offer critiques of our beliefs or who offer competing beliefs, we have no choice but to rely on our own judgment. Sometimes our best judgment will be that we ought to defer to someone else, but that is still a judgment for which we must take responsibility.

Moral Philosophy and Moral Education

As I discussed the issue of nonhuman animals, I showed how the tools and strategies of moral philosophy could aid us in our deliberations and self-examination. Recall that moral philosophy encourages us to:

(i) Check the consistency of our beliefs.

(ii) Theorize about the nature of morality and of its demands and to seek to understand the underlying justification for moral rules.

(iii) Identify the premises we are using as support for our moral claims.

(iv) In identifying our premises, to sort out the moral claims from the nonmoral claims so that we can see where we need to acquire more empirical data or to appeal to experts.

(v) Use thought experiments.

(vi) Put our emotional engagement into a theoretical context.

Not only are we not born with an innate moral sense or conscience, we are not born with the ability to engage in activities (i) through (vi). To learn how to check for consistency and identify our premises, we need to have training in critical reasoning: we need to be able to understand how to construct and to evaluate arguments. To be able to theorize about the nature of morality and to sort out moral from nonmoral claims, we need to have some understanding of what sorts of moral theories are plausible and of the nature of moral concepts. In order to utilize thought experiments, we need to develop imagination and an ability to understand analogies. Finally, to put our emotional engagement into theoretical context, we need to have a theoretical framework to shape and guide our emotional reactions.

All these tasks are complex, and in order to acquire and hone them, we need to have an appropriate sort of education. Of course, given that these are the tools of moral philosophy, some basic education in that field can greatly facilitate our ability to fulfill our duty to due care in moral deliberation. That will not, however, be sufficient: the premises in our moral arguments are often claims about science, engineering, economics, history, and so on, and therefore a well-rounded education in such fields is needed so as to be a responsible moral deliberator. And given how experts and those who report on the views of such experts can themselves have agendas, we need to have training in evaluating sources and in interpreting texts. Exposure to art and literature allows us to further develop our ability to imagine alternatives and to engage emotionally.

But, I think, moral philosophy can provide structure to our moral thinking, showing us how to employ what we garner from, for example, literature and the sciences. And the earlier we are introduced to the tools of moral philosophy, the more natural their use will be for us, and thus the more difficult it will be to avoid moral deliberation and self-examination of the relevant sort.

I hope I have convinced you that engaging in moral philosophical thinking is important and interesting. However, perhaps you are thinking that it is far too time-consuming: *How can we hope to be responsible moral deliberators when we have to take care of our families and earn a living?* I have the luxury of actually being able to make my living thinking about morality, but it is a luxury that few have. Inevitably, a moral question we must all face is how to balance all the demands we face. But at the least, we want to avoid the sorts of failures exhibited by our case studies. Being open-minded about where we might be going wrong and being willing to listen to moral criticism represent the necessary and only starting place.

Notes

Chapter 1

1. Of course, one can quite plausibly view Jefferson's motivation for condemning the introduction of slavery into the colonies not as a statement of a humanitarian opposition to African bondage but, rather, as the expression of bitterness at having been put into a position of having to defend living off of the sweat of other human beings. Now Virginians, to use Jefferson's infamous phrase, had "the wolf by the ears," and England was not offering help in finding a way to release it, where releasing didn't involve being overrun by "wolves" (i.e., being forced to live side by side with a large free black population) and probably having one's hands bit off (i.e., losing the basis of one's wealth or, even worse, facing rebellion on the part of the enslaved).

2. Thomas Jefferson to Edward Coles, August 25, 1814.

3. As Henry Weincek points out, Jefferson was responding to a letter from a member of the younger generation who was proposing to take up the antislavery banner with a concrete plan. So Jefferson's own assertions support aiding Coles to whatever extent an "old man" was capable. Henry Weincek, *Master of the Mountain: Thomas Jefferson and His Slaves* (New York: Farrar, Straus, and Giroux, 2012), 241.

4. Weincek, *Master of the Mountain*, 241.

5. Some philosophers claim that it is actually *impossible* for someone to accept that an action is wrong and yet not have any motivation to refrain from performing that action. Such philosophers are known as *motive internalists*. (See David Brink, *Moral Realism and the Foundations*

of Ethics [Cambridge: Cambridge University Press, 1989], 37–43, for a discussion of various forms of internalism in ethics.) However, even if they are not motive internalists, most philosophers accept that there is some sort of connection between moral judgment and motivation to act. Exploration of such connections is woven throughout the following chapters.

6. Of course, it is a question that we can raise for all those slaveholders who signed the Declaration of Independence, in response to which Samuel Johnson famously asked, "How is it that we hear the loudest yelps for liberty among the drivers of negroes?" See his "Taxation No Tyranny: An answer to the resolutions and addresses of the American Congress."

7. See Weincek, *Master of the Mountain*, for eye-opening discussions of both Jefferson's character as slave master and historians' collusion in propagating the myth of Jefferson as the exemplary slaveholder. All the examples in this paragraph are derived from Weincek's text.

8. This phrase is from Abraham Lincoln's First Inaugural Address, delivered on March 4, 1861.

9. Here I am making the assumption that morality does not reduce to considerations of self-interest. Some philosophers have argued that moral rules are derived from reasons of self-interest, although for such philosophers that derivation is not always straightforward. (See Thomas Hobbes, *Leviathan* [Indianapolis, IN: Hackett, 1994] for the classic statement of this kind of position; and David Gauthier, *Morals By Agreement* [New York: Oxford University Press, 1987] for a contemporary defense of the Hobbesian position that utilizes modern decision theory and game theory.) However, I am going to continue to discuss morality in the way that most conceive of it, as a kind of constraint on self-interest.

10. John Stuart Mill, *On Liberty*, ed. Elizabeth Rapaport (Indianapolis, IN: Hackett, 1978), 37.

11. See Primo Levi, "The Gray Zone," in *The Drowned and the Saved*, trans. Raymond Rosenthal (New York: Vintage Books, 1988), 36–69, for a provocative discussion of the moral responsibility of Jewish prisoners in Nazi concentration camps who colluded with the Nazis in order to gain benefits for themselves. See also Claudia Card's discussion of gray zones in *The Atrocity Paradigm: A Theory of Evil* (New York: Oxford University Press, 2002), 211–34.

12. Thomas E. Hill Jr., "Moral Responsibilities of Bystanders," *Journal of Social Philosophy* 41, no. 1 (Spring 2010): 28–39, 32.

13. Hill, "Moral Responsibilities of Bystanders," 33.

14. Other concepts, such as that of murder, are also moral concepts, but are so in a more, as it were, covert way. Murder means something like "wrongful killing," so its analysis involves one of our paradigmatic moral concepts. We need to always be on the lookout for such covertly moral concepts, because failure to recognize them as such can lead us into bad reasoning. Consider, for example, an argument for the immorality of abortion that takes as a premise the claim that abortion is murder. Once we recognize that murder is a covertly moral concept, we can see that the argument amounts to saying that abortion is immoral because abortion is wrongful killing, and we can all agree that that is not a good argument.

15. I think, however, that it is somewhat misleading to describe Eichmann as a desk murderer, given that he visited Auschwitz. So although Eichmann did not participate in the daily running of the extermination camps, he had first-hand knowledge of what was happening there—the murdered Jews were more than just numbers on paper for him.

16. There seems to be disagreement in the psychological literature on whether these are distinct but overlapping concepts or the same concept. Psychopaths will be discussed further in chapter 5.

Chapter 2

1. See, for example, Robert J. Smith, "The Psychopath as Moral Agent," *Philosophy and Phenomenological Research* 45 (1984): 177–93.

2. This is, as I understand it, what Hannah Arendt meant when she called evil 'banal' in her now famous *Eichmann in Jerusalem: A Report on the Banality of Evil* (New York: Penguin Books, 2006). After observing Eichmann at his trial in Jerusalem, Arendt was struck by how very ordinary Eichmann seemed—just another mindless bureaucrat who had found himself employed by the Nazis. Of course, Arendt herself never interviewed Eichmann and, in fact, did not even stay to witness the entire trial. David Caesarini's *Becoming Eichmann: Rethinking the Life, Crimes, and Trial of a "Desk Murderer"* (Boston: Da Capo Press, 2006) provides a fascinating corrective to Arendt's partial portrait. However,

whether or not Arendt presented Eichmann accurately, I think she was right to remind us that evil people are just *people* who are like you and me in surprising and disturbing ways.

3. Bernard Williams, "Moral Luck," in *Moral Luck* (New York: Cambridge University Press, 1982), 20–39; Thomas Nagel, "Moral Luck," in *Mortal Questions* (New York: Cambridge University Press, 2012), 24–38.

4. Gitta Sereny, *Albert Speer: His Battle with Truth* (New York: Vintage Books, 1996), 201.

5. Sereny, *Albert Speer*, 184. "Duties" here is, of course, a reference to one's job duties. One of my main points in this section is that Speer was in a position to have recognized that his *moral* duties required him to seek out precisely that information that General Order No. 1 was commanding him to ignore. This conflict between duties of role or position and moral duties becomes very important in our discussion of all the Nazis discussed in this chapter.

6. See Sereny, *Albert Speer*, 463, 551, 635.

7. As I pointed out in chapter 1, an important aspect of moral reasoning involves understanding the relationship between nonmoral claims and moral claims. Speer was not prepared or was unwilling to recognize the moral significance of some of his nonmoral beliefs.

8. Sereny, *Albert Speer*, 463.

9. Sereny, *Albert Speer*, 162.

10. Sereny, *Albert Speer*, 23.

11. Sereny, *Albert Speer*, 608.

12. Sereny, *Albert Speer*, 148.

13. Sereny, *Albert Speer*, 222.

14. Sereny, *Albert Speer*, 636.

15. Sereny, *Albert Speer*, 117.

16. Sereny, *Albert Speer*, 228–29.

17. Sereny, *Albert Speer*, 313; emphasis mine.

18. Sereny, *Albert Speer*, 313.

19. Sereny, *Albert Speer*, 379.

20. Sereny, *Albert Speer*, 706.

21. Sereny, *Albert Speer*, 222.

22. Sereny, *Albert Speer*, 13.

23. Sereny, *Albert Speer*, 50. These claims might lead us to think that Speer was in fact a psychopath or, at least, not entirely nonpsychopathic. However, I am inclined to reject that interpretation of Speer because of his interactions with Casalis that I discussed earlier: these interactions seem to indicate that Speer was capable of a kind of emotional and intellectual engagement that would be beyond the reach of a psychopath like Bundy. Further, if Speer had been a psychopath, there would probably have been no motivation for him to avoid the kind of knowledge that Hanke warned him against acquiring.

24. Sereny, *Albert Speer*, 90; emphasis in original.

25. Sereny, *Albert Speer*, 338.

26. Sereny, *Albert Speer*, 567.

27. Sereny, *Albert Speer*, 427.

28. Sereny, *Albert Speer*, 25.

29. Sereny, *Albert Speer*, 633.

30. Many see the Nazis as being overused as examples of evil people. I disagree; they may be used a lot, but that does not imply overuse, because they are so often such good examples and such well-documented ones. Further, for many of them, we have their own testimony about their crimes, which is invaluable to understanding.

31. These institutes were part of the Nazi plan to eliminate so-called useless eaters, the mentally and physically handicapped and the mentally ill. These initiatives, scholars have argued, provided the Nazis with a trial run for the Final Solution. For example, mobile gas vans were used for killing for the first time in eliminating the disabled or mentally ill. The euthanasia institutes were shut down after the public reacted with outrage, an indication that the Nazis were responsive to public opinion and that the German people were not completely terrorized into silence, as so many attempted to claim after the war. The euthanasia institutes, in addition to providing germs of methodology for the Final Solution, provided personnel, Stangl being a prime example.

32. Gitta Sereny, *Into That Darkness: An Examination of Conscience* (New York: Vintage Books, 1983), 163.

33. Sereny, *Into That Darkness*, 228–29.

34. Sereny, *Into That Darkness*, 164.

35. Sereny, *Into That Darkness*, 164.

36. Sereny, *Into That Darkness*, 201.

37. Sereny, *Into That Darkness*, 207–208.

38. Sereny, *Into That Darkness*, 169–70.

39. Sereny, *Into That Darkness*, 164.

40. Sereny, *Into That Darkness*, 55. I find this remark of Stangl's to be a good example of the kind of compartmentalization likely required by many Nazis. Stangl, in talking about this time at the euthanasia institutes, repeats the claim that the policies of the institutes were justified because it was better for those killed—their lives weren't worth living. But if one truly believed that, why would one need to be assured that no one whom one cared about would be subject to euthanizing? Wouldn't one want to put a loved one out of his or her misery? Keeping one's thinking about one's loved ones separated from one's thinking about those dealt with in one's professional capacity was necessary to retain one's self-image as a decent person.

41. Sereny, *Into That Darkness*, 164.

42. Sereny, *Into That Darkness*, 110.

43. Sereny, *Into That Darkness*, 231.

44. We will return to this way of avoiding moral reality when we consider, in chapters 5 and 7, our own support of factory farming through our consumption of meat, while we are unwilling to confront the horrors of factory-farm installations and slaughterhouses. We are often content to ignore wrongdoing and suffering as long as we don't have to see it on a daily basis.

45. Rudolph Höss, *Death Dealer: The Memoirs of the SS Kommandant at Auschwitz*, ed. Steven Paskuly, trans. Andrew Pollinger (Boston: Da Capo Press, 1996), 183.

46. Höss, *Death Dealer*, 124; emphasis mine.

47. Höss, *Death Dealer*, 152.

48. Höss, *Death Dealer*, 50.

49. Höss, *Death Dealer*, 84.

50. See Höss, *Death Dealer*, 153, 171.

51. Höss, *Death Dealer*, 153.

52. Höss, *Death Dealer*, 128.

53. Höss, *Death Dealer*, 139–40.

54. Höss, *Death Dealer*, 142. Very difficult moral questions are raised by the actions of those Jews who inflicted suffering on fellow inmates in order to secure greater privileges for themselves. Are such persons, given the nature of their situation and suffering, to be regarded as fully morally culpable for their mistreatment of their fellow prisoners, are they to be regarded wholly as victims, or are they culpable but to a mitigated degree? Primo Levi, himself an Auschwitz survivor, suggests in his "Gray Zones" that persons such as the members of the *Sonderkommando* (groups of Jews who worked in the gas chamber/crematorium complexes, leading people into the chambers, removing bodies from the chambers after death, or disposing of the bodies) lie beyond our assessment or judgment. It is unclear how Levi intends us to interpret this claim. He could mean that they simply cannot be said to be guilty or to be free of guilt, that we are in no position to be able to assess their guilt or lack thereof, or that, as a matter of humility, we should be careful about judging such people. I do think that it is important to think about these matters because, for many of us, it is our collusion in wrongdoing to maintain our privileges that is our most serious moral difficulty.

55. Höss, *Death Dealer*, 142–43.

56. See also *Death Dealer*, 45 for Höss's reading of the demeanor of the *Sonderkommando*, those Jews assigned to work in the gas chamber/crematory complex.

57. Höss, *Death Dealer*, 83; capitalization in the original.

58. Höss, *Death Dealer*, 153.

59. Höss, *Death Dealer*, 161–63.

60. Höss, *Death Dealer*, 162.

61. Höss, *Death Dealer*, 163.

62. None of this is to deny Höss's obvious and strong anti-Semitic convictions (see, for example, *Death Dealer*, 183). But anti-Semitism does not lead one inevitably to regard genocide as morally permissible.

63. Erskine Clarke, *Dwelling Place: A Plantation Epic* (New Haven, CT: Yale University Press, 2005), 74; see also 103, 133.

64. Clarke, *Dwelling Place*, 89; see also 108, where Jones labels slavery "evil."

65. Clarke, *Dwelling Place*, 90.

66. Clarke, *Dwelling Place*, 96.

67. Clarke, *Dwelling Place*, 90.

68. Clarke, *Dwelling Place*, 89.

69. Clarke, *Dwelling Place*, 77.

70. Clarke, *Dwelling Place*, 103.

71. Clarke, *Dwelling Place*, 96.

72. Clarke, *Dwelling Place*, 105.

73. Clarke, *Dwelling Place*, 133.

74. Clarke, *Dwelling Place*, 138.

75. Clarke, *Dwelling Place*, 126–29.

76. Clarke, *Dwelling Place*, 130.

77. Clarke, *Dwelling Place*, 350.

78. Clarke, *Dwelling Place*, 349.

79. Clarke, *Dwelling Place*, 351.

80. Clarke, *Dwelling Place*, 355.

81. Clarke, *Dwelling Place*, 354.

82. Clarke, *Dwelling Place*, 359.

83. Clarke, *Dwelling Place*, 356.

84. In "Evil as an Explanatory Concept," *The Monist* 85, no. 2 (2002): 320–36, 331.

85. In his final interview just before his execution, Bundy attributed his crimes to his early and continuing consumption of pornography. The interviewer was chosen by Bundy, and was a zealous crusader against pornography. One cannot help but see the interview as one long exercise in manipulation on Bundy's part.

86. Stephen G. Michaud and Hugh Aynesworth, *Ted Bundy: Conversations with a Killer* (Irving, TX: Authorlink Press, 2000), 188.

87. Michaud and Aynesworth, *Ted Bundy*, 137; all emphases in the quotations are as in the original unless otherwise indicated.

88. Michaud and Aynesworth, *Ted Bundy*, 37.

89. Michaud and Aynesworth, *Ted Bundy*, 79, 80, 96.

90. Michaud and Aynesworth, *Ted Bundy*, 120.

91. Michaud and Aynesworth, *Ted Bundy*, 83, 92.

92. Michaud and Aynesworth, *Ted Bundy*, 112–13.

93. Michaud and Aynesworth, *Ted Bundy*, 82, 186, 201.

94. Michaud and Aynesworth, *Ted Bundy*, 69.

95. Michaud and Aynesworth, *Ted Bundy*, 151–52.

96. Michaud and Aynesworth, *Ted Bundy*, 210.

97. Michaud and Aynesworth, *Ted Bundy*, 115, 96, 80.

98. Michaud and Aynesworth, *Ted Bundy*, 95; see also 116.

99. Michaud and Aynesworth, *Ted Bundy*, 145.

100. Michaud and Aynesworth, *Ted Bundy*, 146–47.

101. Michaud and Aynesworth, *Ted Bundy*, 150–51.

102. Michaud and Aynesworth, *Ted Bundy*, 118.

103. Michaud and Aynesworth, *Ted Bundy*, 84, 104.

104. I admit that this is speculation on my part—we may never know whether Bundy took pleasure from inflicting pain on his victims. All that I want to suggest here is that there is at least some reason to seriously consider Bundy's claims on this matter, rather than just regarding them as a feeble attempt to garner sympathy.

105. I will return to the notion of conscience in chapter 7.

106. Michaud and Aynesworth, *Ted Bundy*, 259.

107. Michaud and Aynesworth, *Ted Bundy*, 277, 281.

Chapter 3

1. The "we" here refers at least to the portion of Americans to which I and my American readers belong, I am assuming. Any generalizations about a group as heterogeneous as that of Americans have to be understood quite loosely.

2. Douglas L. Wilson, "Thomas Jefferson and the Character Issue," *Atlantic Monthly* 270 (1992): 57–59+.

3. See Fawn M. Brodie, *Thomas Jefferson: An Intimate History* (New York: W. W. Norton, 2010).

4. Wilson, "Jefferson and the Character Issue," 62.

5. See Alison Dundes Renteln, *The Cultural Defense* (New York: Oxford University Press, 2004), 51.

6. I am not going to be addressing the legal issues here. For a discussion of the cultural defense in law, see Renteln, *The Cultural Defense*.

7. It is also possible to have true beliefs that are unjustified, perhaps because they are based on mere guesses or on the testimony of a generally unreliable informant.

8. I do not, however, think that this task is exclusively the province of the historian. Wilson's attempt to vindicate Jefferson from the charge that he had sex with Sally Heming reveals that he relies on a reading of Jefferson that is dependent on both a vague conception of the nature of moral standards and moral motivation and an underestimation or misunderstanding of the types of evasion that I will discuss in chapter 6.

9. This has the result that an agent can be (epistemically) justified in believing she is doing the right thing but nonetheless not (morally) justified in acting as she does. I'm not sure whether that is the right thing to say or not; as I have said, this issue raises a lot of interesting questions about the nature of right action.

10. I am going to be discussing the simplest version of cultural relativism, one that I think gets employed by quite a few people in thinking about morality. My goal is to point out the difficulties of this simple, familiar version of cultural relativism, not to argue that no more sophisticated version of the view is available and worth discussing. Readers who want to explore cultural relativism and other forms of relativism further can consult *Moral Relativism: A Reader*, ed. Paul Moser and Thomas L. Carson (New York: Oxford University Press, 2000).

11. There is another variant of cultural relativism according to which the context will determine whether S's judgment that T's doing X is right/wrong is to be assessed relative to the attitudes prevalent in S's culture, relative to the attitudes prevalent in T's culture, or relative to the standards of some other culture entirely. (On another version of this view, such judgments will have no meaning, and thus no truth value, until a culture is specified.) Consider as an analogy: I might say of my parents' Chihuahua that she is large, and the truth value of my statement will depend upon whether it is interpreted as claiming that she is large relative to the class of dogs or that she is large relative to the class of Chihuahuas or relative to the class of house pets. Which interpretation is correct will depend on various features of the context

(which may or may not include the speaker's intentions). I will set this version aside because it interprets moral judgments as being systematically ambiguous as between (at least) cultural relativism with speaker-relativity and cultural relativism with agent-relativity.

12. We need to make sure that we do not state cultural relativism in a way that seems to come naturally to both laypeople and some philosophers. Consider the following:

> *Cultural Relativism Mistake*: To say that T's doing X is right (or good) for T is just to say that members of T's culture believe that T's doing X is right (or good).

When philosophers offer an analysis of a concept, they are attempting to offer a way of translating claims involving that concept in order to preserve the meaning of the original claims. So it is obvious that they will not have achieved their purpose if they use the very concept that they are trying to analyze; after all, we all know that a definition of a word ought not to contain that word—circular definitions are bad definitions. So Cultural Relativism Mistake is just that, a mistake.

Further, one can see that Cultural Relativism Mistake lands us in a regress. If to say that (a) *T's doing X is right* is just to say that (b) *members of T's culture believe that T's doing X is right*, then I can substitute the latter claim (b) wherever (a) "T's doing X is right" appears. But it appears in the latter claim (b) itself, which then becomes "Members of T's culture believe that members of T's culture believe that T's doing X is right." Uh-oh, there's the claim "T's doing X is right" again, and so now I get "Members of T's culture believe that members of T's culture believe that members of T's culture believe that T's doing X is right." Uh-oh, . . . It should be clear that there is no end to this, hence the infinite regress. I doubt anyone finds such a view to be a plausible account of the meaning of moral claims. Thus, we always need to remember to state any version of cultural relativism in terms of attitudes such as approval, not in terms of beliefs.

13. Things are actually quite a bit more complicated than my presentation here. It certainly is the case that, in general, members of my culture disapprove of slaveholding, but their attitudes toward Jefferson make it difficult to tell if they disapprove of *Jefferson's* holding slaves. And did members of Jefferson's culture approve of slaveholding? That depends on how broadly we construe Jefferson's culture: Was it composed of

white southerners or of Americans, where at least some of the latter (Hamilton, Franklin, etc.) disapproved of slaveholding. Any cultural relativist has to contend with the difficulties of specifying how we determine the members of any particular agent's culture.

14. One important issue for any cultural relativist is determining what counts as a culture. How do I determine who are the persons who constitute my culture or Jefferson's culture? Are recent immigrants to the United States part of my culture? Were northern abolitionists part of Jefferson's culture? I don't know a good way to answer these questions without stipulation, but I will not address this potential objection to the cultural relativist position because there are other objections that are more interesting for my purposes in this book.

15. It is particularly difficult to make sense of a notion of American "culture," given the diversity of people who live in the United States.

16. This is, of course, a vast oversimplification of antebellum American divisions on slavery. However, here I am describing the view of those who defend cultural relativism, not my own views. The kind of complexity we see upon even the most cursory of studies of antebellum American views on slavery supports my view that the notion of culture is too vague to be able to do any work for the cultural relativist.

17. Again, we can ask, do fundamentalist Christians in the United States belong to a different culture than do, say, atheists? Can we even make generalizations about such groups of people, given that they are likely to differ among themselves along other dimensions?

18. This is not to say that *no one* takes such a line; I have heard people insist that for any given person, her religious beliefs are *true for her*, although it is always unclear what that is supposed to mean. More often, however, the drive for religious tolerance will lead to the insistence that all religions, ultimately, are saying the same thing, just in different ways. This latter claim seems patently false—for example, Christians claim that Jesus Christ is the son of God, while Jews deny that Jesus was the messiah, let alone God made flesh. It is very difficult to see how two people can really be saying the same thing if one says "P" while the other says "Not P." How can two people be saying the same thing if one accepts the doctrine of the Trinity while the other claims that it

is unintelligible? But issues of religious toleration and critique are not my subject.

19. There are some who would claim that religion is a subjective matter, but it is unclear what they mean. I understand most religious people as regarding it as an objective fact that, for example, Jesus was the son of God or that Mohammed was a prophet. I also understand them as saying that those who reject Jesus's divinity or Mohammed's status as prophet have false beliefs.

20. J. L. Mackie, *Ethics: Inventing Right and Wrong* (New York: Penguin, 1991), 36–37.

21. There is a further question about why we should discount the role of socialization in the formation of scientific hypotheses, but I will leave that issue aside here.

22. There are certainly attempts on the part of cultural relativists to offer views yielding the conclusion that slavery and genocide are wrong for all people at all times. I do not think these views can be successful without accepting, at some point, a commitment to some objective moral truths. The reader can evaluate such a view for herself by reading David Wong, *Natural Moralities: A Defense of Pluralistic Relativism* (New York: Oxford University Press, 2009).

23. Gilbert Harman, "Moral Relativism Defended," *Philosophical Review* 84 (1975): 3–22, 5.

24. Harman, "Moral Relativism," 4.

25. Harman, "Moral Relativism," 7.

26. If we were concerned with the details of Harman's views, it would be important to examine the ways in which Harman could allow for competing implicit agreements.

27. On this issue, see Jeffrie G. Murphy, "Moral Death: A Kantian Essay on Psychopathy," *Ethics* 82 (1972): 284–98.

28. This does not settle the issue of what the appropriate treatment of the criminally insane is. In order to answer this question, we would need to address the justification and goals of legal punishment.

29. Susan Wolf, "Sanity and the Metaphysics of Responsibility," in *Responsibility, Character, and the Emotions*, ed. Ferdinand Schoeman (Cambridge: Cambridge University Press, 1987), 46–62, 56.

30. Wolf, "Sanity," 56.

31. Wolf, "Sanity," 57.

32. As is the case with certain sorts of brain tumors—these tumors can cause irrational thinking, reasoning, and feeling in persons who exhibited no such cognitive or affective impairments before the appearance of the tumor. In such cases we would be reluctant to attribute any blame to a victim of such a tumor who engages in wrongful behavior.

33. See Weincek, *Master of the Mountain*, for discussions of the variety of skilled tasks performed by slaves on Jefferson's plantation.

34. For more on the issues raised by Wolf's article and my discussion here, see Michele M. Moody-Adams, "Culture, Responsibility, and Affected Ignorance," *Ethics* 104 (1994): 291–309; and Neil Levy, "Cultural Membership and Moral Responsibility," *The Monist* 86 (2003): 145–63.

35. Levy, in "Cultural Membership," suggests that it would require far more to acquire evidence undermining such a pervasive social practice. It just does not seem that it would require as much as he claims that it would.

36. John Stuart Mill, *The Subjection of Women* (Indianapolis, IN: Hackett Publishing, 1988).

Chapter 4

1. Sereny, *Into That Darkness*, 231–32.

2. Michaud and Aynesworth, *Ted Bundy*, 95.

3. Notice that something could have both intrinsic and instrumental value: something may be worth having for its own sake and also be productive of something else worth having for its own sake.

4. For further discussion about different conceptions of intrinsic value, see Derek Parfit, *Reasons and Persons* (New York: Oxford University Press, 1986), 493–502.

5. See John Stuart Mill, *Utilitarianism*, ed. George Sher (Indianapolis, IN: Hackett Publishing, 2002), 23–24.

6. See W. D. Ross, *The Right and the Good* (Indianapolis, IN: Hackett Publishing, 1988).

7. Immanuel Kant, *Grounding for the Metaphysics of Morals*, trans. James W. Ellington (Indianapolis, IN: Hackett Publishing, 1981).

8. Kant, *Grounding*, 14–15, 31.

9. My application of Kant's Universal Law Formula follows closely that offered by Christine Korsgaard, "The Right to Lie: Kant on Dealing with Evil," *Philosophy and Public Affairs* 15 (1986): 325–49.

10. I am following Kant in limiting the application of the Categorical Imperative to rational beings, a category from which Kant explicitly excluded nonhuman animals. But one could alter Kant's own understanding of the Categorical Imperative and insist that it actually applies to all sentient beings so as to include pigs, cats, and octopi in the category of beings that are ends in themselves.

11. See Shelly Kagan, *The Limits of Morality* (New York: Oxford University Press, 1991), chap. 4, for similar consequentialist critiques of Kantianism.

12. Art, in particular literature, can help us to hone our capacities for sympathy and empathy by aiding us in projecting ourselves into the minds and lives of people very different from ourselves. Engagement with nonfiction narratives, memoirs, and biographies can also help us to expand our understanding of how circumstances shape people and of how people understand their own responses to the pressures of historical and cultural forces.

Chapter 5

1. There is a vast array of literature on emotional intelligence, but the concept was popularized by Daniel Goleman, *Emotional Intelligence: Why It Can Matter More Than IQ* (New York: Bantam), 1995.

2. See Shaun Nichols, "How Psychopaths Threaten Moral Rationalism: Is It Irrational to Be Amoral," *The Monist* 85 (2002): 285–303, and Jesse Prinz, *The Emotional Construction of Morals* (Oxford: Oxford University Press, 2007).

3. I am not making claims about how emotions would function in the moral life of some sort of god-like intellectually superior being – I am concerned about how we are to educate *human beings* in order to prepare them for moral choice and action.

4. Sereny, *Into That Darkness*, 208.

5. I say "for many of us" because I am not making a claim that necessarily holds for all people. In fact, I am extrapolating from my own experience and from the reports of other people, both those I know directly and those about whom I have read. This sort of claim, I believe, is the most that we can hope for with respect to the phenomenology of psychological states.

6. Actually, there do seem to be some people for whom hatred is gratifying, in so far as their hatred of others, be they blacks, Jews, or gays and lesbians, undergirds their sense of their own worth. But it is not clear in such cases whether the hatred is intrinsically pleasant or merely has pleasant causal effects, such as a feeling of pride in one's own whiteness or heterosexuality. I am trying in the current discussion to talk about the nature of the emotions, not about their causal effects; however, in so far as we can experience an emotion and its causal effects simultaneously, it is very difficult to sort these things out via introspection.

7. There is a philosophical question here as to whether emotions are themselves just particular types of pains/pleasures, or whether they are experiences that at least sometimes (or, perhaps, always) have the property either of being pleasant or of being painful to endure. Settling this question is not important for my task here and so I pose it merely to leave it aside.

8. Some philosophers think that the very fact that we seem to locate pains in parts of the body supports the claim that in fact pains (and pleasures) have content – they are, in some way, *about* that part of the body in which we locate them. The phenomenon of "phantom limbs" in which someone feels pain as being in a limb that he or she no longer has can also be employed to argue that pains have content. I remain unconvinced by such arguments, but will not pursue them further here.

9. We can, however, still sympathize with bats, caring, for example, that their habitats not be destroyed because we do not want them to suffer.

10. Quoted by Jeffrey Herf in *The Jewish Enemy: Nazi Propaganda During World War II and the Holocaust* (Cambridge, MA: The Belknap Press of Harvard University Press, 2006), 125, 132, 146, 149, 150.

11. Richard Rhodes, *Masters of Death: The SS-Einsatzgruppen and the Invention of the Holocaust* (New York: Alfred A. Knopf, 2002), 114.

12. Rhodes, *Masters of Death*, 124.

13. Rhodes, *Masters of Death*, 217.

14. See Rhodes, *Masters of Death*, 124.

15. Rhodes, *Masters of Death*, 167, emphasis mine.

16. Rhodes, *Masters of Death*, 162.

17. Rhodes, *Masters of Death*, 182.

18. Rhodes, *Masters of Death*, 91.

19. Quoted in Richard Overy, *Interrogations: The Nazi Elite in Allied Hands 1945* (New York, Viking Press, 2001).

20. For more on 'the socialization to killing,' see Robert Jay Lifton, *The Nazi Doctors: Medical Killing and the Psychology of Genocide* (New York, Basic Books, 1986).

21. Hoss, *Death Dealer*, 162.

22. Hoss, *Death Dealer*, 163, emphasis mine.

23. Hoss, *Death Dealer*, 153.

24. For such an argument, see Jonathan Bennett, "The Conscience of Huckleberry Finn," *Philosophy* 49 (174): 123–34.

25. Daniel Jonah Goldhagen, *Hitler's Willing Executioners: Ordinary Germans and the Holocaust* (New York: Alfred A. Knopf, 1996).

26. This latter may very well be what I will uncover in a lot of cases of guilt, given how at least some of us can continue to feel guilt for what we have been taught is wrong even after we ourselves have intellectually rejected those beliefs.

27. See Nichols, "How Psychopaths Threaten Moral Rationalism."

28. See, for example, *The Psychopath: Emotion and the Brain*, by James Blair, Derek Mitchell, and Karina Blair (Blackwell, 2005).

29. Michaud and Aynesworth, 277, 281.

30. See Theodore Millon, Erik Simonsen, and Morton Birket-Smith, "Historical Conceptions of Psychopathy in the United States and Europe," in *Psychopathy: Antisocial, Criminal, and Violent Behavior*, eds. Theodore Millon, Erik Simonsen, Morten Birket-Smith, and Roger D. Davis (New York: The Guilford Press, 1998).

31. Carl Elliott, *The Rules of Insanity: Moral Responsibility and the Mentally Ill* (Albany, NY: State University of New York Press, 1996), 74–75.

32. Carl Elliott and Grant Gillett, "Moral Insanity and Practical Reason," *Philosophical Psychology* 5 (1992): 53–67; 56–57.

33. H. L. A. Hart, *The Concept of Law* (Oxford: Clarendon Press, 1961), 86–88.

34. Thus, if one internalizes the legal norms of one's society, one will view sanctions for breaches of the norms as justified. However, if one lives in a society that one views as having an unjust legal system, one will reject the legal norms of one's society and will adopt the external perspective on those norms. Of course, one will use those laws as a basis of prediction (if I hide Jews in my home, then I will be punished if I am found out), but will not view the sanctions that others would impose as justified. So the reasons that one has to obey the laws are purely prudential, and can, it seems, often be outweighed by competing moral considerations.

35. Heidi L. Maibom, "Moral Unreason: The Case of Psychopathy," *Mind and Language* 20 (2005): 237–57.

36. See Elliott, *The Rules of Insanity*, 71, 74, and Walter Glannon, "Psychopathy and Responsibility," *Journal of Applied Philosophy* 14 (1997): 263–75; 265.

37. Elliott, *The Rules of Insanity*, 71.

38. This would not yet be any kind of argument for not incarcerating psychopaths; in fact, it may very well be an argument for permanent incarceration for those psychopaths who demonstrate violent tendencies—they should be treated like dangerous wild animals. But, unlike with man-eating tigers, psychopaths have no 'natural habitat' in which, if contained without human encroachment, we could coexist with them on this planet—they would seek us out to prey on us, because other human beings are, in some sense, their 'natural prey.' For further discussion of this issue, see Murphy, "Moral Death."

39. As I mentioned above, much work has been done documenting ways in which the brains of psychopaths differ from the brains of non-psychopaths. So such a difference can provide some evidence for the lack of an ability to empathize, but only if we have sufficient reason for believing that that difference always causes such a lack. There are complicated questions here about how to establish the physical correlates or causes of mental abilities.

40. David Hume, *A Treatise of Human Nature*, ed. L. A. Selby-Bigge (Oxford, UK: Oxford University Press, 1978), 457.

41. Glannon, "Psychopathy," 268, emphasis mine.

Chapter 6

1. This is, of course, a question that needs to be asked about any German citizen during the period of the Third Reich. However, the question is much more pressing in the case of someone who was as highly placed as Speer was.

2. Weincek, *Master of the Mountain*, 17, 172.

3. For use of a similar example, see Herbert Fingarette, "Self-Deception Needs No Explaining," *The Philosophical Quarterly* 48 (1998).

4. Kurt Bach, "An Analysis of Self-Deception," *Philosophy and Phenomenological Research* 41 (1981): 351–70; 358.

5. David Patten, "How Do We Deceive Ourselves?" in *Philosophical Psychology* 16 (2003): 229–46.

6. Patten, "How Do We Deceive Ourselves?" 234–35.

7. Bach, "Analysis of Self-Deception," 360. Note that, in what follows, I use "evasion" to cover the entire range of ways in which we avoid confronting beliefs, desires, intentions, that we do not wish to acknowledge. So my use of the term is different from Bach's.

8. Bach, "Analysis of Self-Deception," 361.

9. Bach, "Analysis of Self-Deception," 361–62.

10. Sereny, *Into That Darkness*, 55, 164.

11. Sereny, *Into that Darkness*, 169.

12. Sereny, *Into That Darkness*, 163.

13. Sereny, *Into That Darkness*, 164.

14. Of course such a wardrobe would have seemed extravagant to the work-Jews who had one uniform in which they toiled 24/7 without access to sanitary facilities. Quote is from Sereny, *Into That Darkness*, 117–18; quotes in next paragraph are both from p. 118 as well.

15. There are some accounts of self-deception as motivated ignorance that take the motivating desire to be a desire to believe (or to not believe).

(See, for example, Dana K. Nelkin, "Self-Deception, Motivation, and the Desire to Believe," *Pacific Philosophical Quarterly* 83 (2002): 384–406.) These accounts, however, do differ from standard motivated ignorance accounts, and, thus, as I suggest in the text, are best kept separate.

16. Sereny, *Albert Speer*, 463.

17. Academia is chock-full of such people, and, in fact, the culture of the contemporary academy encourages the cultivation of extreme dedication to work and careerism. Thus, Albert Speer can stand as a cautionary tale for many academics.

18. See Sereny, *Albert Speer*, 162.

19. Sereny, *Albert Speer*, 117.

20. Sereny, *Albert Speer*, 313.

21. For a discussion of desire "as an informational filter," see Dion Scott-Kakures, "Motivated Believing: Wishful and Unwelcome," *Nous* 34 (2002): 348–75; 352.

22. Kurt Bach says that one way of evading belief in p is to, whenever p occurs, immediately think of not-p and of various considerations that support not-p. He calls this technique "jamming" (Bach, "Analysis of Self-Deception," 361–2). What I am talking about in the text is another method that is similar to jamming, in that both involve cluttering the mind in order to avoid a belief that one does not want to have. But the sort of cluttering that I am describing involves avoiding even thinking about either p or not-p.

23. Clarke, *Dwelling Place*, 90.

24. Clarke, *Dwelling Place*, 96.

25. Clarke, *Dwelling Place*, 90.

26. Clarke, *Dwelling Place*, 89.

27. Clarke, *Dwelling Place*, 77.

28. See Scott-Kakures, "Motivated Believing," 351.

29. Clarke, *Dwelling Place*, 89.

30. Clarke, *Dwelling Place*, 130.

31. Clarke, *Dwelling Place*, 359.

32. Clarke, *Dwelling Place*, 351.

33. Clarke, *Dwelling Place*, 105.

34. One of the important types of moral theory I am not going to discuss is known as *virtue theory*, which takes the fundamental goal of the moral life to be the cultivation of the virtues. However, understood correctly, that does not mean that virtue theory takes an agent's prime concern to be her own goodness because, in developing virtues, the agent will be developing other-oriented states of mind. For an overview of virtue ethics, see Michael Slote's contribution to Marcia W. Baron, Philip Pettit, and Michael Slote, *Three Methods of Ethics* (Malden, MA: Blackwell Publishing, 1997), 175–238. Baron defends a Kantian deontological perspective, Pettit a consequentialist perspective, and Slote a virtue ethics one. Then each responds to the other two, providing a debate concerning the three major approaches to moral theory.

35. Quoted by Weincek, *Master of the Mountain*, 69.

36. Weincek, *Master of the Mountain*, 8.

37. Weincek, *Master of the Mountain*, 210.

Chapter 7

1. It is important to see that I am *not* asserting that blacks are just like nonhuman animals. I am drawing an analogy: the case of Jefferson's actions vis-à-vis his slaves and ours vis-à-vis nonhuman animals are similar in certain morally relevant ways, although they are undoubtedly different in others.

2. For a fascinating discussion of the role of honor in the antebellum South, see Bertram Wyatt-Brown, *Honor and Violence in the Old South* (New York: Oxford University Press, 1986).

3. See Weincek, *Master of the Mountain*, 70–71.

4. Jefferson's at least purported moral view, as expressed in the Declaration, was that of John Locke. See John Locke, *Second Treatise of Government*, ed. C. B. Macpherson (Indianapolis, IN: Hackett Publishing, 1980).

5. Weincek, *Master of the Mountain*, 69.

6. My language here is intentionally ambiguous. I am using the expression "what makes X happy" to mean, ambiguously, either "what constitutes X's happiness" or "what brings about or causes X to be happy." Consider a hedonist, who accepts that to be happy is to experience pleasure; according to the hedonist, what it is for my cat to be

happy is precisely what it is for me to be happy—to be happy is to experience pleasure—but what causes my cat to be happy (Fancy Feast, naps in the sun, a warm lap) is quite different from what makes me happy (reading novels, talking with my friends, thinking about and debating philosophical issues).

7. Nor did Jefferson compare the abilities of his black slaves to those of uneducated poor whites. Doing so might have led him to speculate that lack of education and other resources played more of a role in achievement than does skin color.

8. Of course, our conception of what we need is, at least in part, a result of culture. What middle- and upper-class Americans think of as needs is very different from what poor Americans or persons in Third World countries think of as needs. So we should reflect on our own desires and preconceptions about what we need as we deliberate about how we ought, morally, to distribute our resources.

9. And, of course, experts in fields such as biology, economics, etc. are as susceptible to various forms of evasion, rationalization, and motivated irrationality as are laypeople. So we need to be cautious in accepting the viewpoints of experts who might, unbeknownst perhaps to themselves, be influenced by their own desires in their interpretations of data or formulations of hypotheses.

10. See Weincek, *Master of the Mountain*, 174.

11. We can only wonder what was going on in his mind during his encounters with Sally Hemings.

12. I find it interesting how often cartoon animals are used to sell animal products; for example, I've often seen cartoon pigs in chef's clothing being used to tout the virtues of barbecue. These animals are always portrayed as very cheerful. Is this supposed to reassure us, making us feel that the animals themselves are happy to be meat for us?

13. For one of the best known discussions of these issues, from a consequentialist perspective, see Peter Singer, "Famine, Affluence, and Morality," *Philosophy and Public Affairs* 1 (1972): 229–43.

14. See, for example, Samuel Scheffler, *The Rejection of Consequentialism: A Philosophical Investigation of the Considerations Underlying Moral Conceptions* (New York: Oxford University Press, 1984).

15. See Diane Jeske, *Rationality and Moral Theory: How Intimacy Generates Reasons* (New York: Routledge, 2008).

16. See Henry Sidgwick, *The Methods of Ethics* (Indianapolis, IN: Hackett Publishing, 1981).

17. See Jeske, *Rationality and Moral Theory*.

18. Bundy, of course, is yet again an anomaly. As far as we can tell, his own interests were the only reasons Bundy seemed able to recognize and act upon. Jeanette Kennett argues that psychopaths do not have the ability to grasp reasons at all, but it seems to me that they take their own interests as reason-giving: self-interest guides everything they do, and at the very least, they do not regard themselves as irrational in pursuing their own interests. See Jeanette Kennett, "Autism, Empathy, and Moral Agency," *Philosophical Quarterly* 52 (2002): 340–57.

19. I say "so-called" because some moral philosophers object to the term "charity." That terms carries the implication that when we give to organizations such as the ASPCA or UNICEF, we are somehow going over and above what we are morally required to do. If, however, one thinks that morality or justice requires that those of us in privileged positions aid those in less privileged positions, then one may think that "charity" is misleading, insofar as it suggests that giving is optional rather than morally required.

20. The early modern British moral philosopher Bishop Joseph Butler seemed to hold the view that God imbued each of us with such a moral sense. See Joseph Butler, *Five Sermons Preached at The Rolls Chapel*, ed. Stephen Darwall (Indianapolis, IN: Hackett Publishing, 1983).

Index

animals, nonhuman
  consequentialist reasoning
    with respect to, 234–6
  cultural pressures
    regarding, 228–31
  human emotions toward, 174–6,
    188, 193, 238–9
  moral evasion regarding,
    209–11, 241–3
  Kant on, 140n10
Auschwitz. *See* Höss, Rudolph
Aynesworth, Hugh, 27, 58

Bach, Kurt, 202
belief
  avoidance of, 33–8, 211–16,
    215n22, 241–2
  justification of, 14, 75–80,
    76n7, 84–5, 89, 131
  and moral culpability, 106–12
  relation to emotions of, 160–2,
    170–1, 179–80
  religious, 86–7, 86n18, 87n19
  scientific, 86–9, 88n21
  See also moral belief, nature of

Brodie, Fawn, 71–2
Bundy, Ted, 25–7, 57–70, 117–19,
  145–8, 176–85, 245n18
  excuse, lack of, 101–2
  guilt, lack of, 67–9, 178–80
  moral evasion, lack of, 202–3
  moral rules, attitude to, 182–5
  moral considerations,
    motivation by, 98–9
  as psychopath, 57–8, 176–7
  remorse of, 60–1, 182
  See also concepts, moral: and
    Bundy; emotions: and
    Bundy; empathy: and Bundy

Caldwell, Erskine, 25
Categorical Imperative, 138–40,
  142, 171
circumcision, female, 73–4, 86
Coles, Edward, 1–11, 50, 73,
  101, 202
compartmentalization, 32, 222
  and self-deception,
    198–9, 200
  in Stangl, 45, 45n40, 203